The World of
SHERLOCK
HOLMES

By the same author

IN THE FOOTSTEPS OF SHERLOCK HOLMES
A STUDY IN SURMISE
THE LONDON OF SHERLOCK HOLMES

The World of
SHERLOCK
HOLMES

Michael Harrison

E. P. Dutton & Co., Inc.   New York   1975

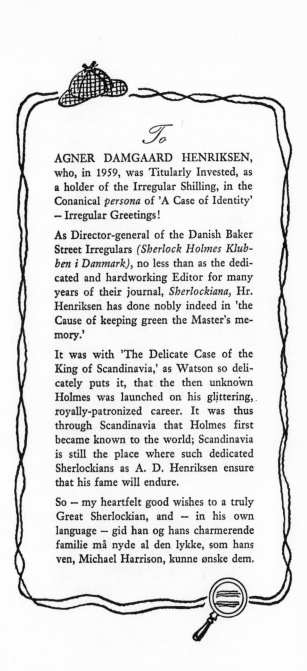

To

AGNER DAMGAARD HENRIKSEN,
who, in 1959, was Titularly Invested, as
a holder of the Irregular Shilling, in the
Conanical *persona* of 'A Case of Identity'
— Irregular Greetings!

As Director-general of the Danish Baker
Street Irregulars *(Sherlock Holmes Klub-
ben i Danmark)*, no less than as the dedicated and hardworking Editor for many
years of their journal, *Sherlockiana*, Hr.
Henriksen has done nobly indeed in 'the
Cause of keeping green the Master's memory.'

It was with 'The Delicate Case of the
King of Scandinavia,' as Watson so deli-
cately puts it, that the then unknown
Holmes was launched on his glittering,
royally-patronized career. It was thus
through Scandinavia that Holmes first
became known to the world; Scandinavia
is still the place where such dedicated
Sherlockians as A. D. Henriksen ensure
that his fame will endure.

So — my heartfelt good wishes to a truly
Great Sherlockian, and — in his own
language — gid han og hans charmerende
familie må nyde al den lykke, som hans
ven, Michael Harrison, kunne ønske dem.

Note

The chronology of Holmes's life, and more particularly, that of his numerous cases, are matters concerning which there has been, and will continue to be, argument of a learned and (alas!) often bitter quality. If the last words on the Holmesian 'who?' and 'why?' have not yet been spoken, be sure that the last word on the 'when?' is equally remote.

Nevertheless, in a narrative history an accepted and acceptable chronology is an essential; and I found my own purpose admirably suited by the chronology to be found in the late William Baring-Gould's *Sherlock Holmes of Baker Street* (New York: Clarkson N. Potter Inc., 1962; London: Rupert Hart-Davis Ltd, 1963). I have also, in the main, adopted Mr Baring-Gould's account of the origins and early life of the Master. Where I differ on any point of research from this great Sherlockian – regretted both as valuable friend and eminent Holmesian researcher – it is never a matter of importance;[1] and I take this opportunity to proclaim, once again, the debt that I, with all other dedicated Sherlockians, owe to an historian who died far too young. *Requiescat!*

[1] See, for example, my *The Blue Blood of the Holmeses* in *The Baker Street Journal*.

Contents

List of Illustrations

List of Illustrations

facing page

All illustrations obtained through Contrad Research Library

The World of
SHERLOCK
HOLMES

I

Background to Youth

On 6th January, year after year, in restaurants, clubs, public halls and private houses all over the world, men and women meet to celebrate the birth of Sherlock Holmes in 1854.

It is Twelfth Night, but the talk at these gatherings is never of the Three Kings, the King of the Bean, the Lord of Misrule, the Boar's Head, and all the other ancient things connected with the Twelve Days of Christmas. The talk is always of something new discovered about the man who raised himself to an universal eminence as the master-discoverer – and it is singularly appropriate, then, that he should have been born on Twelfth Night, on the feast of the Magi.

We remember these 'three Kings from the Orient' principally as bearers of gifts; we should remember them as, if not the first, then the first *famous* Seekers of history.

Their 'evidence' was a Star; and by following up that astral clue, they found the One Whom they sought. They found, indeed, as Holmes would have been the first to point out, because they sought *methodically*. "Let us consider our data," Holmes said to Watson in that singular affair of Shoscombe Old Place. He could have added – save that he considered the fact so self-evident that it was not worth the mentioning – that something sought *methodically* cannot escape discovery.

Holmes was born on 6th January, 1854, seventeen years after Princess Victoria of Kent was roused from sleep in the then shabby old Kensington Palace, to be told by the Prime Minister that she was now Queen of All the Britains.[1]

Less than three years after her accession, the Queen had married Prince Albrecht (Albert) of Saxe-Coburg and Gotha, her cousin; now, after fourteen years of happy and fruitful married life, this iron-willed, indissolubly united couple had imposed a single individuality on their Age.

Less than twenty years had passed since the last of the Georgian dukes, William IV ('Silly Billy') had died; and Victoria's coldly, ruthlessly efficient agents had cleared Windsor Castle of the 'childless' monarch's mistress, Mrs Jordan, the actress, and her brood of fourteen royal bastards.

In fewer than twenty years, Victoria and Albert had made the raffish Georgian Age less than a memory, for all that the majority of the Queen's courtiers and ministers had grown up in that Age. The Georgian Age had gone; and now, in 1854, Sherlock Holmes was born into what, though not twenty years old, was a thoroughly Victorian England.

Holmes will never be completely understood without its being realized that he was, not despite of his individuality; his near-eccentricity; but rather *because* of them, the most typical Victorian of them all.

Holmes was but seven years old when typhoid carried off (at the early age of forty-one) the Prince Consort, who lived long enough to see, with his dying eyes, proof that his most unusual diplomacy had prevented war between Great Britain and the Union Government. Holmes was too young to have known, or been known to, 'Albert the Good', but, as Holmes came to manhood, he was able to serve the Widow of Windsor with that complete dedication of the totally loyal subject which was a phenomenon of the nineteenth century in almost all countries of the world.

We shall see that he was not yet thirty when he was first called upon by the British Government to frustrate the machinations of the Devilish Foreigner; his successful conduct

[1] The royal title on the first coins of Queen Victoria reads: VICTORIA D.G. BRITTANIARUM REGINA – 'Victoria, by the Grace of God, Queen of All the Britains'.

of which Top Secret case inevitably brought his name forward when what the novelists then called 'the chancelleries of Europe' were deeply troubled over 'The Delicate Case of the King of Scandinavia'. Almost anarchistic in his dislike of, and contempt for, the mere mechanism of the social order – judges, lawyers, soldiers, policemen; abstract 'justice' – Holmes yet, all his life, exhibits the profoundest respect for the Well-Springs of Order, as the average Victorian perceived them: the Monarch, the Establishment behind the Establishment, the Nobility and Landed Gentry (not for nothing did the bookshelf at Baker Street hold both *Debrett* and the *Almanach de Gotha*!), and that indefinable but always perceptible sense, in Victorian life, of the quality which gives stability to an existence where a man may expect to reap what he has sown.

Holmes was born, in that bitter winter of 1853–4, as yet one more war was to engage the attention of Britain's soldiers and sailors, but not, apparently, of its ordinary people, save those who had a relative in the battle-zone. I remark, in a life of Charles Dickens that I wrote some years ago, that in his correspondence covering the time of the Crimean War (and of the Indian Mutiny) there is *not one* mention – even the most casual – of the fact that his country is at war. (A job for the soldiers and sailors – isn't that what we pay them for?)

This opinion of the Crimean War persists. I open a modern synoptic history of our times, *Britain and the World in the 19th Century*,[2] and turn up a reference to the affair:

The Crimean War

His need for spectacular success and his desire to follow the footsteps of his uncle led Napoleon III into military adventures. His first was in the Crimea in 1854. Urged on by Great Britain, he supported Turkey against Russia and led France into the Crimean War, and although France's military organization was not much better than Britain's and her losses were heavy, it resulted in victory and was thus a success. It certainly won him some support at home.

[2] G. K. Tull and P. McG. Bulwer; London: Blandford Press, 1966.

Thus, in a short paragraph, is dismissed not only one of the most important wars of the nineteenth century, but one of the most important – some might say the most important – of all the wars of history. If its striking lessons were lost on the average reader of *The Times*, they were not lost on those who realized, as the war ended, that they would now have to fight with entirely new weapons, with entirely new tactics.

And the man who won the war, *in six world-changing, history-changing hours*, was that Napoleon III whose military skill is dismissed so cavalierly in the passage quoted above.

What was more, Napoleon ended both the war and a seven-thousand-year-old pattern of history with a secret weapon of his own invention, which had been developed in his private workshop at his own expense. Before I go on to describe this extraordinary event, in which a secret weapon really *did* win a war – and in a matter of six hours – let us see what changes came out of this 'unimportant' war (that Dickens thinks not worthy a mention in his letters):

(a) The first appearance of the *Blitzkrieg* in modern, 'civilized' times. The attack without the preliminary warning, without the customary ultimatum – and an attack carried through, not only with that ruthlessness, but with that ruthless *speed* which is the whole essence of the *Blitzkrieg*, and is responsible for its name – 'Lightning War'.

(b) The first appearance of the armoured warship – in this case, shell-proof. Its immediate and mind-shocking success made it clear to all involved that here they were gathered at the end of a seven-thousand-year-old era; that they were staring incredulously at

(c) The last appearance of the wooden warship, in which, though with different weapons, men had fought all the great sea-battles of history, from Marathon to Actium, from Lepanto to St Lucia, from Trafalgar to Navarino. In the six hours during which Todleben's 'impregnable' forts at Sebastopol, which had withstood orthodox land and sea attacks for two years, crumbled under the gunfire of Napoleon III's armoured, semi-submersible monitors, the wooden warship was rendered as uselessly obsolete as the sling-stone or the fire-hardened wooden arrow.

(d) The first appearance of the war-correspondent – in this case, Mr (later Sir) William Howard Russell, of *The Times*, who took to his unprecedented task all his Jewish intelligence, his Jewish obstinacy, and his Jewish energy. The Army certainly resented his 'spying', but their sneers and worse had no effect on Russell, conscious that *The Times* was (then, at any rate) more powerful to protect and destroy a career than any Admiralty or War Office. The immediate and long-term effects of *The Times*'s decision to send Russell to the seat of war, to 'get the truth' for the British public, cannot be over-estimated. For the first time, public opinion could operate *during a war* and not long after the battle had been fought, the campaign finished. The institution of the War-Correspondent altered the pattern of war as much – more, perhaps – than any weapon has done. However totalitarian a system, it has never dared *not* employ its war-correspondents, even though, sometimes, in nullifying the effect of his reports, the High Command has had to add one more 'imperative' griminess to the squalid hypocrisy of war. By introducing the war-correspondent, *The Times* took, in effect, the civilian to the battlefield; began the slow transfer of power by which fighting generals and admirals are – theoretically, at any rate – subordinate, *even on the field*, to the politicians. And, by taking the civilian to the battle, *The Times*, in appointing Russell its first war-correspondent, made it inevitable that, fifty years ahead, the battle itself would come to the civilian.

(e) The first appearance of an *organized* medical service – and organized specifically for the care of the wounded fighting man. Hitherto, wives and sweethearts had accompanied the troops, and cared for them: a rough-and-ready system which killed as much as it cured. An extraordinary woman, Florence Nightingale, changed all that. 'Gently brought up', she scandalized her family by training as a nurse; and scandalized the family even more by organizing a band of trained nurses whom, against the open and determined opposition of the Brass Hats, she took to the Crimea. From the *success* of her innovating reforms in army-nursing, came, ten years later, the Red Cross – an organization directly inspired by her wonderful example.

The *social* effect of her innovations were even more important: her care of the sick and wounded soldier implied that the fighting man had some rights *in the field*. We take this to-day so much for granted that it is hard for us to realize that his rights – admitted even by the most brutal of social systems – were secured to him as a result of the Army's permitting Florence Nightingale to set up hospitals in the Crimea and elsewhere before the 'disastrous' implications of her work were realized – and by then, of course, it was too late.

The 'secret weapon' of Napoleon III was a wooden ship of very low freeboard, which, after it had been heavily armoured with 9-inch rolled iron plate, was almost awash. The only superstructure were the conning-tower and the casemates for the powerful guns; conning-tower and casemates being, of course, all well protected by armour. Reciprocating steam-engines gave the 'monitors' a speed of about three knots; not enough to enable them to make the long journey from Brest to the Black Sea, but more than adequate to ensure their manœuvrability as they came within range of the Russian guns at Sebastopol.

Napoleon III had found a French naval captain, embittered through compulsory retirement – the service fault: 'excessive zeal'. The Emperor engaged this man and put him to work experimenting, first with shell-proof armour-plate, and then with model monitors. As the Crimean War went inconclusively on, with neither side winning, and both sides losing, Napoleon hurried his naval assistant towards completion of the three monitors that the Emperor had planned.

The British Government, given the details of the secret weapon, promised to have three of their own monitors ready to join Napoleon's; but the British, though paying lip-service to the new armoured ship, 'didn't believe in it', didn't get on with the construction of the monitors, and let Napoleon 'go it alone', convinced that he would 'make a frightful cock-up of it, old lad: you know what these bloody Frogs are, eh, what?'

Three French steamers towed the three monitors out of Brest, across Biscay, around the Iberian Peninsula, through the Mediterranean and the Dardanelles and the Sea of Marmara into the Black Sea. And so to Sebastopol, its forts still inviolate despite even the poison-gas[3] (*another* first, by the way!) that the British had sent against the Russians.

Drawn up in line abreast, just beyond the range of the Russian guns, was the fleet of the combined Powers – Britain, France, Turkey and Piedmont. The three French steamers moved through the line of warships, and slipped their tows. At three knots the monitors moved forward, heavily shelled by the Russian guns. The monitors slowed down, let go the anchor, and from only a few hundred yards' range, opened fire on the forts. After six hours, the white flag rose above the shattered casemates of Sebastopol, and one French monitor-man was slightly wounded – by a shell splinter which had passed through a ventilating slit.

To be born when Holmes was born was to be born at a time of innovation – and of the change that innovation inevitably ordains.

Even those who 'can't be bothered with' technical change are affected by it, since the world in which they live has been changed as technology produces new things. Holmes, as we shall see, was far from being disinterested in the wealth of invention, mostly (though not exclusively) in the mechanical field, which was to span that period which lies between the world of the stage-coach and that of the interplanetary rocket.

I have had cause to mention and to consider Holmes's apparent dislike of the telephone; but apart from this prejudice, he welcomed innovation in everything – in travel, in communication ("He never wrote when he could telegraph," Watson remarks), in political grouping (he was passionately in favour of the tightest Anglo-American *rapprochement*),

---

[3] Sulphur dioxide (SO_2), to 'smoke the blighters out'. Unfortunately for the British, this ingenious idea was frustrated by a change in the wind's direction, after which the choking British 'outlawed' poison-gas as a 'barbarism'. The Germans, however, caught on, and returned the gas to the British in 1915; *not* relatively harmless SO_2, though!

in education (he admired the system of free, compulsory, national education – the new schools: "Lighthouses of the future, Watson!").

Perhaps Holmes's father, ex-East India Company's cavalry officer Siger Holmes, was a man who read the newspapers aloud; or perhaps Holmes, as did the infant Macaulay, learned the art of reading a page upside-down, as his father read *The Times* and let the top half of the page fall forward.

Yes, but at what age did Holmes learn to read? I think it more likely that either Holmes's father or his half-French mother – the French have lively minds, and are always intensely interested in what goes on about them – pointed out to young Sherlock what wonderful things (and some pretty awful things, too) were happening.

Take, for example, the year 1861, when Holmes was seven.

In 1861, at the year's end, the Prince Consort died, and the Queen was to enter upon that exhibitionistic, necrophile widowhood which, at first encouraging the development of a republican movement in Britain, ended by changing the republican sentiment into an hysterically royalist near-worship of the Head of State.

The Prince Consort's last act, as I have said, was to prevent war between President Lincoln's government and that of Her Britannic Majesty.

Two diplomats, Slidell and Mason, had been accredited to, respectively, the Courts of St James and Fontainebleau by President Davis, whose Confederate States' government had been recognized by Britain and France.

As these men were crossing the Atlantic in a British ship, the ship was overhauled and stopped by a North American warship under the command of Commodore Wilkes, USN, a descendant of the revolutionary-turned-reactionary John Wilkes, of 'No. 49' fame.

Palmerston, then Foreign Secretary, had taken punitive action even before drafting the Note to President Lincoln, protesting against an action which was both an insult to the British flag and a violation of international law. 'Pam', with his usual impetuosity, had despatched 8,000 well-armed and well-supplied troops to the Canadian-American border, knowing that the British people would be whole-heartedly behind a war against the Yankees.

The dying Prince Consort's last act had been to demand to see – and to insist on 'toning down' – 'Pam's' stern note to Honest Abe. The prospect of a small, victory-assured war against the Union Government appealed to most in Britain; the British people were concerned, of course, only with the martial aspects of the proposed war – they neither appreciated the inevitable economic consequences of the American Civil War, nor would they have cared much had those consequences been pointed out to them.

Only the Prince Consort was against the war, and on his death-bed he managed so to revise the Note as to save Lincoln's face – for the German prince understood the make-up of the 'simple' American lawyer better than ever the English nobleman could have done.

For there was no war – and the inevitability of one of the most single-minded imperialisms of history was assured.

Two events of a more – apparently – pacific nature took place in that same year of 1861: the invention of the first successful incandescent electric lamp and the first successful electromagnetic telephone; the former, the invention of a young English civil engineer, Joseph Swan; the latter, that of a young German small-town schoolmaster, who, lacking academic qualifications in the qualification-obsessed Germany of the late 1850s and early 1860s, was to be sneered out of fame and life by the unimaginative professors to whom he described his invention.

Nonetheless, despite the claims of later men, Johan Philipp Reis did invent a workable telephone, and demonstrated it in 1861; and a century later, through a deal of persistence, I was able to persuade the German Government to honour the memory of this pioneer with a postage-stamp shewing his telephone. There were also big exhibitions organized in his memory, again as a direct result of my work for Reis.

Swan, then of Newcastle-upon-Tyne, produced the world's

first incandescent electric lamp in 1861; its filament being of oiled paper coated with powdered carbon. It took Swan (later Sir Joseph) another eighteen years to perfect his lamp, and when he did, he found himself challenged by the go-getting Edison as 'inventor'. Fortunately for common sense, Swan did not waste his substance on the law-sharps – in any law-case, Edison would certainly have got the better of the not-so-sharp Englishman – and, rather than fight, Swan joined Edison, their patents being shared, and their 'joint' incandescent lamp being marketed as the 'Ediswan'.

Another innovation, seemingly unimportant, yet with profound social significance, was the opening, in the London of 1861, of the Aërated Bread Company's first tea-shop. The makers of this 'patent' bread, being unable to sell it to the public through the normal retail outlets – the 'old-fashioned' baker wouldn't consider adopting the process by which his bread became 'aërated' – decided to 'take it direct to the public', and began to open a chain of tea-rooms, many of which are still with us, though the ownership has now passed to a Canadian *entrepreneur*, a Mr Garfield Weston.

But the 'ABC' tea-shop was to do far more than accustom the British – notably the London British – public to the new 'aërated' bread. It was to achieve the tremendously important side-effect of introducing a challenging rival to the tavern – into which no 'respectable' woman above the social rank of the labouring class would, or could, go. The tea-shop, for the first time in the world's history, marked out, as it were, a place in readiness for the 'respectable female' – as distinct from the domestic servant, barmaid or factory-girl – who was (though no one yet foresaw it) about to enter both commerce and industry.

Within seven years of the first tea-shop's opening, Sholes would have invented and perfected[4] the typewriter, and sold

[4] With the exception of the spring-loading of the carriage, to effect 'automatic carriage return', and the shift-key, the Sholes prototype machine was, in all but the two conveniences mentioned, the typewriter that we have today. Substitution of electric for manual power hasn't effected any essential change in design.

it to the Remington Company, then desperately anxious to supplement or replace its market for rifles, needed far less now that the Civil War had ended.

Excellent publicity, for which American Business had already demonstrated its flair, launched the typewriter on a wondering world. Anticipating the advertising techniques that Pond's Cold Cream used in the 1930s, the Remington admen secured a live, for-real Countess to drum their new wares.

Seated before a vast and cumbrous mechanism which looks in its dimensions and apparent intricacy like something out of a spinning-mill, a young lady smiles from the wood-engraving, as she rests her fingers on the keys. A 'dainty' booted foot pokes modestly out of the pleated hem of her tight skirt to press down the pedal which will bring the carriage back to the left-hand margin. The copy explains that the Countess Lydia Tolstoy, daughter of the eminent Russian novelist, acts as her distinguished Papa's amanuensis and 'typewriter', and *always* uses a Remington.

By the mid-'seventies, the typewriter had arrived in Britain and in most of the already highly industrialized countries of Europe. (*The Times* newspaper and the British Royal Household were among the first to adopt the new-fangled mechanical writing-device: I notice that, with the true traditionalism of the enthusiastic innovator, all letters from Buckingham Palace or Windsor are typewritten on machines using the now old-fashioned pica [12-pt] roman face.)

When, with the invention of the typewriter, the New Woman emerged, the tea-shop was ready for her. It had all the required qualities: it was eminently 'respectable', it was 'safe', it was cheap – and it had a 'ladies' room', to which women might retire with modesty and there find privacy. That it was not until after the Second World War that every British tavern or bar had a 'ladies' room' explains the immediate attraction, for 'respectable' women, of the tea-shop.

By 1879, Edison had opened London's first telephone-exchange in Lombard Street, and from the opening, this was staffed, as far as the less responsible work was concerned, by women, as was, indeed, the (Government) Central Telegraph Office at St Martin's-le-Grand. The telegram, the typewriter, the telephone – these three, in chronological order, did more, in a practical way, for 'Women's Lib.' than ever the strident female would-be lawyers, doctors, 'social workers', 'divines' and printers,[5] with their misdirected energy and their topsy-turvy sexuality could and did do.

Comparing the nineteenth century with those which have gone before, the historian is struck by the new element of *impatience* manifest at every level of, and in every activity of, society.

But whether this impatience is the product of the speeding-up everywhere apparent; or whether the impatience encourages the speeding-up, it is hard to say. Perhaps knowing that one's message will be delivered, by post, within, say, twelve hours, or by telegram, within, say, twelve minutes, encourages an impatience with any tardiness on the part of the recipient.

'Cutting corners' now becomes the rule rather than the exception in every aspect of human activity – even where, and (one thinks that one sees) *particularly* where, the corner-cutting saves not only time but more important things: a consideration of the rights of others, a respect for tradition, a submission to protocol . . .

[5] Miss Emily Faithfull, an eminent do-gooder, established a printing-shop completely staffed by females – compositors, machine-minders, proof-readers, 'devils', and the rest. This bold champion of Woman's Rights secured for herself the appointment of 'Printer-in-Ordinary to Her Majesty'. Fate was at its most cynical, one feels, in making this man-hating Amazon the victim of a singularly embarrassing encounter, of an 'intimate' nature, with the elderly Vice-admiral Codrington, a hero of Navarino (1827), who, in his dotage, not only pressed his unsought attentions upon Miss Faithfull, but let the female printer see a proof – of his virility – over which she had hoped never to have to cast her eyes. Despite the publicity given to the Admiral's 'insulting be-haviour', the Greek Government of 1927 had no hesitation in issuing a stamp in honour of his uncle, Sir Edward Codrington (on which he is called 'Sir Codrington'), nor has the Chelsea pub named after Sir Edward suffered a change of title.

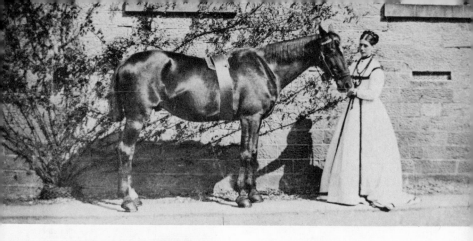

1 Mrs Siger Holmes, with her favourite chestnut gelding, 'Aurungzebe', at Mycroft, 1861 (*Contrad Research Library*)

2 Sir Edward Sherrinford, grandfather of Sherlock Holmes. *Photograph: Henry Rigge, 35, New Bond Street (Contrad Research Library)*

3 Lady Sherrinford, sister of Horace Vernet, and daughter of 'Carle' Vernet (1758–1835), both eminent members of a family of eminent French painters. *Photograph: Fratelli Alinari, Florence (Contrad Research Library)*

4 Siger Holmes, Captain, Honourable East India Company's Service (retired), father of Sherlock Holmes. *Photograph: Lock & Whitfield, 178, Regent Street (Contrad Research Library)*

5 Mycroft Holmes, elder brother of Sherlock Holmes. A clerk in the Foreign Office, this photograph was taken at the time of the Berlin Congress, 1878, that he attended. *Photograph: Elliott & Fry, 55, Baker Street, Portman Square (Contrad Research Library)*

6 Mrs Holmes, of 24, Montague Street, Russell Square, whose relationship to Sherlock Holmes is still uncertain. This extremely rare portrait is, apparently, the only one surviving of this still satisfactorily unaccounted-for element in Holmes's life, though there may be a clue to her origins in the location of the photographer. Was their meeting a typical Victorian 'seaside romance'? *Photograph: H. J. Godbold, Hastings (Contrad Research Library)*

7 Sherlock Holmes, aged six, in the Scotch dress made fashionable by the example of Queen Victoria's young sons. *Photograph: S. Bayfield, 2, High Street, Tunbridge Wells (Contrad Research Library)*

8 An important new field of employment for 'respectable' women was opened up with the establishment of London's first telephone-exchange in Lombard Street, City, in 1879. The country's telephones were not nationalized until 1912 *(Contrad Research Library)*

9 Another all-powerful Woman-liberator: the Typewriter, invented by Sholes in 1873. *Photograph: courtesy of Sperry Rand Ltd (Remington Rand Division)*

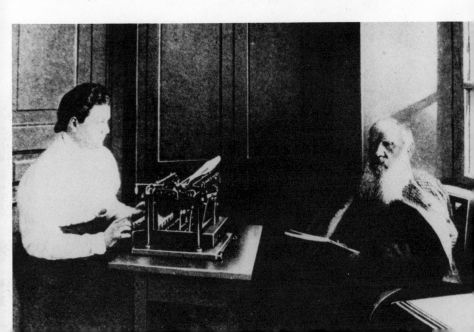

10 A scandal averted, James Kenneth Stephen, tutor to Prince Albert
Victor of Wales, heir-but-one to the Throne, went mad and achieved
murderous immortality as 'Jack the Ripper'. The connection of this
homicidal lunatic with the Prince of Wales's heir was suppressed, and both
Prince Albert Victor and 'Jack the Ripper' died within a few weeks of each
other, the latter in a lunatic asylum. *From a drawing by F. Miller, 1887
(Contrad Research Library)*

The Turkish Black Sea Fleet was at anchor in the roadstead outside the ancient Greek port of Sinope; the port, as Pausanias tells us, which was the last-but-one stopping-place of the Hyperboreans as they brought gifts to Delos.

Turkey was not at war; and the skeleton crews on the warships flying the Crescent and Star slept soundly or took their watches conscious of no sense of danger. On their starboard beam, the ancient town shewed a few lights as early-morning workers dressed for the new day; on their port beam, the night sea was unbroken save for an occasional gleam of starlight from a gently moving wave.

But out of that apparently friendly night ships were coming – they were crossing from the Crimea; from Sebastopol at the 'waist' of the Black Sea – headed, with no lights shewing, for Sinope.

Out of the false dawn Admiral Nakhimov's Black Sea Fleet swept down on the moored, sleeping, almost defenceless Turkish ships. Answering to the orders signalled from shielded lamps, Nakhimov's vessels swung into position, and – the alarm not yet being raised in the Turkish fleet – poured broadside after broadside into the victims of this classically executed *Blitzkrieg* – the first of modern times.

The Turkish fleet was doomed; return fire was almost impossible from the blazing, exploding ships. A few slipped their anchors and fled; militarily, the victory was total. On land, the Russian armies moved into the Turkish *vilayets* of Moldavia and Wallachia – the *Blitzkrieg* Age, in Europe at least, had begun again.

The lesson was not lost on the Prussians.[6] In the year in which Britain, France and Sardinia went to war with Russia over the unprovoked and unannounced attack on Turkey, that agreement which, more than anything else, created the pattern of our present-day world, was signed. This was the

---

[6] Nor, apparently, on the Soviet Russian government. In the first and third years of 'the Great Patriotic War' (World War II), the late Josef Stalin created several new Russian orders of chivalry, naming them after Russian heroes of the past. One such order is named after Admiral Nakhimov.

famous Protocol of London, signed by Great Britain, France, Spain, Austria and Prussia, guaranteeing the sovereignty and territorial integrity of Denmark.

In 1863, Bertie, Prince of Wales, a sad trial to his Mother (who 'could never forgive Bertie' for having caused his 'angel Papa's' death[1]), had married the beautiful but undowered Princess Alexandra ('Alix') of Denmark, and when, in open defiance of the Protocol of London – and in obvious admiring imitation of Nakhimov's treacherous attack on the Turks – Prussia launched a *Blitzkrieg* on Denmark exactly ten years later, Queen Victoria refused to prevent Prussia's breaking her solemn obligation towards the Protocol. Victoria's eldest daughter, the Princess Royal, had married the Heir Apparent to the Prussian throne; and, Victoria explained, she did not wish the British to think that they had been drawn into war on account of Bertie's having married a foreign princess.

Armed with this matchless precedent – plenary authority to sign and break treaties as it suited them – the German rulers subdued Denmark in a matter of weeks, annexed Schleswig-Holstein, and went on to defeat Austria, and to annex and erase (as far as their identity was concerned) those independent German states – including Hanover (ruled by a British duke) – which had been unfortunate enough to join the losing side. The contempt for the British – Royal Family, Government, People – that Victoria's holding back in 1864 had inspired in all German minds is apparent in Bismarck's treatment of Hanover, over which Victoria would have ruled had the German successions not been regulated by the Salic Law.

Not only was Hanover deprived of its identity as a nation, and incorporated into Prussia as a province; the Hanoverian Royal Family, also, were personally punished. Kaiser William I seized all their private estates and personal fortunes where seizable, and they went into exile in Paris as – despite their

---

[1] The Prince Consort went up to Cambridge to remonstrate with his undergraduate son about his affair with the daughter of a local landlady. At some point on this visit, the Prince Consort contracted typhoid, from which he died. Victoria preferred to think that Albert had died 'of grief'.

membership of the British Royal Family[8] – the paupers of European royalty.

The confidence that every German government since has felt that Great Britain would condone every international piracy; shrug tolerantly (and, most would come to think, cravenly) at any treaty-breaking, however wanton; encourage, in every way, every filthy trick, the more so as its victims were the British, 'protected' by the British Government: all this may be traced back to Britain's standing aside, against all treaty obligations, in 1864.

When the 'emerging' States of the world weren't Black but White, *they* needed money, too; and, as in our own days, this money was taken from British investors by (usually) London-based banks – 'British' only in the most highly technical sense of that phrase – and passed on, after the usual deduction of bankers' commission, to the needy borrowers.

When those needy borrowers had spent the money raised on what is laughingly called 'the British market', and spent it not often wisely and not often unselfishly, they had no desire to pay the loan back. If the Russians invented the modern *Blitzkrieg*, and the Germans developed it, the modern Americans of the United States of North America invented the art of national repudiation of debts to cheat a creditor.[9]

Sixty million pounds of debts were thus repudiated. Great Britain was willing to send 'punitive' expeditions to such nations as Syria, Mexico and Chile, chasing debts that those nations hadn't the least hope of being able to pay, but left

[8] The last King of Hanover, the (blind) George V, was H.R.H. the Duke of Cumberland, K.G.

[9] Perhaps it should be pointed out that the repudiations were by State and not by Federal governments. It was in commenting acidly upon this commercial practice that Charles Dickens forfeited, by the publication of his *American Notes*, his personal – though not literary – popularity in the United States, where his pirated works enjoyed an immense success. However, in spite of the hard things that Dickens had to say about the United States in both *Martin Chuzzlewit* and *American Notes*, he did – even if somewhat conditionally – prophesy a future of unprecedented importance for the leading nation of the New World.

the United States of America well alone. *There*, too, the lesson of Britain's pusillanimity was not overlooked.

The rulers who bore Britain's craven nature – I talk here of the country's average politician, and not of its average citizen – always in mind were the German politicians. It made no difference whether these politicians were aristocrats or upper middle-class; *petit bourgeois* or proletarian. Bismarck and Hitler both understood that British politicans were as reluctant to conform to the 'moral', 'solemn', obligations of any treaty as old *Blut und Eisen* and Schickelgruber themselves – though, with far more cynicism and far more honesty, these two treaty-ignorers made no bones about their contempt for the Solemn Promise and the Written Undertaking.

So that, in 1935, when Hitler wished to enter the Rhineland, he went, confident that Britain would not oppose this breaking of yet another treaty. As confident, he moved into Czechoslovakia, Poland . . . and though the British did go to war after Hitler's invasion of Poland, it was rather *post hoc* than *propter hoc*, seeing that British politicians did nothing at all to help their Polish ally. (And protégé!)

Victorian impatience, then, had been inspired by the knowledge that affairs could be speeded up; and this desire for more and more speed (the crack steam-trains of the world were topping 80 mph before 1880; the telegraphic link with America was established by 1858) affected the moral standards in a fashion which is only too noticeable to-day, when, save in the ravings of the romantic novelists or the religious-press hacks, moral standards, as our great-grandfathers knew and respected them, have been sneered or plausibly argued out of existence.

Holmes, brought up partly in the agricultural North Riding of Yorkshire, and partly on the Continent, with his half-French mother, could not have escaped that curiously ambivalent development so noticeable in him as a fully grown man. He tells us, of course, of the French strain in his blood – that his grandmother was a sister of 'Vernet, the French painter'; that is, Emile Jean Horace Vernet (1789–1863), and thus a daughter of Antoine Charles Horace, who preferred to call himself 'Carle', Vernet (1758–1835). The Vernets were an extraordinary family, brilliant, energetic, with an outstanding quality which survived, undimmed, from generation to generation.

They had been distinguished artists from the seventeenth century, and their energy – always surplus to requirements – found its outlets in ways seemingly unconnected with painting. 'Carle' Vernet, for instance, was an ardent Anglophile, as a young man in the golden age before the Revolution of 1789, in which disastrous year his son, Horace, was born.

Known to the *jeunesse dorée* of pre-Revolution Paris as 'English' Vernet, Carle not only imported English horses and jockeys and staged horse-races *à la mode anglaise,* but began that fashionable addiction to English customs which is still common amongst the French.

This was an addiction which survived the tremendous changes of the Revolution, partly because all revolutions, *at their beginning*, are violently anti-nationalistic, and partly because it was from the English philosophers and political writers that many of the Fathers of the Revolution gained their own revolutionary ideas. And, again, as with the Russian revolutionaries, England had afforded them sanctuary. Even during the worsening of relations during the long Napoleonic wars, nothing like a hatred of the English developed in France; and at the height of the hostilities, Sir Humphry Davy and his wife were invited to France by the Emperor, in order to receive a 50,000 fcs awards for Sir Humphry's contributions to Science.

True to his true-blue John Bull principles, the knighted chemist refused to wear the compulsory court-dress designed for Napoleon by David (who had sketched the emaciated, short-haired Marie Antoinette as she had walked bravely to the guillotine).

And, after the Restoration, with the return to France of so many – including members of the Royal Family – who had lived for over twenty years in England and spoke, many of them, its uncouth tongue, English was even more fashionable. Besides, of the armies of occupation, only that of the British behaved with near-decency – the conduct of the Russians and the Germans in the Paris of 1814 and 1815 can still bring a shudder to the sensitive French soul.

Britain was lucky in that she was represented in France, both militarily and politically – to which the distinguished representative added, socially – by His Grace the Duke of Wellington. A French-speaking Irishman (always a popular race with the French), Wellington, with his well-trained, well-disciplined squadron of harlots; with his Irish arrogance towards men and his Irish blarney for the women; with his tremendous presence topped – and as it were, summed-up – in an imperial nose as vast as that of their admired King Henry IV, Wellington, defeater of Napoleon though he might have been, was still a hero to the French. He kept his men in order, and when the Treaty was signed, and the armies of occupation left (the Russians and the Germans, after their traditional fashion, heavy with loot), Wellington stayed on as His Britannic Majesty's ambassador.

The nephew of the Vernets would have been assured of a warm welcome in a France which, then as now, has always a special *bienvenue* for the creative man and his family.

If Holmes had the sort of exceptional memory for his earliest years that I have, he would, in later years, have been able vividly to recall, perhaps not Bordeaux and Pau, that he visited with his parents when he was only a year-and-a-half old, but certainly the France that he knew at four years of age. He would surely have had distinct memories of Montpellier, in the gentle South, where, even today, the visitor can never escape that permeating Roman presence. Here, in the heart of the Roman province of Gallia Narbonensis, both the Greek and the Roman genius remain; in May, 1858, when the inhabitants still wore their distinctive Provençal dress, spoke their more-Roman-than-French Provençal, and the native poets and men of letters were reviving the ancient language in its more literary forms, Holmes first became aware of his grandmother's native land. Not long after the Holmeses had returned from this land of fairy-tale, Robert Louis Stevenson,[10]

[10] *Travels on a Donkey in the Cervennes.*

on his donkey, came to these parts. It had not altered in the thirty years or so since the Holmeses had returned to England in June, 1860, when Holmes was six, and ready for an English dame-school. Europe, with its new Bessemer and Krupp steel, and the new weapons that the high-grade steels made possible, was becoming completely industrialized around the more densely populated centres. But the bicycle and the motor-car had not yet arrived to 'open up' the countryside, first to tourism and then to settlement. And though, in common with all the other European countries, France had adopted the steam locomotive running on metal railways, railway development in France lagged far behind that of Great Britain, Prussia and even industrially-backward Russia. Iron being three times as dear in France as in England, the French railway system was about one-third as long as the English (approximately 1,200 : 4,000 miles), a national deficiency which was to be a principal cause of the rapid and total defeat of the French by the Germans in 1870.

But, in 1860, the golden lands of Provence were untouched by industrialization. Even to-day one may capture something of that serene landscape and seascape, 'white ships sailing by Montpellier and Cette . . . half veiled in sunny haze', of which Stevenson writes.

The ruins of Roman and mediæval times – the castles, the triumphal arches, the amphitheatres (as at Orange, Arles, Nîmes), the soaring aqueducts, the remains of Papal ambition and Papal splendour at Avignon – why did this fairy-tale land, now so busily renewing its glories under the romantic, ruthless direction of State-subsidized Violet-le-Duc, make so little appeal to the imagination of young Sherlock Holmes?

Was there something at home to 'spoil it all'? – some unhappy association which prevented the boy's enjoying what the normal small boy would, in the common phrase, have given his eye-teeth for?

And yet, Holmes, now almost forty – the age at which, if we are ever tempted nostalgically to retrace our footsteps, we open the gates of Memory – returned to Montpellier. It is true that, in November, 1893, Holmes was, so far as the world knew, dead; and that it must have been under his *alias* of Sigerson that he 'conducted researches into the coal-tar derivatives at a laboratory' at Montpellier.

After an 18-year-old English chemist (the later Sir) W. H. Perkin, had synthesized indigo from coal-tar, calling the aniline dye *mauveine*,[11] ruining the French indigo-crop industry almost overnight, and retiring, a wealthy man, before his nineteenth birthday, the German chemists had taken up coal-tar technology, and achieved a near-monopoly in its derivatives, mostly dyes and flavourings. Saccharine (forbidden to be imported into Italy by a law of 1883) and synthetic salicylic acid, marketed by the chemical firm of Bayer under the trade-name 'Aspirin', were perhaps the best-known products of the late nineteenth-century German coal-tar industry.

What would have caught Holmes's inquisitive eye in this admittedly promising commercial field? A new dye . . . ? Hardly likely. A new flavouring for cheap 'gob-stoppers', to ruin what was left of the teeth of the world's milling poor? Unthinkable! A new depressant, anti-depressant, hypnotic, addiction-cure? Far more likely. But what about a new high-explosive – something which, oddly enough, was catching the imagination of a young English writer, Herbert George Wells, soon to become world-famous as one of the most imaginative writers of all time? Wells was fascinated by the new high-explosives, with their sinisterly allusive names. And so, perhaps, Holmes may have been.

But if we look at the chronology – we are jumping in time here, as though in that outstanding product of Mr Wells's imagination, the Time Machine – we observe that, just before Holmes took advantage of the events at the Reichenbach Falls to disappear, he was engaged on that mysterious 'Matter of Supreme Importance to the French Government'. We know

[11] Perkin always claimed that he 'just made this name up', as George Eastman claimed that he 'just made up' the name of his world-altering cheap camera, the Kodak. But I think that, somewhere in Eastman's subconscious was a Kodiak bear, and it is notable that the Turkish for 'blue' is *mavi*, and that French *mauve* appears before Perkin.

no more than may be conveyed in those few words, but later, when I return to the events of December, 1890 to March, 1894, I shall suggest some plausible reasons for thinking that Holmes revisited the golden scenes of earliest childhood not only at the request of the French Government, but also with his true identity being known to, at least, the *Chef du Deuxième Bureau*. The directors of French Military Intelligence knew that Holmes hadn't died at the Reichenbach Falls, even though Dr Watson's sentimental myopia prevented his guessing the truth.

The Holmes family had spent a month more than two years in the balmy climate of the Gulf of Lyons, over which, however, the terrible *mistral* blows, to plunge the human spirit into suicidal gloom, just at that time of Spring when the human heart should be at its happiest, at its most hopeful. Something far worse than mullygrubs or the blue devils remains, permanently lodged in the human liver, after the *mistral* – the Italians know its baneful character as *scirocco*, the Arabs as *khamseen*: but it is its same terrible self wherever it blows – had gone to sour the spirits of peoples father East.

These early wanderings of the Holmeses raise some interesting questions, and, I think, explain, even without those question' being answered, much of the adult character of Sherlock Holmes.

Why did Siger Holmes, late of the Honourable East India Company's cavalry, leave England in July, 1855 (returning to England in June, 1860), and again in October, 1860 (returning to England not before September, 1864, at which time Sherlock, Siger and Violet Holmes's third child and third son, was ten).

Travel, they say rightly, 'broadens the mind'; and so it does; but there is also little doubt that children whose early years are marked with frequent changes of residence do tend to grow up to be restless, even neurotic, adults. And that Sherlock Holmes was both restless and neurotic, his friend Watson's carefully delineated portrait, taken over a period of more than thirty years (1881–1914), makes unambiguously evident.

But why was Siger[12] Holmes so restless – or, to be more precise, why did he find it necessary to take his wife and children abroad so frequently and for such long stays?

According to Mr Baring-Gould, Sherlockian family-researcher *par excellence*, Captain Siger Holmes, HEIC, was invalided home in 1844, though the researcher does not state whether it was a wound or a disease which had cut short the Scandinavian-Yorkshireman's military career. However, the date is significant, and may afford a clue to the facts of Siger Holmes's leaving the service of 'John Company'.

In 1813, the British Government had taken the monopoly of the trade with India from the British East India Company; a monopoly which had been enjoyed and vigorously (some said ruthlessly, and even immorally) defended since the granting of the Company's charter by Queen Elizabeth I in 1600.[13] From 1813 to 1833, the Company concentrated on its China trade, which had not been taken away; but when that also came to an end in 1833, the Company ceased trading alto-gether, and remained in India as a Board of Directors exercis-ing that powerful patronage which comes with a prestige built up over more than two centuries. Though the Board of Direc-tors of the Honourable Company maintained an official existence, the Board no longer met, and all the immense power of 'John Company' was now concentrated into the hands of one man, the President of the Board, who was *de facto*, if not *de jure*, Viceroy of India under any pre-1858 British Government.

There was a Governor-General, appointed by the British

---

[12] Mr Baring-Gould has cleverly deduced the Christian name of Sher-lock Holmes's father from the fact that, after his disappearance, Sher-lock Holmes used the name, 'Sigerson', that Mr Baring-Gould interprets as 'son of Siger'. It appears to be a name of Scandinavian origin, from the root which has given the better-known form, 'Sigurd'

[13] It was to finance the trading operations of the newly-chartered East India Company that the first *dollar* to be authorized by an English government was issued, bearing the head of Queen Elizabeth I and the date, 1600. The new Australian, New Zealand, Caribbean and other dollars are thus wrongly assumed to have 'an American origin'; they have an English origin, before even there was a 'Great Britain'.

Crown, and Tull and Bulwer's[14] statement that the President 'concerned himself only with important policy; in practice, most authority was in the hands of the Governors-General, who were autocrats with more power than any other men either in Great Britain or the colonies' is not in accordance with the facts. The Governor-General had more delegated, more official, authority; it was he who signed Orders in Council. But the Governor-General was a Merovingian king to the President's Mayor of the Palace: the *real* authority lay in the hands of the President; the *real* patronage was dispensed by him. The Governor-General became the Supreme Military Commander under the orders – though always tendered as *advice* – of 'the Man Who Understood the Country', the President.

This advice entailed war after war; and in one of the most important, Captain Siger Holmes received, I think, his physical and military come-uppance.

In 1838, as a counter-measure to combat growing Russian influence in Afghanistan, the then Governor-General, Lord Auckland, re-established a former Amir in Kabul, and maintained such power as the restored monarch had by British arms. Unfortunately, the people of Afghanistan rose against the ruler who had been imposed on them by the British, and, from the safety of India, Auckland ordered the British to abandon their protégé – not the first time that such an order has been given and obeyed; nor, indeed, the last. The return from Kabul to India, however, was through a country now completely hostile to the British: on that fearful retreat through the Khyber Pass, some 3,000 British – soldiers, civilians, women and children – with some 12,000 sepoys and camp-followers of both sexes and all ages, were wiped out, almost literally to a man. The sole survivor was an Englishman: how he escaped, even he could not understand.

A strong punitive force of British returned to Kabul to 'shew the flag' and 'restore prestige'. Their occupation of Kabul was a token one; after a few weeks of pretending to

[14] *Britain and the World in the 19th Century,* op. cit.

35

have reconquered the country, they withdrew on the orders of the new Governor-General, a titled attorney with all the narrow thinking and mean-minded opportunism of his tribe.

Now the British took on the Sikhs, because those Sikhs dwelling in Scind owed allegiance to the Amir of Afghanistan, and the military Government of India wished to 'neutralize' this warlike people, who stood astride the way to Afghanistan (to which the British, fearing the Russian penetration south to India, intended to return).

The Sikhs fought well – but not well enough; and how Sir Charles Napier, in 1843, announced by a famous single-word message that he had conquered Scind used to be a story retailed by every school-history. The conqueror of the Scindian Sikhs sent the single-word despatch: 'Peccavi!'[15] – a message which would be as incomprehensible to any modern Army field-commander or his aides or to any bum-burnishing base-wallah as the news that the Sikhs were being given assisted passages by the British Government to invade Britain would be incomprehensible to Sir Charles Napier (and, indeed, to the defeated Sikhs of 1843).

The territory of Scind was annexed; the military action – because British arms had been successful – was bitterly criticized in the British Liberal press; Governor-General Ellenborough was recalled; and Captain Siger Holmes was invalided out of both Service and sub-continent.

Elsewhere I have written of the Holmes baronetcy, the genealogical details of which are a matter of record.[16] It is Mr Baring-Gould who has been most successful in revealing the Holmes genealogy in the *direct* line; but this notable researcher has omitted to tell us something of the financial background of Sherlock's youth. Let us see if, here, we may not do something to repair that omission.

As a captain on the Bengal Establishment, Siger Holmes would have received an allowance of £51 7s. 6d. a month when in the field (field-service counting with effect from post-

---

[15] Latin for 'I have sinned' (i.e. Scind).
[16] *See* Appendix I.

ing of orders at barracks). Field-allowances were calculated as
at 25 per cent of salaries, exclusive of 'poker money', and all
other emoluments. A 'John Company' captain, then, would
be in receipt of a tax-free salary of £2,466 per annum, increased by field-service to £3,082 10s. per annum, whilst
actually on a war establishment – a distinction very liberally
interpreted in an India in which a Company war was the
rule rather than the exception.

The field-allowance would cease, of course, on Captain
Holmes's wound- or fever-enforced retirement, as would those
generous 'other emoluments', those 'perks', which did so much
to raise one's pay to something comparable with that of the
next highest rank (a major received £4,500 per annum 'basic',
and £5,625 when on active service).

Life-expectancy in the service of the Company being short
– the climate was literally 'killing', so far as the average European was concerned – promotion in all branches of the
Company's service, but notably in the armed forces, was com-
parably swift. All the same, it would have been unlikely that
Holmes would have got his company under ten years' service;
and so we may make a fair guess at what his pension would
be.

The sums granted by way of superannuation allowances to
officers and servants of the Company were fixed by the 53rd
George III.c.155 (*i.e.* 1813). For Captain Holmes, under sixty
and with over ten years' service, the following would apply:

	Proportion of salary
If above 10 years and less than 20	One-half

Captain Siger Holmes, HEIC (retd) would thus be in receipt
of a pension for life of £1,233 per annum; not vast wealth,
to be sure, and affluence certainly not entitling him to be
called a 'nabob', the half-respectful, wholly-envious term
applied in those days (see your Thackeray) to those who came
back from India with a hob-nailed liver and a face as yellow
(with fever) as the *lakhs* and *crores* of golden coins with which
they returned. All the same, a man might bring up a family
respectably, and even travel to the cheaper parts of Europe –

as Siger Holmes did – on far less than 'a cool thousand-a-year' and something over. From her father, Sir Edwin Sherrinford, Mrs Siger Holmes would have received a dowry, and this join-ture would have been protected for her by Sir Edwin's solici-tors. The income from the settlement would, however, have been at the joint disposal of her husband and herself. I think that we shall not be far wrong in thinking that Mr and Mrs Siger Holmes 'rubbed along' (as the phrase then went) on about £2,000 a year.

Holmes's – that is to say, Sherlock Holmes's – need to earn a living when he came down from the latter of his two Uni-versities is explained, not merely by the fact that he was a younger son, and so in no expectation of inheriting anything from the modest Yorkshire estates, but because Holmes Senior enjoyed only income, and not capital.

That there is some connection between Siger Holmes's military service and his journeyings abroad seems indicated by a coin-cidence of dates.

On the outbreak of the Crimean War in 1854 – a war which was followed by the war between India (*not* Great Britain) and Persia in 1856, and the Indian Mutiny in 1857 – Siger Holmes collects his family and goes to Bordeaux, thence to Pau and Montpellier. He returns in 1860, when all hostilities have ended; and in time to assist at the death-bed of his father-in-law, Sir Edwin Sherrinford, who dies in the October of 1860 at the age of 73. A war with China seeming imminent, the Holmes family now sails for Rotterdam, moving on to Cologne, and from there embarking on a Continental tour, which lasts over three years.

Was the reason for this travelling that, as war broke out, Siger Holmes wished to join in, and Authority would not let him? – or that Authority, convinced that the ex-Captain had recovered, wished to call him before a medical board, and Siger Holmes had no more taste for war? And so escaped to Europe, until such time as Authority lost interest in him?

The benefits and disadvantages of this restless life, as far as Sherlock Holmes is concerned, are pretty evident. His schooling, before he entered the Grammar School at Mycroft at the age of twelve, can have been only of the scrappiest sort.

He admits this to Watson in 1881 – though Sherlock does not go as far as to explain it (perhaps he was unaware of the causes of his unbalanced knowledge?). In the light of Mr Baring-Gould's researches and discoveries, the famous 'test yourself' list from *A Study in Scarlet* takes on a new significance. The list, you may remember, was compiled by Watson, to Holmes's dictation. Holmes has, in his usual forceful, be-damned-to-you way, been discussing with his new flat-mate, not merely knowledge, but knowledge considered from the view of its importance to him who possesses it.

"Depend upon it," Holmes said, "there comes a time when, for every addition of knowledge, you forget something that you knew before. It is of the highest importance, therefore, not to have useless facts elbowing out the useful ones."

Holmes has already shocked Watson by, not merely the *extent* of the 'consulting detective's' ignorance, but more, by the *quality* of that ignorance. "His ignorance," Watson reflected, "was as remarkable as his knowledge. Of contemporary literature, philosophy and politics he appeared to know next to nothing. Upon my quoting Thomas Carlyle,[17] he enquired in the naïvest way who he might be and what he had done. My surprise reached a climax, however, when I found incidentally that he was ignorant of the Copernican theory and of the composition of the Solar System. That any civilized human being in this nineteenth century should not be aware that the earth travelled round the sun appeared to be to me[18] such an extraordinary fact that I could hardly realize it."

Watson's condescending astonishment certainly didn't shame Holmes.

"But the Solar System!" Watson protested.

' "What the deuce is it to me?" he interrupted impatiently: "you say that we go round the sun. If we went round the

[17] Then living in Cheyne Row, Chelsea.
[18] *Sic.* Such oddities of idiom are not infrequent in Dr Watson's writings.

moon it would not make a pennyworth of difference to me or to my work." '

And we know that this is true – though we may still sympathize with Watson's being scandalized by his friend's nonchalant confession.

Watson, as we recall, made a list of what Holmes knew – and didn't know. I find the list even more instructive than Watson found it.

SHERLOCK HOLMES – his limits

1. Knowledge of Literature – Nil.
2. Knowledge of Philosophy – Nil.
3. Knowledge of Astronomy – Nil.
4. Knowledge of Politics – Feeble.
5. Knowledge of Botany – Variable. Well up in bella-donna. opium and poisons generally. Knows nothing of practical gardening.
6. Knowledge of Geology – Practical, but limited. Tells at a glance different soils from each other. After walks has shewn me splashes upon his trousers, and told me by their colour and consistence in what part of London he had re-received them.
7. Knowledge of Chemistry – Profound.
8. Knowledge of Anatomy – Accurate, but unsystematic.
9. Knowledge of Sensational Literature – Immense. He appears to know every detail of every horror perpetrated in the century.
10. Plays the violin well.
11. Is an expert singlestick player, boxer and swordsman.
12. Has a good practical knowledge of British law.

How many times this list has been read, no man – even helped by a computer – can now say; it must have been read with approbation as many times as it has been read with a decided feeling of superiority on the part of the more traditionally-educated reader. I wonder how many times it has been read for its *intrinsic* information; as a guide to what we may learn *about Holmes*? I venture to say: not many times.

Yet, better than any detailed description of his appearance, his personal habits, his mode of life in a set of Baker Street rooms, this idly constructed list tells us perhaps all that we can learn of those influences which, as a boy, shaped the man.

Watson says, "When I had got so far in my list, I threw it into the fire in despair . . ."

That was surely the action of a man with little perception; with far too little perception. For consider the list that Watson made, and couldn't interpret. What does it tell us?

In the first place, not only by its inherent imbalance, but by its void at 'important' points, it tells us that it records the imperfect knowledge of the autodidact, the self-educated man. The man who, *studying without experienced control*, learns too much of one subject, too little of another; and learning, whatever he learns, always at the expense of a less favoured subject, which is starved of attention, so that the learner may give an overplus of enraptured interest to a subject more favoured. That Holmes went to school, Mr Baring-Gould makes clear; but by the time that Holmes entered Mycroft Grammar School at twelve, he had not that familiarity with school-learning, lesson-conning (so different from the undisciplined absorption of knowledge) to which his schoolfellows had become habituated since an early age.

That he could learn, we know; he was intensely observant, quick to learn; but not in the manner in which one learns at school. He was a little self-willed Autolycus,[19] learning what he wished to learn – and only that – and spurning all other 'boring' fields of knowledge; and always with the undisciplined, undirected learner's stock excuses – that Holmes was still using to Watson, fifteen years later; by which time the stock excuses had become unthinking habit.

If Mr Baring-Gould be correct, Sherlock Holmes enjoyed only seven uninterrupted terms of regular schooling – from and including the Summer Term of 1866 to and including the Summer Term of 1868, in the September of which year he was again taken abroad by his parents, going by steamship to the busy Norman port of St Malo, and thence, by the still

[19] An interesting name for a 'magpie': Autolycus, 'The Wolf who walks alone'.

sparse railways and the still active and efficient *chaises de poste* system, back to Pau.

Sherlock's schooling, such as it was, had been further interrupted in the winter of 1865–66 by an illness of a severe character, possibly – in view of the bitter winter weather of the Yorkshire moors – of a pulmonary nature. One cannot say; but it could well be that his addiction to cocaine, remarked upon by Dr Watson when the two men met in January, 1881, had developed from an earlier addiction to some 'softer' drug, prescribed, in the reckless manner of the time, by the grammar-school's consulting physician.

That the recovery was slow, or, at any rate, not as quick or as complete as anxious parents might have wished, is doubtless the reason for Mr and Mrs Siger Holmes's decision to take Sherlock from Mycroft Grammar School and remove him to Pau.

Here – and certainly it was to counteract the sequelæ of some affection of the chest and lungs – Sherlock was placed in the *salle d'armes* of Maître Alphonse Bencin, the internationally famous fencing-master. Rowing, archery and fencing – these three branches of athletics were stock recommendations of the mid-nineteenth-century physician for the 'setting up' of any lad debilitated by the all-too-frequent 'chest troubles', which could be anything from incipient 'consumption' to emphysema. Of the three, fencing had an advantage over the other two in that it developed the legs as well as the upper parts of the body, and taught, besides, a general physical agility – one of the characteristics in Holmes which struck Watson on his first meeting Holmes in '81, and that Holmes retained in large measure even after he had turned sixty.[20]

Schooling or tutoring must have been arranged for Sherlock locally: there were then – are still – excellent *lycées*, not only at Pau itself, but also at Bayonne, Tarbes, Orthez, and other neighbouring towns. Yet Holmes's knowledge of French we accept rather by implication than by direct evidence, although it should be noted that when he quotes from memory

[20] He is strikingly active, *physically* as well as mentally, against the enemies of Britain in *His Last Bow*.

– and then incorrectly – his amended version is in far more colloquial French than is the original. Thus, in a letter from Gustave Flaubert to Georges Sand, dated December, 1875 (where did Holmes see this, by the way – and how?),[21] the phrase occurs: *L'homme n'est rien, l'œuvre tout* – 'Man counts for nothing – his achievement for everything.' Recalling this aphorism in October, 1890, during the case of *The Red-headed League*, Holmes changes it to the much more colloquial *L'homme c'est rien – l'œuvre c'est tout*: a trifle longer, but far more as the ordinary Frenchman-in-the-street would express it.

The Latin that he, in common with all other British boys, learnt at the time, was, judging by his two Watson-preserved quotations, strictly school-required-reading stuff; indeed, the two Latin authors among the books mentioned as in Holmes's shelves at Baker Street – Horace and Catullus – sound suspiciously like school editions surviving unread on the shelves of a man who leaves them there out of unthinking sentimentality or mere laziness, or both. The other Latin book, *De Jure inter Gentes* – "a queer old book I picked up at a stall yesterday" – was a seventeenth-century legal work; but bought for its cheap price or 'quaint' binding or elaborate title-page or for all of these things. One feels that it wasn't bought for 'reading', or even to 'keep up my Latin'.

The books at Baker Street do not reflect the fact that Holmes's German – picked up, as six-year-old children will instantly pick up any foreign language, at Cologne in 1860 – was probably as good as his French. He twice quotes Goethe in German (both times in *The Sign of the Four*), and French (four quotations), five times.[22] Twice (in *A Scandal in Bohemia*

[21] By no means one of the least important of the as-yet-unsolved mysteries of Holmes's life.

[22] Whatever the limitations of Holmes's general knowledge – limitations that Watson professes to find 'remarkable' – Holmes's knowledge is often unexpectedly recondite – sometimes startlingly so. As, for example, with the French quotation with which Holmes rounds off an uncomplimentary reference to the Scotland Yard detectives, Lestrade and Gregson: *'Un sot trouve toujours un plus sot qui l'admire.'* In its context, the remark is certainly *ben trovato*, but one wonders why

and *His Last Bow*) Holmes has some remarks to make upon the German language. He recognized the word, *Rache*, written in blood on the wall of the empty house in Lauriston Gardens, without hesitation. *Rache* is the German for 'revenge, vengeance'. And in *The Red-headed League* he treats Watson to a lecture on the superiority of German music to the French or Italian. (But he need not have known a word of German to be able to do that.)

Yet, in order to go up to Oxford, as he did in 1872, he would have had to take and pass Responsions in several subjects, of which, at that time (and for long afterwards) two *compulsory* subjects were Greek and Latin. Mr Baring-Gould states that Siger Holmes hired the services of a tutor to 'cram' Holmes for Oxford, and that this tutor was none other than the brilliant yet criminally perverted James Moriarty, with whom Holmes was to 'cross swords' (how readily the analogy with fencing must have sprung to Holmes's mind) in later years, and clutched in whose murderous arms Holmes was to fall towards the boiling waters of Reichenbach.

Moriarty, born in 1846, was some eight years older than Holmes, and the young tutor was probably happy to spend the fine summer of 1872 in the comfort of the old farmhouse at Mycroft. The duties would have been light; and for all Holmes's dislike of Greek – he makes no allusion to it in the Watsonian record – young Sherlock would have applied himself diligently to the unpalatable task of learning far more than the simple paradigms, knowing that ignorance of Homer's tongue would prove an insuperable barrier to his becoming an University man. But 'cramming' is not intended to teach, to inform; it is simply intended to take young men

– and even *how* – Holmes should have recalled the last line of Canto I of *L'Art Poétique* of Boileau (Nicolas Boileau-Despréaux; 1636–1711): not by any means the best known work of a poet himself almost forgotten in the England of the 1880s. The origin of this quotation was pointed out by the late William Baring-Gould, who has also noted that Holmes, though 'astonishing' Watson by asking who Carlyle was, yet most aptly quotes Carlyle. Baring-Gould suggests, rightly I think, that Holmes was not above making fun of Watson's too evident credulity.

– it was exclusively young men then – through examinations. But, if one learns precious little from 'cramming', one may learn a deal from the 'crammer', and the bent of brilliant, socially immoral Moriarty's mind was not without its effect on that of his almost-as-brilliant pupil.

Moriarty, according to Baring-Gould, 'could teach the boy nothing', because 'between Sherlock Holmes and Professor James Moriarty there flared up instant hatred'.

'As for Sherlock,' Baring-Gould continues, 'he went happily back to his pony and the moors.

'But now the time was approaching when a wider world was to make its call upon him.

'In the October term of the year 1872, Sherlock Holmes took up residence at Christ Church, like his brothers Sherrinford and Mycroft before him – a first-year man at Oxford.'

It was not at all as easy as that. The only undergraduates permitted to join Oxford University without examination were Wykehamists entering New College, because both were founded by William of Wykeham; the Bishop's intention being to found a school at Winchester, and a College at Oxford, to which boys from his school would proceed. It is not suggested that Holmes was a Wykehamist; and so he would have had to be 'crammed' for Oxford, whether or not he disliked his private tutor. He would have had to do some heavy swotting before he 'took up residence at Christ Church'.

And that means that Moriarty did not 'soon leave to return to his academic calling'; Moriarty must have stayed on until it was certain that Sherlock Holmes would be able to go up to Oxford.

Moriarty was a truly brilliant man; and the influence of such on a youth of sixteen or seventeen is weighty indeed. The influence is the more felt as the difference in age between the influencer and the influenced is small – to the ordinary influence that one powerful mind must always exercise over any other is added the wondering respect that the junior *must* have for one who, though but a few years older, has successfully overcome all those academic obstacles that the junior, the tiro, has still to tackle.

45

At the age of only twenty-one; that is, in 1867; Moriarty 'had written a treatise on the binomial theorem which had a European vogue'.

'On the strength of it,' writes Mr Baring-Gould, 'and because of certain connections his West of England family possessed – he won the mathematical chair at one of the smaller English universities.

'There he soon produced his magnum opus – a work for which, despite his later infamy, he will be forever famous. He became the author of *The Dynamics of an Asteroid*.'[23]

To evaluate Moriarty's influence, as a young mathematical genius on an ambitious but impatient younger man, would be desirable; the attempt may be made only by examining what little we know of Moriarty's (not so much character, as) background. I find it significant in this enquiry to note that one of Moriarty's brothers – there were three, all curiously christened with the same name, James – was a station-master. This argues divergent standards within one family, but was the station-master the 'drop out', or was *our* James Moriarty, one day to be called by Holmes 'the Napoleon of Crime', the 'bright boy of the family'?

Mr Baring-Gould's reference to the influence of Moriarty's 'family connections' may or may not be justified, but one has the feeling that there was not a little autodidactic about Moriarty himself; that his learning was not acquired in an altogether orthodox manner, and that such progress as he made in the academic world was due more to his own efforts than to any 'family connections'. If the social status of the station-master Moriarty represented the social level of the Moriarty family, then James the Tutor would be an Outsider (to use Colin Wilson's descriptive term), and thus the most dangerous influence that Sherlock Holmes – himself already heading for Outsidership – could have encountered.

Holmes may or may not have disliked Moriarty – it seems likely that he did; though that dislike may have been no more

[23] The importance of this paper, 'incomprehensible to the scientific critics of the time', has been explained by the late Edgar W. Smith (1894–1960) Sherlockian Extraordinary.

than the spontaneous reaction of an undisciplined mind to one whose teaching had to include orthodox academic rules. But the title of Moriarty's paper is significant, as is the date, for he must have produced it within the five years between his writing his treatise on the binomial theorem and Holmes's going up to Oxford.

Moriarty's work stamps him as a man of his moment. Aeronautics was an obsession with the inventive, the philosophical, the speculative mind of the mid-nineteenth century.

The great name is that of Sir George Cayley, first to lay down the elements of aerodynamics through long and careful experimentation with gliders of his own construction, in one of which he undoubtedly flew – perhaps the first man in the world to do so. By 1847, Phillips had constructed a helicopter which anticipated so many modern 'sophistications' that it is impossible to study Phillips's design without wondering why the first man-carrying helicopter flights (by Bréguet and Cornu) did not occur before 1907.

The Phillips helicopter was steam-driven. Lift was effected by two contra-rotating aerofoils of aluminium, in the trailing edges of which were slits through which jets of high-pressure steam were ejected. The helicopter had no 'prime mover' as such; the high-pressure steam was led to the aerofoil nozzles by a flexible pipe from a stationary boiler.

Did it fly?

On Salisbury Plain, when the inventor fed the steam to the aerofoils, the helicopter rose so rapidly and with such velocity that it broke connection with the flexible pipe, and took off in unassisted flight. It was never seen again.

In the same year, and also on Salisbury Plain, Stringfellow achieved remarkable results with his model monoplanes, powered by lightweight steam engines of his own design. And in 1867, so great and so diffused was the interest in aeronautics, that a band of enthusiasts founded the Aeronautical (now the Royal Aeronautical) Society. Four years earlier, a German inventor had taken out a patent for a lighter-than-air flying machine; an ellipsoid balloon with a *riveted aluminium skin.* Powered by a steam engine, this metal airship was to be *jet-propelled.*

What was needed to make an efficient flying machine was an engine with a high power/weight ratio, which meant, in practical engineering terms, a lightweight metal. Giffard had taken his dirigible balloon from Paris to Chelles in 1852; his lightweight steam engine driving it a somewhere between 2½ and 3 knots. Lightweight steam-engines could be constructed – Stringfellow's are marvels of ingenuity in design and precision in engineering – but the saving in weight was always necessarily achieved at the cost of power.

The metal, in fact, had arrived in 1854. In 1863, Napoleon III put his cuirassiers of the Garde Impériale in aluminium breast- and back-plates; and in 1867, at the Paris Exposition, the first prize for metal sculpture was won by an aluminium statue.

For the rest of the century, men would be experimenting, and coming nearer and nearer to that achievement which awaited the world on 17th December, 1903, when, at Kitty Hawk, the Wright Brothers's powered glider stayed aloft for just twelve seconds.

No man who had had the prevision to imagine and write *The Dynamics of an Asteroid* could have failed to exert the strongest influence on so enquiring a mind as that of the young Sherlock Holmes.

It was left to Mr Baring-Gould's patient researches to reveal the details of Holmes's ancestry, though, in a small article in *The Baker Street Journal*, I myself have added some information concerning the Holmes family, not in the direct line.[24] Holmes himself is remarkably reticent about his ancestry; though that may be explained by the fact that Watson did not commit to paper all that Holmes told him, or that the 'case' in which we might have learnt more of the Holmes genealogy from the Master's own lips has been lost or destroyed. He tells us little. He mentions the French connection – his relationship to the Vernets, and adds that his 'people'

[24] *See* Appendix I.

11 'Headquarters' of the Wilde Set, up to the time of his conviction and imprisonment in 1895 was the old Café Royal, frequented also by far less dubious characters than Wilde – for both Holmes and Watson knew it well. The famous Grill Room, shewn here, has been spared from the post-World War I rebuilding. *Photograph: Greater London Council*

12 King Christian IX, first Danish king of the Glucksburg dynasty, with his two grandsons: a photograph taken by the King's daughter, Queen Alexandra of Great Britain and Ireland. For Holmes's services – he served the Scandinavian Royal Families on at least three occasions, in negotiations extending over a quarter-of-a-century – he was awarded most of Scandinavia's highest decorations (*Contrad Research Library*)

13 Sir Hiram Maxim, French-Canadian engineer, as unsuccessful in designing aeroplanes as he was brilliantly successful in designing the machine-gun which bears his name, and which made him the object of international interest in the power-hungry world of the late 19th Century. The lower of the two orders on his right breast is Chinese, and records the fact that the Chinese Government was the first to acquire the Maxim Gun – firing 666 rounds of ·303 ammunition a minute *(Contrad Research Library)*

were yeomen: small landed gentry; half-farmers, half-land-lords. He obviously resents too searching an enquiry into his origins; and one instantly suspects, encountering such re-ticence, that the reticent one 'has something to hide'. Holmes does not tell us that his father had served with the Honourable East India Company's cavalry, and here we may have a clue to Holmes's reticence generally.

Well-, indeed grossly over-paid by the standards of the Queen's Army and Navy, the Company's huge armed force – officers, non-commissioned officers and men of the army (British and native), 160,000; British officers and native sailors in the Company's naval department in India, 113 officers, 800 sailors – enjoyed so many privileges denied to those who held the Sovereign's commission that only one form of revenge was left to the 'home-based' soldier and sailor: to despise the 'Indian' officer, and to put him into a sort of social purdah.

What the 'home based' Army officer resented, he despised the 'Indian' officer for escaping. Until 1871, British Army officers purchased their commissions – and sold them; a system which generally meant that promotion was not alto-gether unconnected with wealth. Again, no officer was ex-pected to live on his pay. Though many a British officer must dearly have wished that he might, he would have lost caste in trying to do so. A man bent on a military career who had insufficient private means sought a commission in the Indian or Colonial service, where commissions were granted, not sold; where pay was calculated on far more generous scales; and where the 'amenities' were more agreeable, and far less costly.

The comparison between the rates of pay of 'home-based' and 'Indian' cavalry officers strikingly explains the reasons for the jealousy-based scorn in which the latter were held by the former:

Pay and allowance for a Captain (per annum)

Royal troops		Company troops	
Royal Regiment of			
Horse Guards	£691 12s.	Peace	£2,466
Dragoon Guards	£163 16s.	Active	£3,082 10s.

Plus an allowance of £30 p.a. in each case.

In London, the Colonel of the Horse Guards received only £2 1s., gross pay and allowance per diem, and £1 11s. per diem subsistence, a total of £3 12s. per diem, or £1,302 per annum, little more than a third of an 'Indian' captain's field pay and allowances.

I have remarked elsewhere, and notably in my *In the Footsteps of Sherlock Holmes*, on the Master's touchiness, and have argued from this an awareness of social stigma or insufficiency.

If both Siger Holmes and his son were ashamed of the fact that Papa's cavalry commission had been an 'Indian', and not a Royal one, then Holmes's reticence about his family, and his general air of having something to hide, is explained. Snobberies change from generation to generation; incomprehensible to one generation, the causes of embarrassment which trouble another generation cannot be argued away even by the loftiest minds. It is unlikely that Holmes would have been ashamed of the fact that he had attended a grammar-school, rather than a public-school (that particular snobbery began to be apparent only at the beginning of the present century), but it is almost certain that he would have been ashamed of – or, perhaps, only troubled by – his father's commission having been 'the wrong one'.

Had Siger Holmes been an object of universal, or even of merely Continental, attention, he might well have gained for himself the sinister reputation of a storm-petrel. For, whenever he uprooted wife and children, there was a war or the rumour of a war in the neighbourhood. I have suggested that Siger might have had some personal interest in the disturbances between 1854 and 1858 in which Britain was involved; but wars from which Britain stood piously and (as always with neutrals) profitably aloof seemed, in some odd fashion. to be connected with Siger.

Thus, in 1858, the Holmes family left Montpellier for Pau, just before the plot between Napoleon III and Cavour led to war with Austria and her defeat at Magenta and Solferino in 1859. Returning to England, for the death of Sir Edwin

Sherrinford, in October, 1860, the footloose Holmeses were away again within the month, but waited to begin their nearly four-year Continental tour until North and South began hostilities in America. They returned to England as the Prussians and Austrians were mopping-up the Danes, and Sherlock Holmes's illness during the winter of 1865–6 may have some curious psychosomatic connection with his father's restlessness at not being able to move as Prussia launched its shamelessly contrived war of aggression, in 1866, against Austria and the Confederation states.

The return from Pau to Mycroft in April, 1871, somewhat reversed the common order of affairs; here the journey from one country to another was made after the trouble had broken out – and as the Holmeses came north, through a defeated, but not noticeably different, France, Thiers's Government troops, watched by the contemptuous Prussian army of occupation, were trying to relieve a Paris held by Communists who were to burn a quarter of the city before the Government could recapture it.

The Europe of the nineteenth century; that Europe in which the modern 'luxury' hotel had its origin, and travel attained standards of comfort and punctuality never achieved since; was not at all a Europe at peace. I have mentioned that Dickens, writing over a long period to his friend, Beard, never refers to any of the wars in which Britain was engaged; nor, in fact, do the guide-books and travel-advertisements of the time hint at anything but an universal peace, through which the traveller may be whisked, from one hotel to the next, 'tout confort moderne', at the cheapest possible rates with the best possible service.

And, as far as the traveller was concerned, the picture was truthful: wars were short – six weeks for Prussia and Austria to defeat Denmark; seven weeks for Prussia to defeat Austria and the Confederation; rather less than seven weeks (ignoring the lingering resistance until January, 1871) for Prussia to defeat France.

Only in Communist-ruined Paris did the century see the large-scale devastation with which two World Wars and some other frightful misapplications of human ingenuity and energy have made us familiar. But by 1873, France had paid the new German Empire the £200,000,000 fine (in gold francs) imposed by the victors; had rid the country, by that payment, of the German army of occupation; and by 1874, practically all the destroyed part of Paris (about one-quarter) had been restored or rebuilt.

Visitors to the Paris Exhibition of 1878, in which that great friend of France, Bertie, Prince of Wales, took so deep a personal interest, reported that they could find not the least trace of that maniac incendiarism which, only seven years earlier, had destroyed or gravely damaged almost every one of the capital's outstanding buildings.

Recalling what we noted about Siger Holmes's probable income – he was able to send his three sons up to Oxford, remember, and economies effected in *living* abroad were offset by the expense of reaching and returning from distant places – he must have been one of those men who 'manage' to keep within their means only with continual and openly discussed difficulty. Why do I affirm this? Because of the curiously ambivalent attitude towards money that Sherlock Holmes was to display when all responsibility for living had devolved upon himself. He seems, in the later years, not so much disturbed by the thought of money as scared that anyone should think that he *liked* it: worse, that he *needed* it. In his attitudes towards money, in his relationships with his clients, Holmes often strikes us as pretentious, absurd; and so, often, even his contemporaries must have found him. In his abhorrence of adopting a 'sensible' attitude towards money, an attitude which – though he never came to realize this truth – was far more typical of the upper-class and aristocracy than his 'princely' *pecunia olet* attitude, Holmes veers between the foolishness of 'I work for nothing!' and the hardly more intelligent conduct implied in overcharging an influential client.

Yet, as Watson's carefully compiled record shows, the subject of money – though always in relation to his fees – was

rarely absent from Holmes's mind. He mentions his charges in
A Study in Scarlet, A Scandal in Bohemia (three times!), *The
Red-headed League, The Beryl Coronet, A Case of Identity,
The Priory School, Black Peter, Thor Bridge, The Boscombe
Valley Mystery* and *His Last Bow*. He freqyently contradicts
himself, even to the same person – usually Watson, but not
always. At one time he 'sensibly' declares that his fees are 'on a
fixed scale' (whatever that may mean; but here, as in many
other places, we note the not-so-secret desire to be taken for,
to be accepted as, to become, a 'professional' man) – except, he
adds, 'when I remit them altogether'. Then, on other occasions, he likes to affect a 'hard-headed' greed for money worthy
of the most 'hard-headed' lawyer ever to be found in the pages
of a Victorian novelist, and, rapt in this particular aspect of
his ambivalence, Holmes does have the gall to charge the
Duke of Greyminster £6,ooo for having found and brought
back His Grace's odious little heir, Lord Saltire.

We have forgotten, and the history-books do not record
(though the novels do) the almost total preoccupation, the
perpetual mental anguish, of those Victorian social classes
passing through the painful process of 'bettering themselves'.
To define exactly what was meant by an activity's 'profes-
sionalizing' itself might have taxed the skill of the Victorians,
rarely at a loss for a word. Any activity might become 'professional' if it were not too closely allied with Trade, and if it
might obtain Royal Incorporation. This would create a man-
aging, a directing, a disciplinary body, able to charge fees, to
restrict entrance to the new 'profession' by demanding that
applicants for entrance pass examinations, and to grant the
right to proclaim membership by means of the valued 'letters
after one's name'. It is true that Holmes came down from
both his Universities without a degree; the *Registers* of both
make that fact proven. But we may know this without reference to any written record; Holmes betrays all the aggression,
all the diffidence, all the balancing-up romanticizing of the
man who *might* have regularized himself, but failed to do so.

One should remember that, in dismissing what he does not
know as belonging to subjects which are 'impractical', Holmes

is dismissing – albeit with a laugh – and *knows* that he is dismissing, perhaps the very subjects, ignorance of which cost him his degree.

The actual cost of maintaining a son at one of the Universities in the 1870s was small, even trivial – if we regard that cost simply as a matter of University fees. What could – and did – send the cost soaring were the 'extras': conduct money, battels, books, fines, the concealed money-lending of Town shopkeepers and taverners, subscriptions to clubs and social events, as May Week at Cambridge, the Commemoration Ball at Oxford. If one were some deadly swot, concerned only with gaining the best degree in the smallest number of terms, with a country curacy as the goal of one's modest ambition, one could survive at University on the minimum for board-and-lodging and manage to pay all necessary fees for less than £150 a year.

But suppose that one weren't a deadly swot; suppose that the studying of what didn't interest one bored one silly? Suppose that one were not a bookworm; that one liked sport – the sport that one chose oneself, of course, and not the sport laid down by University regulation or undergraduate custom? Suppose that one liked to fence, to box, to go tubbing?

For a good many terms, Siger Holmes would have had to maintain two sons at the University: Sherrinford and Mycroft; Mycroft and Sherlock. Could Holmes the father have done all that two ordinary young men could have wished? It is unlikely. Economy as an undergraduate calls for willing co-operation on the part of the boy; and few young men have the character to resist at least jealousy, envy, self-pity, resentment, when called upon to live a life different from that of their fellow-undergraduates.

And Christ Church – of all colleges! – in those days, before Jowett had properly set his mark upon Balliol and Balliol upon Oxford, Christ Church was the 'smart', the dashing, the independent, the utterly be-damned-to-you! And where no undergraduate – and certainly not for reasons of his impecuniousness – could slink away and bury his nose in a book!

Only a short while before Sherlock Holmes came up to Oxford, the members of Christ Church had struck boldly – even savagely – against Authority, with imprisonment of the staff, barricading of access to the 'undergraduates' part' of the College, and setting fire to the Library, contemptuous of one of the world's most valuable collection of books, many of which perished in the flames. One is so used, to-day, to read of such behaviour amongst (they've given up calling them 'undergraduates', because graduation is no longer the principal reason for their being at the University) 'students' that it may come as a shock to the less historically-minded reader to know that there were Yahoos about in 1870 as there are now. (Though not, perhaps, so many of them; and they *did* wash, *and* wear collars and ties.)

It was in April, 1861, that the Holmes family began its four-year Continental tour. The War Between the States had come and gone by the time that Holmes was preparing to be entered at Christ Church, where more emotionally influential experiences than assisting at an undergraduates' riot were awaiting him. Thanks to the philanthropic (and dying) Prince Consort, Britain had not swept down on the Union from Canada, and the Union had survived. Now, after the victorious North, in the spirit of Liberal Brotherhood, had occupied and plundered the defeated South, Britain's Liberal government, always a sucker for sucking-up to ruthless foreign success, apologized for a Birkenhead yard's having built, in the ordinary way of business, three ships for the Confederacy. I see that an 'impartial' history[25] says, 'During the Civil War, a British ship-building firm had built three commerce raiders for the Confederacy'.

The yard built three *ships*; it did not build three 'commerce raiders'. That the ships, when built and handed over to their legitimate owners, were used to raid the ocean commerce of Honest Abe's harsh 'democracy', had nothing to do with either the Birkenhead shipbuilders or the British Government.

The blockade of Southern cotton by the ships of the North

[25] *Britain and the World in the 19th Century*, op. cit.

put almost every Lancashire cotton-operative out of work, and his family – in those days of inefficiently organized relief – into starvation. The total number of persons involved in the crash of the cotton-spinning industry was conservatively estimated at the time at not fewer than 3,000,000. But the winning North had imposed that blockade, and the winning North, even then, knew how to put the bite on Britain.

The usual hocus-pocus of 'an impartial investigation' was solemnly observed, and the 'delegates' went to Geneva to eat and drink and generally to beat it up on their respective tax-payers' money. The international board at Geneva gave the sort of verdict that international boards have always given when Britain is involved: the North's impudent claim was fully endorsed; 'compensation' was calculated at £3,000,000, and promptly paid by the 'honest' Liberals, only too happy to seek to appease unappeasable hostility.

Of all the wars which have happened in this world, the American Civil War has probably had the most profound effect upon the destiny of Great Britain.

The cotton-industry imperilled by the North's blockading of Southern cotton, the British government, resolving that never again should Lancashire – and, indeed, Britain's cotton-manufacturing industry – be starved of raw material, looked around for an alternative source of cotton. The British government found it in Egypt.

Now, Egypt, which had recently been equipped by French capital and engineering with the Suez Canal, was recognized as having fallen within the French 'sphere of influence'; a little more time, and it would become as much a French colony as Algiers had been since the completion of its conquest in 1847.

But Britain needed cotton from a source that she could control – and the only controllable source was in Egypt. It was decided, as a 'must' of British foreign policy, that the French be pushed out of Egypt, and that the country – nominally a fief of the Turkish sultanate – be seized by Britain. Altogether, counting the Abyssinian expedition of 1868, under Napier, which may now be seen as part of the 'grand strategy' of isolating Egypt by closing access from the south and south-east, the conquest of Egypt and the Soudan took the British exactly thirty years, from 1868 to 1898, the year in which Kitchener routed the troops of the Mahdi at Omdurman, and gave the young Winston Churchill his first taste of real battle.

But 'alternative sources of supply' fit badly into the economic system of the United States of America. Egyptian cotton and – later – Rhodesian tobacco, even if they could not come under the control of Washington, must not be permitted to remain under the control of Downing Street. The carrying out of the American plan was, naturally enough, not effected within a decade; but it was eventually carried through. What made it easier of accomplishment was that, during the re-establishment of the American monopolies in cotton and tobacco, the United States government was always 'the ally' of the British. To-day, Egypt seems to have become a satrapy of Imperial Russia; Rhodesia has been alienated from the Mother Country and seems to be destined to form a powerful state in the rapidly-approaching Federal Union of South Africa, Portuguese East Africa, Portuguese West Africa, Rhodesia and an ex-German West Africa which will certainly become officially what it has never ceased to be in fact: German.

Holmes's attitude towards the United States of America was always as friendly – and admiring – as that of the Prince Consort. Holmes always asserted his belief in the eventual union of Great Britain and the United States of America – a wish-inspired prophecy which has been accomplished fact since 1941. Later, I shall examine the (more emotional than intellectual) reason for Holmes's pro-American sentiment.

2

University Years

The Dean of Christ Church, in the year in which Sherlock Holmes went up to Oxford, was the Very Reverend Dr Henry George Liddell, DD (1811–1898), to-day remembered only as the father of the original 'Alice' of *Alice in Wonderland* and its sequel, but in the 1870s very much a bigwig in his own right. Before becoming Dean of Christ Church, Dr Liddell had been Headmaster of Westminster School, and before that Chaplain to the Prince Consort. Talent and charm were never enough, in the mid-nineteenth century, to secure plum appointments to respectable and pious gentlemen of the Cloth; birth – or, at least, a good 'connexion' – was essential; and Liddell had both.

Henry George Liddell, Dean of Christ Church, was a cousin of Sir Henry Thomas Liddell, Baronet, 2nd Baron Ravensworth of the second creation; presently – in 1874 – to be raised two ranks in the peerage, and created Earl of Ravensworth, with an additional barony, that of Eslington, thrown in for good measure.

Dean Liddell's wife – Lorina Reeve, of Lowestoft – was of no particular birth, but like many women of a social rank far inferior to that of her husband, Mrs Liddell could, and invariably did, play the Grand Lady. *She* was the aristocrat of Allington – not the easy-going Dean.

Coming up to Christ Church in the autumn of 1872, Sherlock Holmes missed, by a few months, one of the most remarkable episodes in Oxford's long history – not even excluding the riot of a year or two back at Christ Church.

France had been defeated, and ruined Paris had at last been liberated from the Communist destroyers. Britain had come out of the Franco-Prussian affair with sadly diminished prestige: for all that the Prince of Wales begged his Mother, in tears, that she would order Britain to go to the help of France, Victoria, only too keenly aware that her eldest daughter and principal confidante was the wife of the German Crown Prince, refused. Only the grand harlots, both English and of mixed Continental nationalities, literally kept the flag flying in beleaguered Paris – the Union Flag flew proudly and defiantly over Cora Pearl's splendid mansion at 101 rue de Chaillot, which had been converted into a military hospital by its well-kept owner. Sarah Bernhardt made the same patriotic use of her own mansion; and altogether, the *grandes horizontales* came out of the disastrous war with far more credit than the respectable heads of government earned.

Two of these *poules de luxe* – Caroline Hassé and Caroline Letessier – were, though exceedingly good-natured (a contemporary described Letessier as 'one of the sweetest of the gay ladies'), also so exceedingly shameless that neither bothered to pretend to a stage-career. They were just whores – though most expensive ones. Letessier enjoyed a semi-permanent protector in the Crown Prince of Monaco; Hassé went from one excessively rich 'protector' to the next. The year 1872 saw them in England, to which dull but wealthy and immoral place the two young ladies had come whilst the authorities cleaned up battered and burned Paris.

One day, the two young ladies signed the register at what was then Oxford's best hotel,[1] the Randolph; they had arrived amongst the dreaming spires at the invitation of some precociously worldly undergraduates. The management of the Randolph knew the trollops who promenaded the High; it did not know the gay ladies of Paris – and what English whore ever had such clothes, such presence, such manners, such self-possession? exhibited so few of the outward signs of inward disgrace?

A day or two later, we find the two Carolines – straight

[1] It has had a change of ownership since then.

from the more exciting atmosphere of the Cremorne Gardens in London – playing croquet on the lawns at Allington; guests of Dean and Mrs Liddell. They had, so the story goes, been introduced as two young refugees, of the highest respectability, from France. The Dean and his lady made Caroline Letessier and Caroline Hassé welcome. They had tea *à l'anglaise*, they made themselves agreeable, as only the French consciously may, to Mrs Dean, and they were happy to be taught the rudiments of croquet by the four Liddell girls, Lorina, Alice (of *Wonderland* fame), Rhoda and Violet. Seven-year-old Frederick and four-year-old Lionel must assuredly have gathered about, attracted, as children (but especially male children) always are by female beauty. The afternoon was a complete success, and if the practical jokers who had brought the two glittering tarts thought to have embarrassed the Liddells, they had reckoned, not only without the *savoir faire* of the two Carolines, but also without that of the two Liddells.

The story is always told as though the joke resides in the fact that the Dean and his lady had no idea of the nature of their two beautiful French guests; but I have cast doubt on the innocence of the Dean and his lady in another book.[2]

The Dean's cousin, Lord Ravensworth, a privileged royal servant, had married, in 1820, Isabella Horatia, daughter of one of the most notorious rakes of all time, Lord George Seymour, MP, brother of the 1st Marquess of Hertford. Not only had Paris known Lord George well since just after the end of the Napoleonic Wars; Paris even now recalled him as a vigorous voluptuary of over seventy, who would have kept his son-in-law, Lord Ravensworth (and through him, Ravensworth's cousin, the Dean) completely *à la page*, so far as the gay life of Paris was concerned. Dean and Mrs Liddell can have had no doubts as to the identity and occupation of their French guests – as I have explained in another place, no one more admired the successful strumpet in the Golden Age of Harlotry than the Utterly Respectable.

But not, I maintain, from any 'innocence'. The Victorian

[2] *Fanfare of Strumpets*, London: W. H. Allen, 1971.

woman knew as much of the 'facts of life' as her 'liberated' descendant of to-day – perhaps more. Mr Baring-Gould tells us that, soon after reaching Oxford, Holmes struck up a fairly close friendship – as close a friendship as may subsist between a freshman and an established don – with the Reverend Charles Dodgson; Holmes being attracted to the man by his ingenious mathematical mind. If Mr Baring-Gould has not exaggerated the closeness of this friendship, it must have been the one certain way to put Holmes into the bad graces of Mrs Liddell – and so prevent Holmes's coming to be accepted by Oxonians as 'one of us'.

Mrs Liddell had a broad-minded attitude even towards some of the more thought-provoking clerical celibates who came to take tea with her and the Dean; but she drew the line, as they say, at the 'saintly' author of *Alice in Wonderland*, not only forbidding Alice Pleasance (a pretty name for a pretty little girl!) to walk or even speak with Mr Dodgson, but banning 'Lewis Carroll' from her house.

What Oxford made of this open ostracism of Dodgson, we are, curiously enough, not told by any of Dodgson's contempories; even his enemies ignore the situation in their letters and diaries. But Mrs Liddell's 'innocence' was not such that she could not see, in Dodgson's habit of taking very small girls away with him for a seaside holiday, and photographing them naked in his rooms, something not merely eccentric but perverted – and dangerous. Holmes could not have made a worse choice than in taking Dodgson for a friend.

Already equipped by his informal education and picturesque upbringing to qualify for the mistrust with which Oxford, then, tended to regard all nonconformers, Holmes, in embarking on an 'irregular' friendship – as all between undergraduate and don was likely to be thought, in the 'hearty' Oxford of the day – was putting himself outside the possibility of recognition as an acceptable newcomer.

As he said to Watson, one night in the winter of Golden Jubilee Year, as they sat before the coal-fire in Baker Street, he had made few friends at Oxford. "You never heard me talk of Victor Trevor? He was one of the only friends I made during the two years I was at college." A remark in which I find the first sentence the more significant: "You never heard me talk of Victor Trevor?"

As they sit before the fire, with the cold brown fog pressing against the window-panes, but heightening the sense of intimacy for all the other side the fog-beleaguered windows, Holmes and Watson have lived together now for six years; shared each other's private lives; learned, in how many such 'confabs' over the blazing fire, how much of each other's secrets! And yet, "You never heard me talk of Victor Trevor?"

Why? As Holmes, prompted by we know not what to recall one of his few Oxford friends, goes on to tell Watson of Victor Trevor and the first essay in 'professional' detection that Watson is to record under the name of *The 'Gloria Scott'*, we see that there is nothing shameful or even indiscreet connected with the memory of Trevor. Far from it: Holmes not only brilliantly demonstrates his congenital (but also consciously trained) 'ratiocinative' gift – as Edgar Allan Poe would have called it – he does more: he relieves Trevor's father of the burden and terror of blackmail. The fact that the transposition cipher 'broken' by Holmes is even simpler than that substitution cipher which reveals the pirates' treasure in Poe's *Gold Bug* can cast no demerit on the young criminologist – it is possible that in both cases, the cipher-crackers could have dealt with cryptograms ten times more complicated. (It is noteworthy that Holmes was rarely called upon to 'crack' codes or ciphers; when he had to, they turned out always to be of the simplest kind – luckily for Holmes!)

In any case, it was less the 'ratiocinative' side of Holmes's puzzle-solving talent which was on display at Donnithorpe Manor – the home of the Trevors – than the observational capacity that no one valued more highly than he.

Holmes asks the elder Trevor a few questions, which change imperceptibly into statements; though, curiously for a man still little more than a boy, Holmes is not guilty of the desire to mystify which has become a habit by the time that Holmes meets Watson in 1881. ("How are you? You have been in

Afghanistan, I perceive . . .") In telling Trevor Senior certain hitherto hidden facts in Trevor's life, Holmes not only explains how he knows these facts – or, rather, why he thinks them probable – but explains as he goes along.

"You boxed a good deal in your younger days."
"Right again," says the elder Trevor. "Did you know it by my nose?"
"No, by your ears. I am a boxing man myself, and I have observed how the sport can flatten and thicken the ears."
"Anything else?"
"By the callosities on your hands, I should say that you have done a great deal of digging."
"I made my money in the gold fields."
"You have been in New Zealand and you have visited Japan."
"True."

The trouble – as others were later to find out – was that, once a questioner had permitted Holmes to start asking questions, and from there, to start making statements, sooner or later a statement would emerge that the questioner would rather had stayed unspoken. As here . . .

"And you have been closely associated with someone whose initials were J.A. It is someone you were afterwards eager to forget."

When old Trevor has recovered from the mild syncope into which the recollection of 'J.A.' has plunged him, he is courageous enough (or Holmes is persistent enough) to ask the reasons for Holmes's having mentioned 'J.A.'. Holmes, still only eighteen, and aware that he is the Trevors' guest, enquires solicitously,
"I hope I have said nothing to pain you?"
"Well," said Trevor, ruefully, accepting the fact that Holmes will continue, whether Trevor likes it or not, "you certainly touched upon a rather tender point. How do you know, and how much do you know?" (Watson, as chronicler, observes here that the old man 'spoke now in a half-joking way, but a look of terror still lurked at the back of his eyes'.

Even at eighteen, Holmes must have been a terrifying, as well as an unusual, house-guest.)

"You'll remember," Holmes explained, "that the other day we were all three of us out on the lake with the boat. You bared your arm to draw in a fish, and I saw that the letters 'J.A.' had been tattooed in the bend of the elbow. The pink pigment used is peculiar, known only to Japanese artists. The letters are still perfectly legible, but an attempt had obviously been made to obliterate them with acid."

Holmes is correct. This, by the way, is not the last time that Holmes's investigatory activities will bring him into contact with acid. It is, however, the first and last time that he encountered the peculiar pink pigment, known only to Japanese artists. The mystery here is that Holmes should have recognized it for what it was. How did a boy of twenty make himself so expert on Japanese tattooing? But that he was greatly interested in the subject of tattooing we know, and that may account for what strikes the ordinary man as quite exceptional knowledge in one so young. Six years later – in 1878 – Holmes wrote and published a monograph, *Upon Tattoo Marks*,[3] which indicates – and vindicates – his deep interest in the subject.

Out of this first 'professional' venture into detective work, Holmes emerged not only with credit, but with a firm resolution to regard the Detective Art (or Science) as his vocation. From that resolution, Holmes was never to budge.

At eighteen, after having spent nearly eleven years on the Continent of Europe – seven of those eleven years exclusively

---

[3] *Upon Tattoo Marks*, by W. Sherlock. London: privately printed, 1878. This, though Holmes's first published *book*, was not his first printed writing. In the September, 1877, number of *The British Antiquarian*, Vol. XXIII, No. 9, there is an article signed by Holmes, 'Upon the Dating of Documents'. Mr Baring-Gould points out that this article 'deals in the main with the problem of handwritings from the sixteenth century onwards'. With regard to *Upon Tattoo Marks*, the same eminent Sherlockian critic remarks that it 'includes one of the first scholarly examinations of the pigments used extensively by Japanese and Chinese artists'.

14 Chancery Lane Safe Deposit. Not the oldest, but still one of the most famous safe-deposits in the world. Holmes was amongst the experts invited to test the deposit's security, and that he used it to store his most confidential papers speaks highly for his opinion of 'the Chancery Lane' *(Contrad Research Library)*

15 Holmes the Motorist. Caught fortuitously as a passing photographer 'snapped' Marble Arch – shining clean after its wash-up for the Coronation of the previous year – Holmes, at the (English near-side) wheel of his 89.5 H.P. Darracq turns to speak to a passenger at the back. The lady by his side, in the motoring cap, is almost certainly the Countess von und zu Grafenstein, whose husband's honour Holmes was about to save (October, 1903) *(Contrad Research Library)*

16 Sidney Paget's sketch of Sherlock Holmes, probably made about 1891 – the first time that the immortal features of the world's greatest detective were committed to paper by a competent artist. The sketch clearly shows the results of the nervous breakdown that Holmes suffered from 1887 onwards. This, or variants of it, are most popular in Britain (*Contrad Research Library*)

17 The American artist, Frederic Dorr Steele's equally well-known portrait of Sherlock Holmes; the most popular of all the portraits of Holmes outside Great Britain. Though dated some twenty-five years after the Paget sketch, it is intended to shew Holmes as a young, and not a middle-aged, man. *From the original sketch in the possession of Mr Vincent Starrett (Titular Investiture, 1944: 'A Study in Scarlet'), by whose kindness it is reproduced here (Contrad Research Library)*

in the South of France – it must be assumed that, whatever the *negative* evidence, Holmes spoke French fluently. It may also be argued that, since he did not get on particularly well with the English, his manners were 'foreign', and from that we are, I think, justified in deducing that Holmes preferred the French way of life.

Though he was not yet at Oxford when the famous visit of the two *grandes horizontales* to Dean and Mrs Liddell took place, I regard it as probable that this was not the only visit that Caroline Hassé and Caroline Letessier paid to England, and there are certain indications in the record which make it seem more than probable that they revisited Oxford at least once more, in which case, Holmes would have known about this second (and possibly there was even a third) visit. Letessier was certainly out of France when Cora Pearl sold her mansion in the ultra-respectable rue de Chaillot to Blanche d'Antigny, then being kept by – principally – Raphaël Bischoffscheim, partner in Bischoffscheim,[4] Goldschmidt & Cie, bankers, 39, boulevard Haussmann. That was in February, 1873; the first definite date for Letessier's presence in Paris after the flight in 1871 is 28th June, 1874, when, with Serge Narischkine, she attended Blanche d'Antigny's funeral, for which (since Blanche had lost her wealthy banker protector) Narischkine had paid.

If Hassé and Letessier – or one or the other – had revisited Oxford, it is more than likely that French-speaking Holmes, popular or not, would have been recruited as interpreter, since neither Hassé nor Letessier spoke English. If Holmes only saw the two *cocottes huppées* from a distance; or even if he had

---

[4] The anglicization of so many banking families of non-British origin was a notable phenomenon of the fermenting social 'mix' of the later nineteenth century. The bankers, in establishing branches of their businesses in London, established British branches of their families also. One of the Bischoffscheims – Henri Louis – of Bute House, South Audley Street, Grosvenor Square, married his daughter, Amelia Catherine, in 1882, to Sir Maurice Fitz-gerald, 2nd Baronet of Valentia and 20th Knight of Kerry, and an Extra Equerry to the Duke of Connaught. Bischoffscheim's eldest daughter, Ellen Odette, married, 1881, the 4th Earl of Desart, as his second wife.

merely heard of their visit to Dean and Mrs Liddell, no two persons could ever have had a greater influence on Holmes than did these two outrageous tarts.

Holmes's apparent insensitivity in respect of women puzzled Watson, himself no womanizer. It wasn't that Holmes despised or hated women or Woman. Rather the contrary; he was much given to eulogizing them – or Her – in a general kind of way ("Evil is the man for whom no woman mourns!"). But, in the personal sense, Watson observed; in the sense in which Woman really *matters* to Man, and Man to Woman: in that sense, women mattered nothing to Holmes. Watson, though no psychologist; and certainly no psychiatrist; was yet trained to clinical observation, and Holmes's attitude towards women seemed to Watson, in the years immediately after the men's meeting, so ambivalent, so contradictory, that Watson noted them all in his carefully-kept record.

He noted that Holmes seemed to dislike women, and that Holmes 'disgusted' them.[5] Elsewhere, Watson notes that Holmes was 'not an admirer'[6] of women; and that he had 'no interest in women' beyond the problem in hand.[7] Yet, with all this, Watson could not help but be struck, not only by Holmes's 'ingratiating way with women',[8] but also by his invariable 'gentleness'[9] with them. Holmes 'values their instinct',[10] and has such respect for their 'cleverness',[11] that on at least *five* occasions, when he was beaten by a woman, Holmes permits Watson to record the humiliating facts. Holmes is firm on certain opinions regarding what were then called 'the Fair Sex'. Women, said Holmes, were never to be trusted – not even the best of them[12] – and this opinion is

[5] *Dying Detective, Reigate Squires.*
[6] *Valley of Fear.*
[7] *Copper Beeches; Sign of the Four.*
[8] *Golden Pince-Nez.*
[9] *Case of Identity, Veiled Lodger.*
[10] *Twisted Lip, Boscombe Valley, Lion's Mane.*
[11] *Scandal in Bohemia.*
[12] *Sign of the Four.*

surely accounted for elsewhere, when Watson records Holmes's dictum that the motives of women are 'inscrutable'.[13]

From all this, it might have been gathered – and certainly Watson did so gather it – that Holmes, if not altogether a misogynist, was at any rate one of those neuters, those *Wallachen*, that the English climate seems so readily to engender. So far as England is concerned, this sexless type is very common; the sexual drive in such a type being, not so much sublimated as transformed into an energy of a different class, operating with a different end in view.

Such people make energetic politicians, social workers, lawyers, accountants – indeed, it may well be asked if such do not make up the majority of the English employed class, above the level of the day-labourer. Watson cannot be blamed for thinking that his friend belonged to this abnormally undersexed type. This explains Watson's unconcealable astonishment when Watson thinks that his friend has been 'attracted' for the first time in his life – to her whom Holmes (we think a little fatuously) called 'The Woman.'

Words have changed, since Golden Jubilee Year, not so much in semantic content as in usability; that is, though the meaning of certain words may not have changed, it is regarded as a solecism to use them in a certain way. Thus, what sounds to us to-day what Sherlock Holmes, in *his* day, would have called 'bleat',[14] had no such sound in Watson's or other contemporary ears when Sherlock summed up his marvelling opinion of Irene Adler in the declaration that the lady was 'the daintiest thing under a bonnet on this planet'.

Irene Adler outwitted Holmes – and inspired nothing but admiration in him by the feat. Holmes was trying to prevent Irene Adler's causing the gravest embarrassment to Wilhelm Gottsreich Sigismond von Ormstein, Grand-duke of Cassel-Felstein and hereditary King of Bohemia, by sending the King's passionate love-letters and an exceedingly compromising photograph to the future Queen. Mr Baring-Gould

[13] *Second Stain.*
[14] "Bleat, unmitigated bleat . . ." – *Red Circle.*

thought that the 'Wilhelm Gottsreich, etc . . .' was Watson's cover-up for a notorious womanizer of the day – Bertie, Prince of Wales; and others besides Mr Baring-Gould have thought the same.

Ingeniously as Holmes tried to trick Irene, she was too good for him. And she was, says Watson, the only woman of whom he had heard Holmes speak with affection.

Watson, too, moves 'tactfully' around the fact that Irene was no better than she should have been. He calls her an 'adventuress', which was the politest Victorian euphemism for 'Grande Horizontale'. Watson would have us believe that Holmes loved Irene despite the fact that she was a well-kept whore; had Watson known about the visit of Mesdemoiselles Hassé and Letessier to Oxford, he might have wondered if Holmes had not rather been attracted to Irene because, and not in spite, of her whoredom.

In admiring a successful whore, Holmes was in the very spirit of his age. As I have pointed out in my *Fanfare of Strumpets*,[15] the idolized heroine of the quarter-century from about 1850 to 1875 was the Grande Cocotte – especially the Grande Cocotte who came from the most humble origins; women such as Marie-Anne Detourbay, illegitimate daughter of a Rheims cloth-burler. As a young girl, the daughter of the cloth-burler earned a few centimes a day as a bottle-washer, ran away to Paris, changed her name to 'de Tourbey', and, as 'Madame de Tourbey', became one of the *grandes dames* of the Paris stage. She married Comte Edgard Victor de Loynes. There were dozens of stories of a similar plot: the enchanted onlookers saw dream after dream of Cinderella come true . . .

No one admired these women more than the Respectable, from the servants' hall to the Throne itself. I suggest that this admiration was based on a respect for these emancipated servant girls (one, Rosalie Léon, married Prince Piotr Wittgenstein, a multi-millionaire), who had defied, not merely convention, but the restrictive social forces of which purely artificial convention was the most apparent creation. I said in my book

[15] London: W. H. Allen, 1971.

on these extraordinary women, and the even more extraordinary admiration that they aroused; the envious respect that they commanded; that they were seen as the justification of a revolt against conventional marriage – an institution that, whether she admitted it or not, the average Victorian woman, of no matter which social class, was heartily sick.

The world of 1850 onwards saw them for what they really were – not something to be dismissed as mere whores; but the very spirit of Revolt; shewing others how to defy convention and grow rich on the defiance. Perhaps only subconsciously but still clearly, the convention-fettered age saw them as the successful revolutionaries, who would fracture the pattern of society, as philosophers, socialist politicians, *feuilletonistes* such as Henri Rochefort, Trades-union organizers and other agitators had been unable to do. The influence of such women came when, for the first time, contemporary society saw them, not as Outcasts, but as Outsiders – brilliant parasites whose intelligence had permitted them a life of complete individuality; which had permitted them to stand aside from the mainstream of habit-doomed human existence.

Holmes was such an Outsider. To him, more than to anyone else, these incarnate Spirits of Revolt would have made an irresistible appeal. What he saw – or perhaps only heard about – at Oxford in 1872 fixed his sexual pattern for ever; he admired the Golden Harlot – and when he met one, he was instantly her emotional slave . . . and (as Watson tells us) for ever.

Mr Baring-Gould, who has gone deeply into the events at this period of Holmes's life, explains that Holmes changed his University from Oxford to Cambridge; his College from Christ Church to Caius; not only because 'Cambridge offered a greater opportunity to study all the branches of science', but also because there had been a distinct break in normal academic routine when Holmes had telegraphed his brother, Mycroft, in London: 'Please find me London rooms. Enter my name for study of organic chemistry, Bart's. Explain all when we meet. Sherlock.'

Sherlock, Mr Baring-Gould explains, had decided that organic chemistry was one of the many subjects that he must now study if he was to fit himself for his chosen 'profession' of private consulting detective. Mr Baring-Gould says that Siger Holmes was 'furious'; that the father, hearing of this new Holmesian crotchet, agreed to make the son an allowance, but wrote to say that 'I wish never to set eyes upon you again'.

There is something decidedly mysterious about all this; and I feel that Mr Baring-Gould's researches have left much – far too much – to be explained.

Baring-Gould's carefully constructed time-table makes it appear that Holmes did not, as has sometimes been thought, 'cut and run' from Oxford in order to take up 'Stinks' at Bart's. Holmes kept his University terms from October, 1872 to August, 1874: the implication being that he 'studied organic chemistry' at Bart's during the Long Vacation.

But how . . . ? The great teaching hospitals of Britain keep the same terms as the Universities – in several cases, the hospital is actually a college of the university (London's University College Medical School and Hospital are excellent examples). Yet Holmes did manage to study organic chemistry at Bart's during the Long Vacation; but *where* did he study?

Did 'influence' open up the 'Path-Lab' to him during the Long Vacation, or did he make some advantageous arrangement with the hospital authorities, whereby he was allowed a run of the chemical labs in return for work as cleaner or nightwatchman? Perhaps it was this arrangement, already known and accepted in America, but still (in 1874) alien to the British way of doing things, which so angered Siger Holmes. (It would explain the promised allowance as an alternative to Holmes's filling carboys or admitting late-night callers through the splendid eighteenth-century gate . . .)

The proper way of studying organic and other chemistry would have been to go to Cambridge, then the 'scientific' centre of England, as, in many ways, it still is. (It was here, in 1919, that Rutherford first 'split the atom'.)

And this, precisely, is what Sherlock Holmes did. He became a freshman of Gonville and Caius, kept six terms, and left, a Junior Soph, without – inevitably, in the circumstances – a degree. However, his recollections of Cambridge are a great deal warmer than those of Oxford. Cambridge, in any case, not only didn't mind swots, it encouraged them; and Cambridge (as the history of the Boat Race makes clear) cultivated a special type of undergraduate who was supposed to be both a swot *and* a sportsman.

Cambridge, as it had done many times before in its close-on-a-thousand-year history, was again shewing the way; indicating the pattern that society would conform to for the next few centuries to come. Only a decade or so after Holmes had gone down from Cambridge, one of its most brilliant classical scholars, James Kenneth Stephen, of whom I shall make mention in another connection later, would be passionately arguing the case for compulsory Greek and Latin in our universities – the more passionately, as Stephen knew that he was defending an already lost cause.

The Era of the Practical had arrived; the Scientific Age had come – and Cambridge was its guidon-bearer.

That the Pattern-watchers had accepted this fact is seen clearly in the changing attitude towards, not only the *creative* scientists, but to their relatively non-creative ancillaries: the engineers, quantity-surveyors, analytical chemists, builders, and so on. The test of an inventor's quality, judged by the standards of the Era of the Practical, was that his invention should have proved itself by the supreme 'practical' proof: that it had made money (or saved avoidable expense).

The award of Honours always indicates new trends in developing importances. The men whose inventions were about to enrich the State were rewarded with knighthoods, soon improving to baronetcies; before the century (and Victoria's reign) were ended, the baronetcies would have improved to baronies: the inventor-peer would have arrived.

Doyen of these new-type favourites of fortune was Lyon Playfair, son of a Scotch Chief Inspector-general of Hospitals in the Presidency of Bengal. The Scotch, as Dr Johnson morosely (but accurately) commented, have always done well in England, but Lyon Playfair did even better than usual.

In contemporary reference-books, he is entitled, 'the eminent scientist', and so he was. He was lucky, too; being at Cambridge when Bertie, Prince of Wales, arrived as a reluctant undergraduate. Playfair's chemical 'conjuring tricks' interested the not-so-bright Bertie where Greek paradigms had lamentably failed to capture the Heir's never-very-fixable attention. It was Playfair who persuaded the Prince of Wales to let his hand be powdered and then plunged into a pot of boiling lead. General Bruce, the Prince's 'governor', violently protested; but Playfair assured all that the hand would come to no harm, and asked the Prince to trust that there was no danger. The Prince, either to oblige Playfair, or to spite Bruce – far more likely – plunged his hand into the boiling lead, withdrew it, and – as Playfair had predicted – wasn't a penny worse for his experience. Afterwards, the young Prince conceived a somewhat patronizing regard for 'my scientific friend', the rewards of that friendship being considerable, even by modern standards: a knighthood, baronetcy, peerage as Baron Playfair of St Andrews in the county of Fife, the Grand Cross of the Bath and a Privy Councillorship.

When Holmes arrived at Cambridge, the place of Playfair as 'Chief Scientist' had been taken by the even more brilliant John William Strutt, who had succeeded to the title, as the 3rd Baron Rayleigh, in Holmes's second year at Oxford; Strutt, Professor of Experimental Physics at Cambridge, was already Lord Rayleigh when Holmes arrived, to hasten, like some hitherto-faulted homing-pigeon, to the feet of this scientific Gamaliel.

Where Playfair had been a Scotchman, with an inventiveness always somewhat braked by a Scotchman's instinctive need to 'play canny' with life, Strutt was an Irish aristocrat, great-grandson of the 1st Duke of Leinster (James FitzGerald, 20th Earl of Leinster), whose daughter, Lady Charlotte, married to an obscure Army colonel, was created Baroness Rayleigh, with remainder to the heirs male of her body born in lawful wedlock.

Through Rayleigh's veins flowed the turbulent blood of the FitzGeralds, but modified, in an advantageously 'practical' fashion, by that of his mother, whose father was an officer of Royal Engineers. Rayleigh was a 'philosopher' in the old aristocratic tradition of Worcester, Boyle, Cavendish, Lavoisier – the seeker after pure knowledge, neither retarded by poverty nor hurried by greed. To this – which explains Rayleigh's success and influence *at the time* – he added that 'practical' attitude towards research and discovery which shewed him to be, at some point, a convert to his own period.

Rayleigh was one of the three simultaneous discoverers of the element helium (already perceived in the spectroscopic band of the Sun). Rayleigh, indeed, had already named it by the time that he and two other inventors – all three unknown to the other two, and working independently – discovered that helium was to be found on Earth. He also discovered argon.

Rayleigh, too, concerned himself with more 'down to earth' substances than helium. A vigorous opponent of bad or adulterated food, Rayleigh bred a herd of cattle to give milk which was non-tubercular and better-than-normal in other ways. Meeting with some opposition in the marketing of this superior milk, Rayleigh founded a limited liability company, Lord Rayleigh's Dairies Limited, which established tea-shops – 'dairies', they were called – to sell a glass of milk and a 'rational' bun to girl-clerks and typists for three-half-pence. From a well-designed and well-built 'central depot' near the British Museum, the milk-floats and bun-filled vans of Lord Rayleigh's Dairies Ltd left several times a day to stock up his tea-shops. If, to-day, the shop attached to the 'central depot' is a dim Italian espresso-café, one may blame the times, not Lord Rayleigh's vision. Not even God could have foreseen what could have happened to Britain when it was ordered, by the Faceless Ones, to become the unflushed privy of the world . . .

That Holmes was as happy at Cambridge as he had been unhappy at Oxford, we have his own testimony to prove. At last, so Holmes believed, he was the round peg in the round hole

– an undergraduate of an University where every eccentricity was welcome, provided that it were of the *constructive* sort.

At Cambridge, Holmes emerged from his shell; we may imagine that, at first, taught painful lessons by the snubbing of Christ Church, Oxford, Holmes was timid in putting forward his views; in asserting himself. But, soon, the eager-to-learn Cantabs recognized an unusual mind; a mind with, in the modern expression, 'something to offer'. Holmes was not snubbed; he was accepted. "During my last year at the University," he told Watson, "there was a good deal of talk there about myself and my methods."

'Grand' as was Christ Church in the 1870s – a contemporary *University of Oxford Register* reads like a digest of *Debrett* – it was at Caius that Holmes made the first friend who was, in the English as well as in the general meaning of the word, an aristocrat: Reginald Musgrave, a member of one of those few families which may trace unbroken descent from the earliest days of the Anglo-Saxon invasions. The note (in *Debrett*) that the family 'came over with the Conqueror' was misunderstood to mean that the family had not settled in England before 1066.

The Musgrave of Holmes's Cambridge days belonged to a family whose main branch, settled at Edenhall in Westmorland, had been baronets since 1611. By the 1870s, this old family had connected itself by marriage with very many of the most influential families in the Kingdom, among which were several prominent as members of the 'Marlborough House Set' – the friends of the Prince (and sometimes of the Princess) of Wales.

Reginald Musgrave's aunt, Augusta, was first married to Henry Bonham, colonel of the crack 10th Hussars (Prince of Wales's Own), in which both the Prince of Wales and his son and heir, Albert Victor, Duke of Clarence, had held and were to hold commissions. On the colonel's death, Aunt Augusta married the 2nd Earl of Stradbroke. One of her daughters, Lady Sophia Rous, married George H. Heaviside, late 6th Dragoons, whose family name has been immortalized by his more scientific cousin in the Earth's atmospheric layer named after him, 'the Heaviside Layer'. Lady Stradbroke lived in London at 33 Belgrave Square.

The widow of Sir Richard Courtenay Musgrave, 11th baronet, was to marry, in 1882, the 3rd Baron Brougham and Vaux; this lawyer-founded title was not then dispossessed of its wealth, and Lord and Lady Brougham and Vaux's three residences: Brougham, Penrith; Château Eléonore, Alpes Maritimes; and 36 Chesham Place, London, SW, must have been visited by Holmes – for he maintained his friendship with Reginald Musgrave for many years after Cambridge days. The connection between the Musgraves and the Prince of Wales was further to be tightened in 1895, when Sir Richard George Musgrave, 12th baronet of Edenhall, was to marry the Honourable Eleanor Harbord, daughter of the 5th Baron Suffield, Lord of the Bedchamber to HRH the Prince of Wales since 1872, and Superintendent of HRH's Stables after 1889, following the enforced flight abroad of the incumbent, Lord Arthur Somerset.[16]

It would – and could – not be held against Holmes that, 'holding his own' in the company of the aristocratic Musgrave, Holmes was not to dismiss his family (as he did later to Watson) as mere 'yeomen', but rather to dwell overlong on the two baronetcies and several peerages in the Holmes family.

'Musgrave,' says Baring-Gould, 'was not generally popular at Caius, although it always seemed to Holmes that what was objected to as his pride was really an attempt to cover extreme natural diffidence' – in which respect Holmes and Musgrave had much in common.

> 'In appearance, Musgrave was exceedingly aristocratic – high-nosed and large-eyed, with languid and yet courtly manners. He was indeed a scion of one of the oldest families in the kingdom, though his branch was a younger one which had separated from the more celebrated northern Musgraves in the early years of the sixteenth century, and had at length established itself

[16] For details of this scandalous affair, *see* my *Clarence*, The Life of the Duke of Clarence and Avondale, KG (London: W. H. Allen & Co., 1972.)

in West Sussex, where Hurlstone, the manor house of the Musgraves, was said to be the oldest inhabited building in the county. Something of his birthplace seemed to cling to the man. Holmes could never look at him without thinking of grey archways and mullioned windows.

'Now and again Holmes and Musgrave would drift into talk, and more than once Musgrave expressed a keen interest in Holmes's methods of observation and inference.

'It was an important acquaintanceship for Sherlock, for only four years later he was to handle the strange case of the Musgrave Ritual, a chain of events so singular that it was the first to arouse national interest in Holmes as a solver of mysteries.'

What, in fact, made the case of the Musgrave Ritual so influential, not so much in shaping Holmes's chosen career, as in working inevitable success into that shaping, was the link between the mystery's solution and the contemporary Royal Family, one of whose most notable characteristics was an interest, both sentimental and antiquarian, in their own history.

At Hurlstone Manor, Holmes revealed the hidden significance of the mysterious Musgrave Ritual: the location of the ancient Regalia of England, supposedly destroyed by Cromwell's orders, or sold by his venal men, but buried for safekeeping against the day when regicides should have passed away (as all evil things, in their time, pass away) and a King should once more sit on the throne of Alfred the Great. Some parts of the Holmes record are missing, and the Musgrave papers do not mention the fact: but certain it is that the restored Regalia were not rendered up to their rightful Owner without her having graciously commanded the presence of the two young men who had been instrumental in bringing back from supposed oblivion treasures of such worth. This private audience of Her Majesty to which Holmes was commanded in the October of 1879 was almost certainly his first meeting with his Sovereign. There were to be many more such audiences before her death, twenty-two years later.

The pattern of Holmes's life called for his passing through some lean times between his coming down – degreeless, of course – from Cambridge in the July of 1877 and his establishing his unique detective skill in the matter of the Musgrave Ritual; indeed, as Holmes later confessed to Watson, the lean times did not end with Holmes's bowing his grateful thanks for his Sovereign's warm praise.

Perhaps, though, something of the sad nature of that year 'brushed off' on Holmes, even in his hour of success.

The year 1879 was no bright one for Britain. Not only had the nation's arms suffered severe and humiliating reversals in South Africa, at the hands of King Cetewayo's Zulus; the young Prince Imperial of France, only son (and only child) of the late Emperor Napoleon III and his beautiful Empress, was killed in circumstances which heaped shame on the conduct of his British brother-officers.

The Prince, who was a cadet at the Royal Military Academy ('The Shop'), Woolwich, had developed a schoolboy 'crush' on a slightly older officer, K. G. ('Kaygee') Slade, from whom the Prince Imperial was inseparable. When Slade was ordered out to South Africa, the Prince pleaded to be permitted to accompany him, and, against the earnest and personally argued objections both of his mother, the Empress,[17] and of Queen Victoria. The Prince would not listen: he wished to be with (particularly) Slade, Harrison and his other favourites.

One night, the Prince joined a routine patrol, which was ambushed by Zulus; the Prince, pierced by an assegai, was killed. The others, in a manner which did more credit to their horsemanship than to their manhood, escaped. Not for some days was a patrol organized to look for the body, which was brought back to England for a State funeral.

The two widows, Victoria and Eugénie, had grown very close since the collapse of the Second Empire had driven the Empress into exile in England. On appearances alone, it was an unlikely intimacy: Eugénie was much younger, extra-

---

[17] Not the '*ex*-Empress' Eugénie, as I have read even in the works of careful historians. The Third Republic was proclaimed on 4th September, 1870, but no instrument of Abdication was ever signed by Napoleon III. He died, at Camden House, Chislehurst, in 1873, still *de jure*, if not *de facto*, Emperor of the French.

ordinarily beautiful, one of the best-dressed women in the world, and not too intelligent. Victoria, on the other hand, had lost what small claims to beauty she had ever had; her figure was bad, and her face was disfigured with what the dermatologist call *acne rosacea*, and unkind people, 'gin blossom'. (Gladstone, staying at Balmoral, wrote back, scandalized, to his wife to say that the Queen laced her port with *whisky*!). Again, though Albert the Good, so far as is known, never looked at any woman other than his wife (and sometimes, to her openly expressed annoyance, not even her), Napoleon III not only had a number of mistresses, but made no secret of their existence, though he did send the Countess di Castiglione away from a Court ball because her 'see-through' dress – as Salammbô – was 'disrespectful to the Empress'. The women's memories of their husbands must have been different indeed!

Yet they met and liked each other. And the Empress's tragedy – the loss of her only son and child – pained the Queen almost as much as it tortured the now completely solitary mother.

It can have been no very cheerful monarch who offered her small hand to Mr Sherlock Holmes, and congratulated him, in a guttural voice, on his 'cleverness' in having found the Regalia that 'those dreadful people' had caused to be hidden so many years before.

In that part of the histories reserved to 'inventions, social improvements, etc', the year 1879 is marked as one of singular importance. After having annexed the Transvaal in 1877, the British Governor of Cape Colony, Sir Bartle Frere, demanded of the Zulu King, Cetewayo, that he disband his well-trained army of magnificent fighting men. Cetewayo refused, and the Zulu War broke out in 1879, two years after the annexation.

With the advantage of an intimate familiarity with his own country, Cetewayo struck first, struck hard and struck victoriously. The British expeditionary force, though equipped with the latest Martini-Henry repeating rifles, the Gatling machine-gun and quick-firing two-pounders, were no match for the Zulus, who surrounded and massacred them at Isandhlwana, leaving the way completely open for a Zulu invasion of Natal.

The defence of Rorke's Drift – a stone-built farmhouse with some screening yard-walls – stopped the Zulus, giving time for the British to assemble a superior force, and defeat Cetewayo at the battle of Ulundi, which effectively destroyed Zulu independence. This war, one must remember, was only one of the *one hundred and thirty* wars fought by the British between 1870 and 1900, and, like all the others, excited little interest in Britain. The British people expected wars; they expected that 'we' should win every one; and (since they never recognized a defeat when it happened) were convinced that 'we' always had won. Except for those bereaved by the various battles – they included the Empress Eugénie – people, as they say to-day, 'couldn't care less' about the wars that it profited generals to fight, and that Tommy was paid to fight in. So that the column headed 'Trade, Commerce, Social Improvements, Inventions, etc' in the histories could spare no thought for such ephemeral trivialities as the Zulu War.

What the column did have of importance were a pair of 'social improvements' which, regarded as mere novelties at the time, are now seen to be amongst the most world-changing of all inventions: the Telephone and the Incandescent Electric Light.

As a mere provider of illumination, the new lamp was not essential: gas, coal-oil and candles could still provide illumination for all ordinary purposes, as, in so many parts of the world, those older illuminants are still doing satisfactorily.

But the incandescent electric lamp – a light *which did not consume oxygen* – was the third essential when the invention of the Greathead Shield made deep tunnelling possible, when the electric lift made access to and departure from the low-level tunnels possible. The gas and oil lights used on the shallow Metropolitan and District lines – the first was opened in May, 1863 – could not have served to illuminate stairs, platforms and carriage on the 'tubes'.

And, since one thing leads to another – especially in the

79

world of invention – the Telephone, first realized in practical form by Johan Philipp Reis in 1861, and made practical (using Hughes's carbon microphone) by Bell, Gray and Edison, by 1878, was developed into wireless telephony by the Forgotten Man of electrical communication, Aubrey Fessenden, who broadcast speech over a distance of a mile in 1900.

Then there was that other great world-changer, the 'horseless carriage', made practical by Gottfried Daimler in 1877, and put on the market, as far as Britain was concerned, in 1879.

The internal combustion engine had occupied the attention of inventors since the middle of the seventeenth century, when the Honourable Robert Boyle, first Secretary of the Royal Society for the Advancement of Science, experimented with a gunpowder-powered internal-combustion engine. Imitating him, but replacing the Boyle gunpowder by nitro-glycerine, Edison nearly blew his hand off, two centuries later.

The oil-fired i/c engine was, in fact, 'perfected' in 1826; 'perfected', that is, in so much as it 'worked', and could act as a prime-mover to some fairly complicated machinery. The i/c engine was set up in what was then a remotely suburban part of Paris, with few inhabitants, and – one would have supposed – few to object to the noise. But even 'uninhabited' Parc Montsouris in 1827 had sufficient inhabitants to be offended by the noise of the i/c engine, and on complaints from the neighbours the pioneering user of the engine had to revert to older and less noisy power-providers.

Then, in 1877, came the relatively quiet Daimler engine, using the Otto 'four-stroke cycle'; the engine which, with only the most trivial modifications, is in universal employment to-day.

The first Daimlers were on sale in 1879, true 'horseless-carriages'; benzine-powered with the dangerous 'hot coil' ignition (the electric spark was to come later). Yet, within twenty-five years, the 'motor-car' was to race at over 100 mph, and triumphantly survive the rigours of a Paris-Madrid journey.

Once again, Royal interest and patronage accelerated the development of the invention – as, in later and less happy

18 The Genius of Disguise. Only the hawk-like nose, the piercing eyes and slitted lids (compare the Paget sketch, above) enable us to recognize the Master in this contemplative old 'Arab,' as he sat smoking his *chibouk* in the forbidden city of Mecca. Cameras were as disallowed as Infidels in the Mecca of 1893; after 'the Return,' Holmes posed for this photograph, one of the few to have survived from Watson's otherwise vanished album *(Contrad Research Library)*

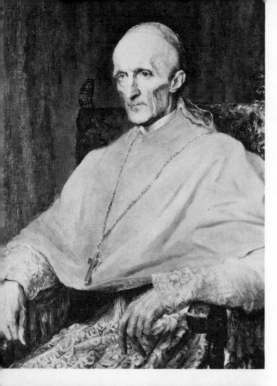

19 Cardinal Edward Manning, one of the most notable figures of the Victorian Age, equally popular with the Queen as with her voluptuary son, neither of whom was repelled by Manning's 'Leftish' championship of still-unorganized labour. It was he who called the Vatican's attention to Holmes's skill and discretion, and who was primarily responsible for the great detective's having been employed to solve the several Vatican-orientated mysteries described in this book. *From the painting by George Frederick Watts; copyright of the National Portrait Gallery*

20 King Edward VII. A graceful compliment to the private consulting dectective who had done so much to avert scandal and the consequences of indiscretion from Europe's Royal families? Or merely a natural tendency to imitate those whom we admire? King Edward VII's dress—inverness in Glenuquhart over-check and billycock hat—could almost have been copied from Holmes's dress in the original *Study in Scarlet* illustration. The King, though, presumably drew the line at a *meerschaum* pipe. Incidentally, the tweed inverness was made by Stovel & Co. (now Stovel & Mason), of 23, Conduit Street, W., the billycock hat came from Herbert Johnson, of 38, New Bond Street, and the cigar came from Benson & Hedges, of 13, Old Bond Street. *Photograph by Lafayette (Contrad Research Library)*

years, warfare was to do. Driving the 'crack' expresses of the main railway lines was then a top aristocratic sport[18] – the Prince of Wales, the Duke of Sutherland, Lord Claud Hamilton (who had the advantage of being a railway director) were star-names amongst the rich amateur engine-drivers – but as interest in engine-driving faded, the potential of a new form of fast travel struck the ex-engine drivers as 'just the thing'.

I have already mentioned the first practical submarine, invented in 1878 by the Reverend Mr George William Garrett, curate of Holy Cross, Manchester. Seven years later, in the year in which – note this well – the crisis developed that Holmes was to handle in the following year, and which is noted in Watson's records as *The Delicate Case of the King of Scandinavia*, the Prince of Wales went to Landskrona.

We shall come to this 'delicate' case later; here let it suffice for me to say that the Prince's visit to Landskrona, ostensibly to attend the launching of the submarine – the *Nordenfeldt II* – that Mr Garrett had designed and built in partnership with Nordenfeldt, inventor of the machine-gun named after him, was regarded at the time as paying too much honour to even an English clergyman. If, people asked at the time, the British Government was interested in submarines, why didn't they leave the inspection of the Garrett-Nordenfeldt submarine to an Admiralty expert? There was, contemporary opinion decided, something somewhat fishy about the visit. Holmes could have told them better.

Then, to round off the list of notable inventions, there was the Phonograph, an invention which had an inbuilt appeal for the Victorians, in that it was both a novelty and 'scientific'. Crowds packed the Royal Institute to hear Professor Tyndall explain the working of the Phonograph, and demonstrate how

---

[18] It was possibly the growing objections of the passengers which killed the 'sport'. It survived on the Continent into our own generation, the last notable amateur engine-driver being the late King Boris of Bulgaria, who consistently drove the engines of the Bulgarian State Railways unti his death in 1944.

the machine, given the spoken line, "Come into the garden, Maud", would repeat it – rather tinnily, it was true, but accurately, none the less.

Holmes came down from Cambridge in the summer of 1877, leaving behind a record which is as full of unanswered questions as it is of certified facts.

One question: why did Holmes not join the Cambridge University Volunteer Rifle Detachment? The subscription was small, and the less wealthy members could be supplied with rifles out of the funds. It can hardly have been because of the large proportion of more aristocratic undergraduates – Prince Albert Victor of Wales was to join the 'Cambridge Rifles' in 1883 – for by now Holmes had made at least one aristocratic friend, Reginald Musgrave, who would have stood sponsor for Holmes had he wished to join the 'Rifles'.

Before me, as I write, is the first edition of my book, *In the Footsteps of Sherlock Holmes*. The pictorial dust-jacket has a simple but effective design of a part of the Ordnance Survey map for Surrey, on which are the three objects which have come to be symbolic of Holmes: a deer-stalker cap (but known as a 'tweed helmet' in the days of Holmes's emergence as a private consulting detective), a curly tobacco-pipe and -- *a magnifying-glass*.

We have become, we tens of millions of us,[19] so used to that magnifying-glass as a *collector* of evidence that we have quite failed to consider it *as evidence in itself*.

If one were to ask the average person why Holmes used a magnifying-glass, one would almost certainly have some such answer as, "Well, to see something; to examine something; to examine a clue . . ." To how many has it occurred to wonder why a young man of twenty-seven (which was all that Holmes was when Watson first met him in January, 1881) should need a glass to see anything? In that historic case that Watson has titled, A *Study in Scarlet*, and dated for us as on 4th

[19] Oh yes! Perhaps 'hundreds of millions' would be more accurate. In America alone, the adventures of Holmes sell 5,000,000 copies a year.

March, 1881, Holmes was, as I have just remarked, only twenty-seven. You will recall that, Holmes's help being called upon by Inspector Tobias Gregson, of 'A' Division, the three men, Holmes, Watson and Gregson, hail a cab and are driven off to Lauriston Gardens, Brixton Road, where, in an otherwise empty house, a man has been found dead.

I have remarked (*writes Watson*) that the wallpaper had fallen away in parts. In this particular corner of the room a large piece had peeled off, leaving a yellow square of coarse plastering. Across this bare space there was scrawled in blood-red letters a single word –
RACHE
"What do you think of that?" cried the Scotland Yard detective, with the air of a showman exhibiting his show.

Now, if a *large* piece of wallpaper had peeled away, then an equally *large* 'yellow square of coarse plastering' must have been left. And, not improbably, the word *Rache* was written in 'blood-red' characters not small.

Holmes remains unimpressed by the two Yard men's 'deductions', that I have omitted as irrelevant here.

". . . I have not had time (*said Holmes*) to examine this room yet, but with your permission I shall do so now."
As he spoke, he whipped a tape measure and a large round magnifying glass from his pocket. With these two implements he trotted noiselessly about the room, sometimes stopping, occasionally kneeling, and once lying flat on his face . . .

Why Watson, the fully-qualified medical practitioner (MD (Lond), MRCS, LRCP) never remarks upon the oddity of a young man's carrying around the sort of high-powered single lens with which shaky old men read newspapers in public libraries is that Watson has, of course, noted Holmes's defective eyesight – and, naturally, the cause – but sees no reason to mention it in the record. It was Holmes's precocious presbyopia which must have prevented his joining the 'Cambridge Rifles' – something else to make heavier what the Americans call his 'chip on the shoulder'.

That Holmes was unduly sensitive about his defective vision

83

now explains that sense of exaggeration, of over-emphasis, that we feel when he is talking of himself: "Observation is my business!" he declaims; the force of his utterance having served to conceal, for nearly a century, the triteness of the remark. (For how could he have even begun to be even a third-rate detective without having been able to observe?)

What caused this optic deficiency? Was it hereditary, the result of disease, traumatic? Had it been induced by drugs? Was this the professionally-respected secret that Holmes shared with Watson, and perhaps with no other living person?

Like the majority of human beings, Holmes 'compensates', and – again like the majority of human beings – tends to over-compensate. He doesn't produce his magnifying-glass furtively, but with a flourish – merely keeping well away from any *verbal* suggestion that he needs it. He treats it as the toff treats his single eyeglass – as an otherwise useless adornment: but an adornment, none the less; and as something more – what to an Hindoo is a caste-mark. The toff of the past used the functionless eyeglass to proclaim to the world that he *was* a toff; Holmes used the *necessary* magnifying-glass to proclaim his status of detective to the world. (And no one thought to ask him if he really *needed* the glass!)

3

The Bleak Beginnings

Was Holmes married? Did he leave – by mutual consent – a Mrs Sherlock Holmes in order to set up housekeeping with Watson in Baker Street?

These are serious questions, and I ask them not without some strong evidence that the answer to both may well be 'yes'.

A search of the registers at Somerset House ought to yield the final evidence in a matter of minutes; and here let me say that diligent search has failed to reveal any marriage of which the male partner was 'Sherlock Holmes'.

But, as Mr Baring-Gould has usefully shewn, Holmes's baptismal names in full are 'William Sherlock Scott', and there was, in the 1870s and 1880s, and there is to-day, no law of England which demanded the *full* names of the contracting parties on the marriage certificate – or even the true names (marriage even under two aliases being held lawful, if there are no legal or religious impediments to the union).

I have a note of some twenty-five Holmeses – all Williams – married in the Home Counties (eleven in London or one of its suburbs) between 1872 (when Holmes was eighteen, and went up to Christ Church) and 1877 (when he was twenty-three and came down from Cambridge).

The reason for supposing that Holmes may have been married when he came down from his second University – and it would explain so much, might we assume that he was – is a discovery that I made when doing some research into that part of the Parish of Bloomsbury in the environs of the British Museum.

On 1877, on coming down from Cambridge, Holmes, as he told Watson, went to live, not with his parents, or even with his brothers, but by himself in Bloomsbury.

The words that Holmes uses to describe his move from Cambridge to London call for close attention.

When I first came up to London I had rooms in Montague Street, just round the corner from the British Museum . . .

Now, even the present writer has interpreted that 'I had rooms' as 'I took rooms'; but, in fairness to Holmes's precision (and also his honesty), he does not say so. It has been *assumed* that he said so, and, in this respect, I have not been without my share of that guilt which comes from not paying sufficient attention to what has been written. What Holmes told Watson was, 'I had rooms', But Holmes didn't say in whose house, and as Bloomsbury was as much a district of boarding-houses then as it is to-day, Watson accepted the words as he was intended to accept them: as meaning that Holmes had taken lodgings in Montague Street.

And there the matter would doubtless have remained, unchallenged as to fact, for a long time, had I not come upon an entry in the *London Post Office Directory* for 1878, which records changes of address, occupancy, etc, for the previous year. And the entry shewed that, from the Michaelmas Quarter of 1877, the tenant of No. 24 Montague Street, Russell Square, had been a *Mrs Holmes*. The lease from the Duchy of Bedford Estate was for seven years. Mrs Holmes would have been asked to provide satisfactory social, banking and commercial references, and these would have been taken up and proved acceptable to the Estate before a lease could have been drawn up. We know, then, that Mrs Holmes, whoever she was, was considered to be a person of 'respectability'.

The Bedford Estate were unable to provide me with more information than is contained in the *Directory*'s minimal entry. In the Bloomsbury rate-books, the tenant of No. 24 Montague Street is still plain 'Mrs Holmes'.

Who, then, was she? If we may credit the lady with a pre-
ciseness of etiquette, of social form; and provided, too, that we
may assume the entry to be as she dictated or wrote it for the
Directory, then, as *Mrs Holmes* (and not Mrs Sherrinford
Holmes or Mrs Mycroft Holmes or Mrs Sherlock Holmes) she
must have been the Wife – or Widow – of *Siger* Holmes. The
wife of the Head of the Family does not assume her husband's
Christian name; she is always, correctly, Mrs Holmes (or whatever the family name may be).

But may we rely on the entry as evidence of her status?
Directories are notoriously prone to error, since those who
gather the facts will always have access to servants or neighbours if the tenants be out – it 'saves another call'.

I have a copy of the GPO Telephone Directory's *London
Yellow Pages Classified (Central)*. Under the bold-face heading, *Do-It-Yourself Shops*, are three entries. The third entry
is that of 'Macmillan & Co. Ltd, 4 Little Essex St, WC 2 . . .
01–836 6633'. Macmillan & Company is the world-famous
firm of publishers. Yet, turning up this carelessly inserted
entry, might not some diligent researcher of a century hence
take it as proven that Macmillan & Company ran a do-it-
yourself shop on the side?

So that I had to accept the 'evidence' of that *Directory*
entry most cautiously. On reflection, and failing to add any
facts to the central fact that a Mrs Holmes had leased No. 24
Montague Street for a term of seven years from Michaelmas,
1877, I decided that what deductions could be made would
have to be made from what I had discovered about Mrs Holmes
and what Holmes had said or hinted.

Valid deduction the first: that there was something either
irregular about Mrs Holmes or about Holmes's association
with her. Why? Because Holmes had concealed her name
(and thus her identity) from Watson, and had hinted – though
not explicitly stated – that he had taken rooms in a lodging-
house in Montague Street. (A statement that Watson would
be most unlikely to check. Why should he? Bloomsbury was
full of boarding houses.)

Valid deduction the second: that Mrs Holmes was *not* Sherlock's mother – he would not have concealed that fact from Watson. But this deduction is not so certain as the first. If Sherlock had quarrelled with his father, his mother might have rented a house, *in her name*, to provide her youngest son with a 'roof' denied to him at the family home in Yorkshire. I think this deduction unlikely; but I feel bound to mention it.

Valid deduction the third: Holmes was unhappy at No. 24. Why? ". . . I had rooms in Montague Street . . . and there I waited, *filling in my too abundant leisure time*[1] by studying all those branches of science which might make me more efficient. Now and again cases came in my way, principally through the introduction of old fellow-students . . ."

Valid deduction the fourth: something – some legal tie or emotional link too strong to be severed by even someone as selfish as Holmes – bound him to No. 24, to Mrs Holmes. Why . . . ? Unhappy in his location, in a district of boarding-houses and hotels, he doesn't move away from No. 24 until some crisis in his relationship with Mrs Holmes forces his hand, or gives him his freedom, or both.

It certainly looks like an 'unfortunate' marriage, of the sort that, for instance, the Earl of Euston, heir to the Duchy of Grafton, contracted with Kate Cooke, in 1871.

Such a marriage would explain much of Holmes's behaviour not otherwise easily explicable. It would explain why his father broke with him – I find Mr Baring-Gould's reason, that Sherlock expressed his intention of becoming a detective, an insufficient reason for Siger Holmes's 'casting Sherlock out'. The cutting off of money, too, would explain why Holmes had to 'fill in his all too abundant leisure time by studying all those branches of science which might make me more efficient'. The proper place for that sort of study would have been Cambridge; one wonders why Holmes left a University that he liked, except that he could no longer afford to stay there. A marriage – 'unsuitable' or 'unfortunate' or even 'disastrous' – would also explain why Holmes, a loyal servant of the Crown, even when, as in the case of Edward VII, he ob-

[1] My italics – M.H.

jected to the character of the Monarch, refused a knighthood. One may control the entries in *Who's Who*; entries into *Debrett*, *Burke*, *Jack*, *Dodd* and the other reference-books are not so easily edited. Had Holmes consented to receive the accolade and rise from his knee as 'Sir Sherlock', there would have been that awkward situation involving *Lady* Holmes. One of the ha'penny newspapers would have ferretted out the fact that there was a Mrs Holmes, and . . . no no, it was impossible. Holmes asked to be graciously excused from accepting this signal mark of his Sovereign's favour, but . . .

They must have got the truth out of him, and sought a solution which would take all difficulties, all perils, into acount. And as I suggested in *The London of Sherlock Holmes*, but now restate here with far more confidence in my theory, it was to surmount the *impasse* of the knighthood which couldn't be accepted – and not only in the case of Holmes – that King Edward's advisers suggested the creation of a new order of chivalry, though one which conferred no title: the Order of Merit. At a private audience in the latter part of 1902, after the King had recovered from his dangerous attack of appendicitis (postponing the Coronation for two months), Edward took the badge of the Order, handed to him by an equerry, and, motioning Holmes to draw near, hung the decoration around his neck. As Holmes bent down, the King whispered, so quietly that not even the attendant and attentive equerry could hear: "I'm afraid, Mr Holmes, that I know your opinion of *me* – but this will shew what I think of *you*!"

No one heard what the King had said to one of his most famous – indeed, world-famous – subjects; but Watson, later, was heard to marvel that, ever since that investiture of 1902, Holmes's attitude of frigid respect for his hedonist[2] Monarch had changed into something a great deal warmer.

---

[2] Kipling, in America, described the King – then Prince of Wales – as 'a corpulent voluptuary', a remark which suited much contemporary American sentiment, but which went down badly with the British. Despite a 'crawling' elegiac poem written on the King's death, Kipling never managed to get himself forgiven for this gratuitous insult to the Throne.

My own view is that Mrs Holmes was Holmes's wife; that they had been married before he was twenty-three (the age at which he left Cambridge); that the lady, for reasons that I have not as yet been able to determine, was considered 'unsuitable', immediately by Holmes's father, and, not so long after, by Holmes himself. His distaste for her company must have been augmented by his having had, for perhaps as much as three years after his coming down from Cambridge, to be dependent upon her. To a man of Holmes's fastidious pride, this must have been the last humiliation; and would have rendered impossible any revival of that attraction which had caused the hasty and soon-to-be-regretted marriage.

Holmes's 'practice' began during the Montague Street period; but slowly, and certainly not very profitably. Ambition came very near to submitting to despair – perhaps the cocaine-taking began at this time: "You can hardly realize how long I had to wait," he told Watson.

There is no record of Holmes's having 'done' amateur dramatics at either Oxford or Cambridge; but it was an age when almost everyone was interested in amateur dramatics – the Royal Family especially – and Holmes, as a man of his age, could hardly have avoided contact with the amateur stage. At any rate, his despair of attaining his ambition in becoming a private consulting detective was such that he did, for a while, put that ambition aside. On Monday, 13th October, 1879, having joined Michael Sasanoff's company on the introduction of a stage-struck Cambridge acquaintance, Holmes made his first appearance on the boards, as Horatio in *Hamlet*. The theatre-goers, looking through the programmes, learnt that the – at any rate, 'professional' – name of the accomplished young newcomer was 'William Escott', a *nom de guerre*, derived from, as Baring-Gould points out, Holmes's three Christian names, 'William S. (for Sherlock) Scott'.

'And critics,' says Baring-Gould, 'are generally agreed that "William Escott" made an amazing success as an actor. This was partly due to Holmes's impressive figure and to his face: the high forehead, set off by strongly marked and exceedingly flexible eyebrows, the large, positive nose, the narrow, sensitive lips, the strong, thin jaw, the keen and piercing grey eyes – and, to crown all, the thick, slightly wavy, dark brown hair, which Holmes as an actor wore rather long.'

In the rapid climb from inferior social status, the 'acting profession' has mostly treated Shakespeare as a handy 'vehicle' for many an actor's and actress's self-advertisement, the various 'interpretations' of Olivia, Hamlet, Lady Macbeth, Othello and so on necessarily differing as violently ('subtly' is the theatrical jargon) as possible from preceding 'interpretations' – and each 'interpretation' leaving Shakespeare, who obviously never quite understood what he ought to have had in mind, more and more forgotten as the origin of the performances.

In a remark credited to Laurence Olivier by Kenneth Tynan, the actor put forward an interesting suggestion that we might perhaps revise our traditional acceptance of what have long been held as the relative importances of the *rôles* in Shakespeare's plays. Olivier, according to Tynan, as they argued over *Othello*, insisted: "The big part is Iago. Othello is just the stooge . . ."

Now, all the 're-thinking' in the world can't reverse the relative importance, as *rôles*, of Horatio and the Prince. The 'big part' is, and will always be, that of Hamlet; whilst Horatio's will always be what Shakespeare planned, that of the 'stooge'. All the same, Horatio is a stooge with a difference, and though he is what, on the lower level of the music-hall, is termed the 'feed', when Horatio is given a longish passage, it is always a passage which expresses the individuality of the man, not obscured by his attendance on Hamlet as a sort of superior servant, and expresses, too, the undimmed originality of his thinking. In the hands of a really talented actor, the part of Horatio may be made to seem of an importance rivalling that of the Prince.

There is a short three-line answer, made by Horatio to Hamlet, which must have rung strangely in the young actor's ears – and in the ears of those members of the cast who knew something of Holmes's background. The lines occur in Act III,

Scene 2, in reply to, and comment upon, Hamlet's long speech which begins:

> Nay, do not think I flatter;
> For what advancement may I hope from thee
> That no revenue hast but thy good spirits,
> To feed and clothe thee?

Thee long speech ending:

> It is a damnèd ghost that we have seen,
> And my imaginations are as foul
> As Vulcan's stithy. Give him heedful note;
> For I mine eyes will rivet to his face,
> And after we will both our judgements join
> In censure of his seeming.

On which the play calls for the utterance of these words by Horatio – words with so curious a personal relevance, so far as Holmes was concerned –

> Well, my lord:
> If he steal aught the whilst this play is playing,
> And *'scape detecting*, I will pay the theft.

Actors have commonly the reputation for being superstitious; it would have taken a harder-headed man than I believe Holmes, at twenty-five, to have been, not to have seen something 'eerie' in the lines that Shakespeare put into the young would-be-detective's mouth.

And the London audiences must have stared with a sense of seeing the perfectly 'cast' actor, when Holmes was playing his first important part as Cassius in *Julius Caesar*, and Caesar grumbled –

> Let me have men around me that are fat;
> Sleek-headed men, and such as sleep o' nights;
> Yond' Cassius hath a lean and hungry look;
> He thinks too much: such men are dangerous . . .
> . . . .
>
> Seldom he smiles; and smiles in such a sort,
> As if he mocked himself, and scorned his spirit,
> That could be moved to smile at anything.

Such men as he be never at heart's ease,
Whiles they behold a greater than themselves...

After the first night, they must have remarked to Holmes, back-stage, "Why, William, the lines might have been written by Shakespeare with you in mind!"

At no time in the history of the Theatre could anyone have joined 'the Profession' and been more impressed with the splendour and – an important point where the actors and actresses were concerned – the *convenience* of the new theatres which were springing up all over the world, but especially in England, France, Germany and America. For the first time, it seemed, the players, no less than the audience, had been borne in mind by the architects. There was magnificence in front of the proscenium; there was also a respect for human dignity behind. Dressing-rooms were now being provided which came up at least to the standards of the modern flat – itself proliferating everywhere (and introduced to London in the 1860s, based on the successful Viennese models).

A sudden interest in the Theatre – not, I think, unconnected with the universal interest in the *Grandes Horizontales*; many of whom either were, or affected to be, actresses – had even reached the point at which Great Britain decided to have a National Theatre. A site was chosen on Bazalgette's new Thames Embankment; funds were raised, plans drawn up, an architect commissioned, and, the basement having been completed (including the modern type of dressing-rooms), the foundation-stone was laid by Queen Victoria's sailor son, the Duke of Edinburgh, in 1874 – the year in which the Duke married Her Imperial Highness the Grand Duchess Marie Alexandrovna, only daughter of Alexander II, Emperor of All the Russias.

The stone must have been laid when the auspices were unfavourable; as I have told in more detail in another place, work ceased on the building, and for nearly twenty years it lay unfinished and neglected at the back of Parliament Street. Then, in 1890, as the Metropolitan Police were seeking new headquarters – Old Scotland Yard and Whitehall Place having grown too cramped – plans for a Police HQ were entrusted to the eminent architect, Norman Shaw, who built the still-standing baronial keep at Derby Gate. (It was opened in 1892, and extended in 1912.) But beneath the now superseded building are the dressing-rooms of the never realized National Theatre, even to the star cut in the door of the principal dressing-room. From these rooms it will be seen what a leap forward theatre-design had taken by the early 1870s.

Theatre-building was universal, but in London, Paris and New York, standards of design were reached which have never since been excelled – hardly equalled. Such works as, for instance, Richard Southern's *The Victorian Theatre*,[3] will give those unacquainted with the splendour in which our grandfathers saw the great successes of the Legendary Names a startling glimpse of now forgotten luxury. To the glories of the architects and interior decorators, the stage-designers and scene-painters – such men as Telbin, Hawes Craven Green and Joseph Harker, to name the most famous three – added their own unrivalled mixture of pictorial artistry, mechanical ingenuity and entrancing 'effects' of illumination in which they took full advantage of the new electric light.

A glance through any history of the late Victorian Theatre will demonstrate what can be – and actually was – achieved when unlimited capital might be called upon to raise standards in an industry which could rely on almost complete public support. There was no 'outside' competition of any moment; what competition there was was vigorous but 'internal' – the competition that every ambitious player presented to another. And there is no doubt that every player, from stars like Irving and Terry, Tree and Anderson, to bit-players and second spearmen, 'lived up' to the implicit flattery of the new luxury. Against such a background of crimson plush, gold leaf and prismatic lustres, new brilliancies of acting appeared. Even the corniest melodrama, transformed by the unselfconscious dedication of an Irving, and acted against the most impressive stage-sets ever to be seen in any playhouse, appeared, to the hard-headed critics of the time, to be 'genuine theatre' – *The*

[3] Newton Abbot: David & Charles, 1970.

Times, in no spirit of ridicule, mentions (approvingly) 'some burst of passion at the Lyceum', for, no matter how the acting of Irving may strike us now, it was impossible for his contemporaries to take him otherwise than seriously.

For an example of the new standards of luxury which were transforming the world's theatres in the last quarter of the nineteenth century, look at the auditorium of the rebuilt Princess's Theatre, in 1880, or the impressively elegant (and still almost unaltered) Grand Foyer of Covent Garden, with its vast pier-glasses, huge velvet drapes and pelmets, and enormous crystal gasoliers. And, for an example of the ambitious and beautiful sets against which the actors played, what could excel that of, say, the Telbin-designed Vault Scene from the 1882 Lyceum production of *Romeo and Juliet*; a symphony of shadows, created about the recumbent alabaster luminance of the sleeping Juliet?

European actors and actresses were assured of a warm welcome by American audiences of the expiring century, not only in the big cities of the East and Middle West, but in the still raw Western 'cities', developing to serve the requirements of wealth based on cattle, silver, gold, fruit and wine.

The welcome, it seems, was as warm as it was uncritical; Baring-Gould mentions that 'Tommaso Salvini, who had enjoyed the advantage of early training in Ristori's company, came to the US for the first time in 1873, and gave one of the greatest performances of all time as Othello, not in the least handicapped by the fact that he had to play the role *in Italian*, while all his fellow-actors replied in English'. For any actor or actress touched with self-doubt, a tour of the United States in the 1870s and 1880s could only prove the finest confidence-inducer in the world.

Holmes was not unique in that, an actor, he was also a University man. But the big rush from the Universities to the footlights had not yet gathered momentum, and it was to be some years before the implicit approval of this entry in

Debrett was to become commonplace in dealing with actors from the aristocracy or the upper classes:

ROSSLYN, EARL OF. (St Clair-Erskine)

JAMES FRANCIS HARRY ST CLAIR-ERSKINE, 5th Earl, and a Baronet; *b.* March 16th, 1869; *s.* 1890; ed. at Eton, and at Oxford Univ.; formerly Lieut. Roy. Horse Guards, and Captain Fifeshire Light Horse Volunteers; is a Justice of the Peace and a Deputy Lieutenant for county Fife, *a member of the dramatic profession*[4] and editor of *Scottish Life* . . .

But approval was on its way; a Royal Family, headed by the enthusiastic Queen, who arranged elaborate amateur theatricals almost every week of the year, could not withhold plenary approval from the 'pro's'. The day of the dramatic Peer was not yet; but its advent was inevitable.

Thus, it was as no 'strolling player', far less as a 'vagabond', that Holmes embarked on the White Star liner *Empress Queen*, from Southampton, sailing on 23rd November, 1879, and arriving in New York ten days later. Following Sasanoff's success with the London *Julius Caesar*, the Russian impresario decided to launch his American tour with *Twelfth Night*, not, one would think, the 'easiest' play with which to tempt a new audience, but one having the advantage of plenty of 'action' to compensate for the subtlety which is too often missed by producer, stage-director, players and audience alike. As Malvolio, Holmes offered, Baring-Gould tells us, 'the most adequate presentation of that character that America had ever seen up to that time'.

The New York run was a long one for those days, when a hundred performances was considered 'record-breaking'; and Sasanoff's company went on from New York to 'play' no fewer than one hundred and twenty-eight one-night stands in as many of the United States' principal cities and towns.

Holmes had accepted an invitation to 'walk on' from his old college friend, 'Langdale Pike', a *nom de guerre* which concealed that of a scion of England's oldest nobility, to earn 'bread and butter money'. But the newcomer's London suc-

[4] My italics – M.H.

21 Buckingham Palace. As it was, before the re-fronting, on the day in 1902 when Holmes was commanded to a private audience of the new King, and there received the Order of Merit, a distinction created specially for the great detective. (*Contrad Research Library*)

22 Wire-tapping in the National Interest. No time for elaborate disguise as an electrical artisan – just the doffing of a jacket, the rolling-up of the shirt-sleeves, the hasty affixing of the Clarkson false moustache always carried in a waistcoat pocket; and Holmes is high above the Central Telegraph Office, St Martin's-le-Grand, tapping the German Embassy's private wire. His assistant in this dubious but patriotic enterprise is not Watson but one of Lord Holdhurst's more enterprising young men from the Foreign Office. *Illustration for an account by Watson, intended for publication in* The Strand Magazine, *but suppressed 'in the National Interest'* (*Contrad Research Library*)

23 A selection from the principal awards bestowed on Mr Sherlock Holmes:
(left-hand page, reading vertically down) Palmes Académiques, Mérite
Agricole, St Gregory the Great, Order of the Bath, St Michael & St George,
St Anne, Vasa, Medjidie; *above,* Legion of Honour, St Olaf, Polar Star.
Collection brought together especially for this book by Mr David Spink,
of the world-famous fine-art dealers, Spink & Son Ltd, St James's.
Photograph: Tony Mann (through Contrad Research Library)

24 Pablo de Sarasate.
This eminent violinist,
who signed this
photograph for Holmes,
was the great detective's
favourite male violinist,
as Madame Norman-
Neruda (Lady Hallé)
was his favourite female
violinist, and the two
brothers De Reske his
favourite singers.
*Photograph: Gerschel,
23 Boulevard des
Capucines, Paris
(Contrad Research
Library)*

24a St James's Hall,
Piccadilly. A London
audience of 1890 leaving
what was London's –
and Holmes's – most
popular and successful
concert-hall until its
demolition in 1904, to
make way for the present
Piccadilly Hotel. Note
that the respectable
middle-class audience
have just been listening
to Sarasate. A
*contemporary drawing
by W. D. Almond
(Contrad Research
Library)*

cess in the *rôle* of Cassius, followed by his even greater success as Malvolio, earned him something over and above mere subsistence. He did not 'splurge' this extra money, but saved it; and it was this reserve fund which, there is no doubt, enabled him to make himself independent of Mrs Holmes and Montague Street, and to set up a separate establishment – though a completely innocent one – with Watson in Baker Street, six months or so after Holmes returned to London in the summer of 1880.

Holmes, on his first visit to the United States of America, spent only eight months there – from 3rd or 4th December, 1879 to 5th August, 1880. He came back a young man far more experienced than the Sherlock Holmes who, pressed for money and emotionally disturbed by his 'irregular' social position, had escaped, first into another mode of life, and, through that avocational escape, into another Continent.

The energy necessarily repressed by his having cut himself off from Family, University, preferred work and, of course, the normal friendships of a young man, burst out, once he had landed in America, with renewed and redoubled force. Not only did he conform willingly and successfully to the demanding discipline of the Theatre; he managed – somehow – to 'work in' spare-time returns to that talent that he had demonstrated so brilliantly in the case of the Musgrave Ritual, the mystery of which was solved by Holmes eleven days before he first trod the boards as Horatio.

In New York, either by design or happy accident, Holmes met one who had already established himself as a private consulting detective, Wilson Hargreave, whom Holmes was to meet again – and this time, professionally – eighteen years later, in the singular case of 'The Dancing Men'. ("A most interesting and unusual case . . . A very pretty case to add to your collection, Watson.") On that first meeting with Hargreave in New York, Holmes found that the detective had already been retained by Vanderbilt – almost certainly the great Commodore himself – in a matter involving the rifling of the multi-millionaire's private safe. Holmes, by the generosity of Hargreave or (more probably) by the dominant force of Holmes's own character, made some suggestions which led to the revelation that the job was an 'inside' one, and that the safe-cracking yeggman was a Vanderbilt footman. (Not British, one hopes!)

A play that the Sasonoff company were presenting in Philadelphia called for a shotgun as 'property', and Holmes was asked to borrow this weapon. He visited a gunsmith's, looked over some of the stock, and there noticed (and memorized) the distinctive mark of the Pennsylvania Small Arms Company, storing this piece of information away until he recalled it and used it to advantage in the case of *The Valley of Fear* – "I can hardly recall a case where the features have been more peculiar". That was eight years later; but Holmes had an excellent memory, especially for the proofing and maker's marks on firearms.

By this time, Holmes had demonstrated his natural ability as a problem-solver on three occasions – in the case of *The 'Gloria Scott'*, whilst he was still up at Oxford; in the so-called *Mullineaux Case*, where the details must still be treated as unrevealed, since I here cannot accept Mr Baring-Gould's conclusions as to the case's nature; and that of *The Musgrave Ritual*, satisfactorily concluded hardly two months before Holmes sailed for America.

In the eight months' stay abroad, Holmes contrived to solve two more mysteries, one *The Case of Vanderbilt and the Yeggman*, in some sort of partnership with the professional private-eye, Hargreave; the other, *The Dreadful Business of the Abernetty Family of Baltimore* – so Watson records it – presumably on his own. One would wish that Watson had described this early case in elaborate detail, for it involved the solution of a classic 'locked room' mystery; in this case, by Holmes's pointing out to the Baltimore police the depth to which the parsley had sunk into the butter.

A passing reference, in *The Six Napoleons*, to "my knowledge of the crooks of Chicago", shews that, despite his theatrical engagements, Holmes contrived to secure some firsthand acquaintance with the already flourishing organized gansterism which has been one of the most notable exports from Italy to the New World.

What, perhaps, was of the most benefit to Holmes in all this eight months' travel to almost every part of the now re-established Union[5] was the unalterable pro-American senti-ment with which he left the Land of the Free. He read Thoreau, perhaps the best introduction to a sympathy with the distinctive American temperament that any foreigner may be given; he read and greatly loved the works of his eminent American namesake, Oliver Wendell Holmes; and, full of a pythonical spirit which owed its origin as much, doubtless, to a noble heart as to cocaine or whisky, he uttered, in 1886, this laudatory and prophetic sentiment:

> It is always a joy to me to meet an American . . . for I am one of those who believe that the folly of a monarch and the blundering of a minister in far gone years will not prevent our children from being some day citizens of the same world-wide country under a flag which shall be a quartering of the Union Jack with the Stars and Stripes.

Quartering . . . ? Surely, all which will be needed will be an extra star . . . ?

Across the world, in far-off Afghanistan, not the folly of a monarch, but certainly the blundering of several ministers, had once again put British soldiers in needless peril. To 'counter the Russian threat to India', Afghanistan had been invaded for the third time in the century; and the British were doing, apparently, no better than they had done earlier. On 27th July, 1880, a week before Holmes left New York for Southampton, the inconclusive but costly battle of Maiwand was fought between a combined force of British and Indian troops and the 'murderous Ghazis' of the Amir of Afghani-stan. Historically, the battle is of little importance; but it was of major importance in the life of Holmes.

[5] Though, that old prejudices still remained, over twenty years after the signing at the Appomattox Court House, Holmes did not need the case of *The Five Orange Pips* to remind him.

For, during the battle, an Army surgeon named Watson, temporarily attached to the Berkshires (66th Foot), was wounded by a bullet fired from a *jezail*. The slug, which hit Watson in the shoulder, 'shattered the bone and grazed the subclavian artery'. "I should have fallen," Watson remembers with gratitude, "into the hands of the murderous Ghazis had it not been for the devotion and courage shewn by Murray, my orderly, who threw me across a pack-horse, and succeeded in bringing me safely to the British lines." So was John Hamish Watson, MD, saved to become, for Sherlock Holmes, what another Scotchman became for Samuel Johnson. Perhaps, had Watson not met Sherlock Holmes in the 'Path Lab' at Bart's (as Boswell met Dr Johnson in the back-parlour of Tom Davies's book-shop), we might still have heard of Johnson and Holmes – but surely as no more than footnotes in the sort of dust-gathering histories that only scholars read.

The subject of any dedicated biographer is as much a creation of that biographer as of Almighty God; God breathed the spirit of life into the subject; the biographer it was who blew that spirit into the living flame.

We shall come to Watson presently; art of the finest kind goes unnoticed – *ars*, they say, *celare artem*; and Watson's art is of the perfect kind which does, which must, escape notice. That silence, says Emerson, which accepts merit as the most natural thing in the world is the highest praise.

Such biographers as Boswell and Watson, who work on the living material, rather than the dead, cannot remain objective observers; after a time, they must affect, by their intense study, the subject studied. It is this fact which generated the statement of Heisenberg's famous 'Uncertainty Principle': that the processes of observation necessarily have their effect upon the spatial co-ordinates of the object observed. In simpler – but perhaps less precise – terms, one moves something just by looking at it. (Try it.)

Upon the basic material so patiently and lovingly collected, over a period of some forty years, by John Watson, a multitude of further-researchers such as I have been able to erect what are often vast structures of comment and correction. We have been able to expand what Watson has merely sketched in briefly; to tell in detail what, in the Watsonian record, is but hinted; to reconcile seeming contradictions in chronology and other matters; to supply that information about Holmes that Watson either did not have or did not consider worth the recording.

Mark that I have said, 'lovingly and patiently'. The latter adverb is as important as the former. Watson has never, not even by me, been given the credit that he deserves for his patience – a patience which becomes all the more remarkable when we consider (as almost no one yet has done) the implications of a few words in Watson's scanty autobiographical interpolation; a 'throw-away' line; a few words stating a fact, made bare and unremarkable and completely immemorable by its absence of self-pity. Here are the words: "I . . . landed a month later on Portsmouth jetty, *with my health irretrievably ruined* . . . " They are my italics; but the truth is Watson's. The statement is free from exaggeration; it is a qualified medical practitioner's unemotional assessment of the physical situation; the diagnosis and prognosis which inform him of major physical damage, with no possibility of cure. We shall see, shortly, that Watson's own financial condition was more disturbing even than Holmes's had been before the latter's journey to the United States; but, despite physical and mental troubles, Watson got down to his self-appointed task of recording for us the history of the remarkable man with whom Watson was to share the greater part of his remaining life.

I stress the *patience* of the observer, because, since the close observer must always influence the subject, Holmes, in time, came to be patient, too. He even learned to develop – though never in Watson's depth of emotion, in his capacity for feeling – something of a knowledge of love.

4

The Exciting 'Eighties

Apart from the two wars – Zulu and Afghan – with which the 1870s ended (and the new decade was about to begin with another: the first South African War), there was a 'better' reason why people were glad to see the back of a decade which had begun with the Franco-Prussian War and ended with 'strained relations' in South Africa between the British and the Boers. The 1870s had ended in a world-slump, where the worst effects were seen in Britain and the United States.

Slumps, however, were not so long-lasting in those days, and already, by the first year of the new decade, trade and commerce were beginning to look up, and people began cautiously to reassure each other that 'the worst seems to be over'.

It was. Holmes could not have returned to England, to tackle, this time with total effort, the problem of making himself the world's first professional private consulting detective, at a more favourable time.

You could say (and you'd be right) that calendar-dates are purely arbitrary; that calendars themselves are purely arbitrary – otherwise people like Solon and Julius Cæsar and Dionysius Exiguus and Mohammed and George III and Marat (or whoever it was who gave France the world's first astrology-based calendar since Babylonian times) and Lenin couldn't change calendars overnight and expect things to go on pretty much as they had done before. But, say, what you like, there is something about a calendar, arbitrary or not, which does seem to pump optimism into people at regular intervals, with the steady dependability of a double-acting pump. New day, new month, new year, new century – they all give us a chance to begin again; to have another go; to change our luck. This is a very valuable human insanity: the addiction to optimism has enriched stockbrokers, religious teachers, politicians, news-paper-owners – anybody with a glib line of patter, nothing to sell but lies, and the easiest of consciences in the undeviating pursuit of the fast buck.

So everyone welcomed the 'Eighties, glad to turn the col-lective back on the dismal, slumpish 'Seventies. And because everyone hoped such great things of the decade, the decade itself didn't let everyone down as much as it might have done.

The Queen of England, now Empress of India as well (since 1876), was still only sixty-one – no great age, even for those days – and had begun to emerge from her widow's seclusion a little. The fact that the Prince of Wales's two sons, Eddy and Georgy, were sailing around the world on a battleship shewed that the Prince and Princess of Wales (whatever the open scandals of the Prince's private life) believed in the good, old-fashioned principles of bringing up children – for what could be tougher or more toughening than the spartan life of two lads before the mast?

One claim of the 'Eighties to recognition that history has endorsed was its demonstrated ability to take up old never-quite-got-there inventions, and make them work. (Well, really, most of this happened in the better-forgotten 'Seventies, but the 'Eighties skilfully marketed these second-time-lucky inven-tions, and made them the disagreeable indispensabilities that they have been for some time now.)

The typewriter (Queen Anne), the half-tone process (1827), the internal-combustion engine (1667), the electric-train (New York, 1836), the electric-light (Herodotus mentions that Cyrus, King of Persia, had it, *circa* 500 BC), the submarine (1557 – London to Greenwich), the jet-propelled boat (Heron of Alexandria, *circa* AD 100), and so on – old inventions which had failed, but out of which the unprecedently practical inventors of Victoria's latter days extracted the riches, as, to-day, modern metallurgical techniques can extract metal from the waste of ancient mines.

And there was peace throughout Europe and – save for the usual South American garlic-and-gold-lace 'struggles for freedom' – through most of the rest of the world. A happy accident in 1883, though it killed a few thousand people, postponed World War I a further thirty years.

Establishing claims to 'spheres' of influence in the Pacific, by 'planting the flag' on islands hitherto peacefully inhabited by the innocently hedonistic Polynesian, came the armed patrols of the Great Powers. Most actively aggressive in this area were emergent Imperial Germany and resurgent imperialistic Republican France. But there were other 'interests' represented, too – and not lagging so *very* far behind the others in the aggressive-acquisitive spirit. There were Great Britain, the United States (whose acquisition of Midway was to pay off almost fifty years later), Spain – then still with that 'Ne Plus Ultra' acquisitive itch – Portugal, Holland and Italy. And it came to pass that all – or most – of these nations' representative warships were assembled in Apia Harbour, Samoa, to which island most of the nations' real owners were laying claim. It was like Navarino Bay again, only worse: gunpower had taken some diabolically long strides since 1827. And they'd invented cordite, too . . .

No one can say now who would have fired first, or, indeed, if any commander would have fired at all. But there came a diversion. That pressure-cooker we call the Earth blew one of its steam-cocks. Krakatoa exploded – and a vast tidal wave advanced on Apia, broke through the lagoon, and began to boil up the harbour and the ships within. There was just one small chance, and only the commander of HMS *Calliope* was willing to take it – to dash, at full speed, through the narrow gap of the coral-reef, into the relative calm of the open sea, and there ride out (he hoped) the most terrible storm that any sailor there had ever seen, in even the storm-racked waters of the southern seas.

He declared his intentions by flag-signal, and, as he drove

through the reef, the ships' companies of the onlooking vessels 'dressed ship' in *Calliope*'s honour, the doomed men waving their straw hats and cheering as the British warship cleared the reef and came into the safety of the open sea. After that, no one thought of war . . .

It was essentially the decade which introduced the Electrical Age, a fact symbolized and assisted to be by the two great Electrical Exhibitions, of Paris (1881) and London (1882). It was the decade which saw the introduction of 'the electric light' into theatres, restaurants, hotels, public assembly rooms, government buildings, churches and railway stations. At the end of the decade, 'the electric light' had reached railway-trains and ocean-going liners as well.

The electric-tramway has vanished from Great Britain, but it survives in popular usefulness in many parts of the world; it was in the 'Eighties that it was introduced. When Holmes and Watson went down to the Brixton Road, in the case of A *Study in Scarlet*, they took a cab; a year later, and they would have been able to go from the Embankment to Brixton by tram – for a penny.

To this decade, too, belongs the introduction of that other world-shaker, the Cinematograph, which, as its natural development, Television (for which a patent was taken out in 1847),[1] has become a world-changer, no less.

'Moving pictures' were first introduced about 1820 as the Zoetrope, in which hand-drawn pictures broke down action into successive 'stills', which were then run rapidly behind a slit, the eye seeing the series of 'stills' as action.

The next step – the substitution of drawings by photographs – was taken by Muybridge, an American, who wished to learn how the legs of a horse behaved whilst the animal was in motion. Muybridge arranged for the horse to run in front of a series of cameras, the horse's hooves 'tripping' wires

[1] The 1847 patent was based on the property of the then newly discovered selenium to change its electrical conductivity according as light fell on it or was withdrawn. The real ancestor of the modern TV system is the 'screen' (1827) by which the half-tone process of reproducing pictures was made possible.

controlling the cameras' shutters, thus providing a series of 'stills' recording the successive movements of the animal.

By arranging these photographs in a zoetrope, Muybridge produced the illusion of action – the 'moving picture' of a galloping horse.

The transfer of photographs to a continuous strip of celluloid (another invention of the 'Eighties) seems so obvious that it is a wonder that the step occurred to only three men, two French, one English: the Lumières and Friese-Greene. (Edison was an early experimenter with the cinematograph, even devising the first 'sound track', but he cannot be considered in any way its inventor.)

By the closing years of this most important of all modern decades, 'animated pictures' were being shewn in the music-halls of London, Paris, Berlin and New York.

Changes were occurring at the Top Level, too. Outwardly, things seemed to have altered little; but that was mostly because the pomp and circumstance associated with Royalty and its armed forces had, if anything, grown more assured, more emphatic, more eye-catching. State pageantry and court ritual in Imperial Germany outshone anything which had been known when Prussia was just one kingdom amongst many.

In January, 1881, the position of the two men destined to form the world's most memorable private and professional partnership had been reversed in the two years which separated them from 1879. *Then*, Watson, newly established in the unassailable Victorian status of 'professional' man by the MD degree taken in the previous year, could – and did – look forward to establishing a steady practice. He had immediately taken consulting-rooms – apparently the whole house – in what was then called Southampton Street, Bloomsbury Square, but which is now known as Southampton Place. The house, built about 1750, has lately been 'remodelled', to use the 'developers'' jargon, but its exterior shews no changes from the day that the newly-qualified doctor put up his plate on the front-door:

JOHN WATSON, MD

Watson talks almost as though he had taken his medical degree in preparation for – to fit himself for – Army life; and this may well be so. He says, "In the year 1878 I took my degree of Doctor of Medicine of the University of London, and proceeded to go to Netley to go through the course prescribed for surgeons in the army. Having completed my studies there, I was duly attached to the Fifth Northumberland Fusiliers as Assistant Surgeon . . ."

This seems plain enough : Watson intended an Army career for himself, but not, I think, one which would have caused him to dedicate his whole life to the Army. As a Doctor of Medicine, his training would not have 'majored' on surgery; and it was evidently to obtain extensive practice in, and experience of, surgery that he joined the Army Medical Service (soon to be fully militarized as 'The Royal Army Medical Corps'). Then, as now, no would-be surgeon could find more, and more diverse, practice than in war; and Watson had the choice then of only two theatres of war : Zululand, where resistance from the Zulus was obviously ceasing; and Afghanistan, where hostilities had hardly begun. (He implies, though in a somewhat ambiguous wording, that he had gone out to India in order to join in the second – or third – Afghan war.[2])

On his return to England, by the troopship *Orontes* (of the Orient Line), he was, he tells us, 'as free as air – or as free as an income of eleven shillings and sixpence a day will permit a man to be'. By 'income' he means his pension of £4 0s. 6d. a week (£210 10s. per annum), and not, one must assume, his total income from – as the Income Tax hominids say – 'all sources'. I have explained in my *The London of Sherlock Holmes* that, in 1881, a single man could live comfortably on less than four pounds a week; but I have pointed out, in that book and elsewhere, that it was plain to see that Watson was not economizing. The Criterion Bar, though ridiculously

[2] Elsewhere I have referred to this campaign as 'the *third* Afghan War'. If one regard the war of 1838, with its terrible defeat of the British, as an affair separate from that of the punitive campaign waged against the Afghans later, then one says 'three Afghan Wars'. If one regard the affair of 1838 and its immediate successor as one war, then one ought to say 'the second Afghan War'.

inexpensive by present-day standards, was still, by contemporary reckoning, not one of London's cheaper bar-restaurants. And by 'free as the air', Watson can have meant only that his 'irretrievably ruined' health would not permit him to continue with a practice which had hardly had time to start before he went to Afghanistan. As for selling that practice, it is obvious that there was nothing to sell; Watson must have been more concerned with finding someone who would be willing to take the lease of No. 6 Southampton Street off his hands.

Whereas Holmes, who had clearly been pressed for money – and the freedom that money alone may buy – in the last months of 1879, returns in August, 1880, if not rich, then at least rescued from the despairing state of eight months earlier.

Holmes cannot have managed to put by more than £10 a week from his salary, if as much; and that would give him a maximum of £300 saved; yet this relatively small sum would, prudently managed, have capitalized him for a year; and, in any case, as he tells Watson on their meeting, "I have my eye on a suite in Baker Street which would suit us down to the ground", 'Young Stamford' – who introduced Watson to Holmes – already having said to Holmes: "My friend here wants diggings; and as you were complaining that you could get no one to go halves with you, I thought that I had better bring you two together."

That was in the January of 1881, but more arrangements are implicit in the men's decision to take rooms together at Baker Street than are mentioned, or even hinted at, in Watson's account. I think that Holmes, though aware of his new friend's 'irretrievably ruined' health, offered him the job of assistant, amanuensis, research-man – at least until some improvement in his health should make it thinkable that Watson go back to practice.

For, in addition to what he had brought back with him from America, Holmes, in the five months or so since his return to England, had proved his professional capacity in no fewer than nine cases; none of any great social importance; though the opal tiara of Mrs Farintosh suggests that she might have had some worthwhile connections. Watson gives no more than the titles of these nine cases, so that it is impossible to say in any one of them exactly what was the problem to be solved, who commissioned Holmes to do the solving, and who, then, paid the bill. Did some public-spirited person hire Holmes to track down and convict 'Ricoletti of the Club Foot and His Abominable Wife'? Perhaps they were blackmailing someone who had heard of Holmes – Mr and Mrs Ricoletti sound the sort of persons who wouldn't have been above a bit of blackmail.

But that the nine cases had brought not only payment but a sound prospect of Holmes's extending his 'practice', is evident, it seems to me, in Holmes's *manner* on the occasion of his first meeting with Watson. Holmes is so obviously *elated* – and I don't mean elated because he has just proven an 'infallible' test for the presence of human blood on an object. Nor is this elation, I hasten to say, consistent with a 'lift' from cocaine, though it might well be consistent with the periodic 'upswing' of a manic depressive. It appears to me simpler, and, all things considered, more reasonable to accept Holmes's cheerfulness as the normal good spirits of a normal young man who is finding that, after some initial disappointments, things are going his way.

Obviously, some satisfactory arrangement has been reached with Mrs Holmes – they need not, he must have informed Watson, expect *her* to come calling around . . .

And Watson, concluding the working arrangements with Holmes, must have found means to break the tenancy of No. 6 Southampton Street. At any rate, Watson's name, at that address, disappears from the *Post Office Directory* after 1882, which implies that he ceased to lease the house after 1881, the year in which he met Holmes.

By the end of 1886, in addition to the fourteen cases already mentioned, Holmes had successfully handled another sixteen cases, and though these are still very mixed in type (as well, we may understand, in intrinsic importance), there is, nevertheless, a distinct upward trend noticeable, especially as we approach the end of this five-year period.

Holmes, as we have seen, had already rendered a service to an ancient English family – the Musgraves – and been brought to the notice of his Sovereign as a result of his success in recovering part of the presumed lost Regalia of the Realm.

But after March, 1881, it is obvious that Holmes's fame has reached the ears of what, to use a common generic term, we may call 'Society'. Not only do we find Holmes called upon to serve three Royal Families – those of Scandinavia, Russia and Holland – but, as might be expected, eminent but lesser persons now shew themselves anxious to secure the services of one whose professional discretion, no less than his professional ability, must have strongly recommended him to those with secrets to keep. What Sir William Gull had become to the Royal Family, Nobility and Aristocracy of Great Britain, in the field of medicine; Sir George Lewis in the field of litigation; Sherlock Holmes – even by the mid-'Eighties – was well on the way to becoming in the field of protecting the Great from their enemies' malice or their own indiscretions.

And not only in Great Britain, but in Europe, also.

My much regretted friend, the late 'Archie' Macdonnell, pointed out, in an article, 'The Truth about Professor Moriarty', in *The Incunabular Sherlock Holmes*, that Holmes must have suffered a breakdown of his mental and perhaps physical abilities in the year 1887 – the year of the Golden Jubilee. Archie certainly made out an excellent case for our believing that Holmes went through a period of intellectual stagnation between 1887 and 1894. He blundered, as Macdonnell pointed out, in the three cases of A *Scandal in Bohemia* (20th–22nd May, 1887), *The Five Orange Pips* (29–30th September, 1887) and *The Greek Interpreter* (12th September, 1888), which last, 'a singular case', could hardly be considered satisfactorily concluded if it could be said that 'the explanation . . . is still involved in some mystery'.

Watson, as Holmes's medical attendant – unsummoned, unpaid, but his medical attendant, none the less – noted regretfully in April, 1887 that, about this time, Holmes had become 'a self-poisoner by cocaine'. But – and who should know this better than Watson, the doctor? – drug-addiction is, in the majority of cases, a symptom of trouble, not a cause. Addictions, whether to alcohol or any of the other 'addictive' drugs, are the result of some psychic imbalance. Human beings mostly drink or drug, not so much to 'put matters right' (they know, in their hearts, poor devils, that drink or drugs won't – can't – do that), but to make things *seem* all right . . . for the time being. But once an addictive pattern has been established, the drugs' own inherent capacity for mischief will add their dangerous influence to the already troubling psychic disturbance.

That Holmes eventually rid himself of his addiction to cocaine we know; and, in his defence, it must be reiterated here that nineteenth-century medicine prescribed the 'dangerous' drugs where the modern general practitioner might hesitate to prescribe anything stronger than aspirin. It is clear that – though Watson warns Holmes against cocaine-addiction in what sound like modern terms – contemporary medical opinion did not share Watson's fears; heroin, the 'Big H' of the international drug-smugglers and drug-peddlars, was fashionably prescribed at the end of the century as a *harmless, non-addictive* substitute for cocaine!

But in the latter part of 1886 and during the first four months of 1887, not only had Holmes's mind suffered no temporary impairment, his mental powers now were at their most forceful. It was as well; he needed all the brilliance of mind, the resilience of will-to-win, the contempt for the insoluble puzzle no less than for the unconquerable foe – he needed all these great gifts, which had brought him to the High Place, and were now (though with a pause, a breathing-space, imposed on him, who would never have imposed them on himself) to take him even further . . .

Watson gives no details; these were plainly confidential matters at the most exalted level. Yet, knowing what we do of the internal and external difficulties of Holland at the end of the last century, we may surely make what have now come to be called 'educated guesses' as to the problems that the reigning Family of Holland called Holmes to solve.

There were, mentioned by Watson, two problems connected with Holland – the first, what Watson calls *The Delicate Affair of the Reigning Family of Holland* (this happened almost certainly in December, 1886, perhaps hanging over until the January of the following year); the second, beginning in February, 1887, and probably lasting until the April of that year, when Watson noted the alarming change in his friend's physical and mental condition, inducing or resulting from the use of cocaine.

But no crisis had come to impair Sherlock Holmes's faculties when, at the end of 1886, he was summoned to exert his peculiar talents on behalf of the Dutch Royal House.

The end of the nineteenth century saw Holland – its Crown, its People, its Economy, its general sentiment as a nation – in that neurotic condition always inspired in a small, rich country by the sight of bigger, often poorer, neighbours embarking on a policy of grab.

Nearly a century before, Holland had been invaded by the French revolutionary troops, and incorporated into the French (Revolutionary) Empire as 'The Batavian Republic', which did not get its liberty when France became an Imperial empire. Instead, the Batavian Republic became the Kingdom of Holland – but with a Bonaparte as King, and French as the official language.

On the final fall of Napoleon and the second restoration of the Bourbons to the throne of France, the Congress of Vienna decided to create a 'barrier state' against any resurgent French ambition by incorporating the former Austrian Netherlands and the now free-once-more United Provinces (Holland) into a new Kingdom of Holland.

Formerly –that is, prior to the French invasion of 1793 – Holland had had a curious, indeed a unique, constitution; though, in some ways, not unlike the crowned republican constitution of Venice. But from 1815, it was intended that the new, enlarged Netherlands should be a kingdom on the new, 'constitutional', model, under King William I.

25 Abd ul-Medjid, Sultan of Turkey, whose unsuccessful attempts at social reform – the promulgation of the *Tanzimat* – so alarmed the other absolutist monarchs of Europe that Turkey became Designated Victim of the sinister *Dreikaiserbund*, 'the League of the Three Emperors.' It was Abd ul-Hamıd II, ill-fated son of Abd ul-Medjid, whom Holmes tried vainly to help *(Contrad Research Library)*

سلطان عبدالمجید خان

26 Baron de Maupertuis. Dutch descendant of a French family settled in The Hague when Louis Buonaparte ruled Holland, the Baron's ambitious scheme for a Dutch-controlled oil-empire threatened Europe's peace, and Holmes it was who – regretfully, for he liked and admired De Maupertuis – frustrated the scheme. *Photograph: courtesy of the Royal Netherlands Institute of Technological History, Amsterdam, through Mr Peter Blau*

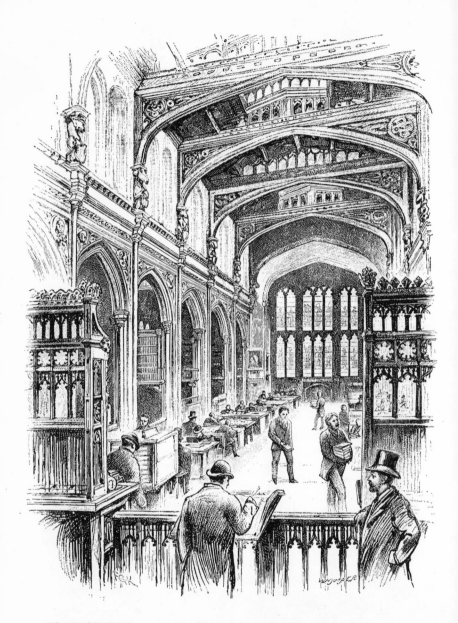

27 The Guildhall Library. Originally founded by Sir Richard ('Dick')
Whittington in the early 15th Century, the present splendid building was
opened in 1872. Housing City of London records dating back to before the
Conquest of 1066, it was in the Guildhall Library that Holmes spent much of
his time in research connected both with 'the Ferrers Documents' and certain
'Early English Charters' *(Contrad Research Library)*

However, as we have seen in recent times, post-Great War settlements are never distinguished by their wisdom. The Dutch, who had fought for their freedom from the Spaniards, at the same time as they were building up a rich overseas empire and conducting (usually successful) foreign wars, had become, by 1815, a people united in language, religion and a fierce (though never loudly proclaimed) chauvinistic pride.

By incorporating the former Austrian Netherlands into Holland, the 'master-minds' of the Vienna Congress put under Dutch rule people who, historically, had come to be very different from the Dutch. The Flemings of the Austrian Netherlands certainly spoke Flemish, a language differing from Dutch only in the most minute particulars; but the Flemings were Catholic, the Dutch were Reformed. And the Walloons, the other people now incorporated into the expanded Kingdom of Holland, were not only Catholic, but spoke French into the bargain. We talk today of 'inbuilt obsolescence'. Certainly, obsolescence was inbuilt as the new Dutch kingdom was proclaimed at Vienna.

And to make the obsolescence more certain, the Dutch treated the newcomers as valueless immigrants worthy of no consideration. Though the incorporated Austrian Netherlands had a population 50 per cent greater than that of the 'original' Holland, both parts of the new Holland sent the same number of representatives to the Assembly. More, Belgium – as the former Austrian Netherlands came to be called – had only one minister in the government. All the plum jobs in the civil service, army, navy and church went to the Dutch; and to provoke further the unrest among the 'Belgians', the Dutch-dominated government ordered, in 1822, that Flemish would be the sole national language. There were other affronts to the French-speaking – incorporated – population, and Belgian resentment led to armed insurrection in 1830, when the Dutch garrison was driven out of Brussels. The creation of an independent state of Belgium was now the concern of the Great Powers, and, at a conference in London, Palmerston declared the dissolution of the post-1815 Kingdom of Holland. The Kingdom of Belgium was erected, and British authority presented the crown to Prince Leopold of Saxe-Coburg, widower of George IV's daughter, Caroline (who had died in 1817) and now married to a daughter of Louis Philippe. Leopold (Queen Victoria's 'dear Uncle Leopold') was a £50,000-a-year pensioner of the British Government, a relative, by marriage, of the British Royal House, and a son-in-law of the King of the French.

The Dutch refused to accept the settlement, and went to war against Belgium; the Great Powers intervened, and, by 1839, had imposed acceptance of the new kingdom of Belgium on a reluctant but realistic Holland.

Holland, then, was something of an outcast in European affairs from 1830 onwards; enduring the contempt which is invariably the lot of the protesting loser; and never quite convinced, as Germanic wars raged around her small territory, that she would not be gobbled up.

Fortunately, relations with Britain in the Far East had evolved into what was, in effect, a mutual defence-and-trade pact. Rivalry in the area around the Malay Peninsula had been amicably settled in 1824, when the Dutch ceded hotly-disputed Malacca to the British in return for British territory in Sumatra. Henceforth, neither Dutch nor British interfered in each other's affairs. The British concentrated upon developing Singapore – founded by them in 1819 – and the whole Malayan area; the Dutch, now separated from British interests by the Malacca Straits, concentrated on building up their Far Eastern empire into a source of income rich enough to compensate them for the politics-imposed constriction of the home country. It must be admitted that, as colonial administrators, the Dutch shewed more greed than compassion; but that could be said of most colonial administrators of the time.

Liberal sentiment – which, really, means interference with the man on the spot by the more carping of the home-country critics – has never acknowledged the enormous debt that it owes to the overseas telegraphic cable. In 1830, when the Dutch, after having suppressed a number of native revolts, dramatically raised the yield from the Indonesian colonies by the forced culture system, Holland's Liberals were too far away to be able to criticize what went on in Java or any other of the Dutch Far Eastern possessions.

Holland had managed, too, to retain her hold on her American colonies: Dutch Guiana and the Antilles – and this, miraculously, despite circumexplosive mainland revolutions, and the developing rapacity of Washington's brand of imperialism, 'Pan-Americanism'.[3]

To keep away from notice; to cultivate a new 'image' of the minding-its-own-business, the industrious cultivator of its own garden, the happy-with-its-own-possessions, completely-harmless-to-its-neighbours, small country – this was what *Realpolitik* counselled for the good of Holland; and this the not inconsiderable talent of Dutch statesmen contrived very largely to accomplish. Except for one thing, which prevented Holland's acquiring that total invisibility in which her whole safety as a nation reposed. She had a 'playboy' Crown Prince who cultivated the wrong sort of publicity as ardently

[3] Given what now seems its inevitable growth into a Great Power, the United States of America was bound, as inevitably, to permit the Monroe Doctrine to develop into 'Pan-Americanism'. The doctrine itself was propounded as part of the deal by which – three years after the War of 1812 had officially ended with the Treaty of Ghent (1815) – Great Britain and the USA both fixed and demilitarized the boundary between the USA and Canada. In return for this pacification of an old trouble-spot, Canning proposed to Monroe and Adams that Great Britain should oppose any Spanish attempt to recover, by force, their former Latin-American colonies. In December, 1823, Monroe, claiming the Doctrine as a purely American invention, uninspired and uninfluenced by the proposals of the British Foreign Secretary, Canning, expounded it to Congress. The essence of the Doctrine, named now after the President who first propounded it, was that any attempt to upset the existing *status quo ante*, undertaken by any Power as regards North or South America, would be regarded as an attack upon the USA. The Doctrine thus 'froze' the then political situation; maintaining the right of the existing colonies of European Powers to survive, but preventing the attempt by Spain to regain her former colonies, and preventing the spread of Russian settlements from Alaska and California. It did not, of course, prevent the Texans from upsetting the *status quo* in a Mexican state, in which the Texans were assisted by British regular naval officers and men specially detached for duty with the Texan insurgents. (*See* Foreign Office Papers: *Texas*; Public Record Office, London.)

as the politicians of his country avoided even the right sort.

William, Prince of Orange, Heir to the Dutch throne, was a rival, in his addiction to pleasure, of that other pleasure-mad Heir, Albert Edward, Prince of Wales. Both frequented the same pleasure-centres throughout a Europe then inspired to cater for the most expensive tastes; both enjoyed the favours of the same *Grandes Horizontales*; both neglected their public duties for their private (but never secret) enjoyments.

When William – nicknamed 'Citron' by the pleasure-loving (and more than a little insane) Duc de Gramont-Caderousse – died on 11th June, 1879, *The Times* primly commented, on the following day:

> He was neither exceedingly arrogant nor exceedingly affable. He easily made friends, and still more easily unmade them, and he seemed born to be one of those joyous meteors who appear and disappear on the horizon of the Parisian Boulevards . . . He took no pleasure in any serious question.

The *Annual Register* added that:

> The Prince of Orange became estranged from his own family, from the general circle of the Royal families of Europe, living more the life of a Paris student, and at times as short of funds as that class is represented to be. He made Paris his home, and the Boulevards the limit of his ambition.

Certainly the most expensive *cocotte* to have been supported by the taxpayers of Holland was the notorious Cora Pearl (real name, Emma Crouch), unreservedly admitted to be the most successful whore of the Parisian *demi-monde* under the Second Empire. Despite his intimate friendship with the Duc de Gramont-Caderousse, the Marquis de St Cricq and Lord Henry Seymour[4] – all notable wits – 'Citron' seems to have been a dull, boorish kind of fellow. Queen Victoria turned him down as a suitor for the hand of Princess Mary of Cambridge on the grounds of his scandalous reputation; the Queen's son avoided 'Citron' because of his infinite

[4] *See* page 60. Lord Henry was a nephew of Lord George.

capacity to bore the too-easily-bored 'Bertie'. The Prince of Wales wasted no tolerance on 'Citron', and was wont to cut short the Dutchman's tedious talk with the sharp command, "*Va donc, Citron!*"

Old King William III, 'Citron's' father, was easily consoled when 'Citron' died; the dead Prince had a still-living, much younger, half-sister, Princess Wilhelmina, who, partly by her own notable qualities and partly by some happy accidents of history, gave Holland her greatest sovereign and the world one of its most respected women of modern times.

In June, 1879, at the time of 'Citron's' death, Holmes was preparing to solve the mystery of the Musgrave Ritual, to enter upon a London stage-career, and to take ship for the United States. What then, seven years later, caused Holmes to be summoned hastily to The Hague, on that vaguely named 'delicate affair' that Watson mentions in two of the fully-described cases?

The King of Holland's health was failing, and though he was to survive for a further five years, it was a sick man who laid some disturbing problems before Sherlock Holmes. Though Watson is understandably reticent about the nature of the problems, I think that we may venture a guess or two as to their identification.

Obviously 'Citron' – the late 'Citron', now – was mixed up in the problems, and that remark of the *Annual Register's* may yield one clue. If 'Citron' was short of funds and pursued by that rapacious harpy, Cora Pearl, then he might well have resorted to some shabby and indeed dangerous expedients in order to raise the wind. Cora's hunger for gold was insatiable, and her dominance of a man was such that there were literally no lengths to which he would not go to get the money without which her 'favours' were unobtainable. (Prince Achille Murat even perjured himself to cheat one of Cora's creditors.)

The dates provide us with a clue, I think. Cora Pearl died (of cancer of the intestine), in her third-floor flat, 8 rue de Bassano, Paris VIIIme, in the dawn of 8th July, 1886. Though her illness had lost her her 'custom', and thus her princely income, she was remembered by the world's press, which united in giving her a (not always kindly) literary send-off. *It was no secret that Cora Pearl was dead.* And one or two persons must have pondered the newspaper reports and wondered how they might turn that lightly-announced death to profit . . .

Two quotations from contemporary reports seem to me to furnish master-clues to the nature of 'the Delicate Affair of the Reigning Family of Holland'.

The first comes from a moralizing obituary in an English newspaper – I have italicized the important passage.

> This is a portrait of the woman who was once one of the darlings of Paris. She is dead, and she died in destitution, though she was the mistress of a prince and the paramour of a millionaire. Yet Cora Pearl, as she called herself, possessed neither beauty, wit, nor culture.[5] What was the secret of the fatal influence she exercised over men? There is no clue to the mystery in the dreary pages which record the history of her miserable life. She was not only vile and vulgar, but vain and vapid. *Perhaps the papers she left behind her, which it is said will be published, may throw some light upon the secret of her fleeting success.*

So that we know – or, at least, we know that it was rumoured – that there were 'papers', of a doubtless compromising kind.

The other – and far more important – quotation is from a contemporary account of the funeral, which took place at the Batignolles Cemetery on 10th July, 1886.

The accounts of the funeral – or, to be more precise, of the *attendance* at that funeral – vary as to the number of mourners: the *Daily News* (13th July, 1886) says twenty; the literary collaboration of Jacques Offenbach, Henri Meilhac and Ludovic Halévy says five, including their three selves. It is with a different account, claiming only three mourners, that I am most concerned here.

[5] That this is malicious nonsense I have made, I trust, clear in my study of Cora and her fellow harlots in *Fanfare of Strumpets*; London: W. H. Allen & Co., 1971.

118

According to this other account, the three mourners who followed Cora's coffin were:

– an Englishman, Mori (sic), who came out of humanity; a Spaniard, Perez, who came out of curiosity; and an unknown man who came to pass the time away.[6]

Mr Holden, from whose excellent life of Cora Pearl I have quoted this brief passage, does well to note that 'Mori' seems an odd name for an Englishman – at any rate, an Englishman of the 1880s.

But, for all its oddity, it strikes a curiously familiar chord in the memories of all who have followed the career of the Sleuth of Baker Street. For what is 'Mori', but the shortened form of 'Moriarty', that man to whom Holmes ungrudgingly conceded 'one of the greatest brains of the century',[7] yet whom Holmes also unhesitatingly described as 'a Napoleon of crime'.[8]

The trail of Moriarty the Criminal again crossed that of Holmes in 1887, in the cases of The Five Orange Pips and The Red-headed League; the actual face-to-face encounter came in the January of 1888, in the case of The Valley of Fear.

Mr Baring-Gould claims that the first encounter between Holmes and Moriarity – that is, as between Thief-taker and Thief – happened at some quite considerable time earlier; but I do not think that Holmes can have met – in person, that is – or even seen Moriarty the Criminal[9] when the latter, as 'Mori', came to Paris to attend the funeral of Cora Pearl and to abstract the compromising papers that rumour said were still in the flat, au troisième, in the rue de Bassano.

That Mori-Moriarty possessed himself of them seems possible, but by no means certain. The ex-tutor needed no more than a child's power of deception to persuade King William of Holland that there had been indiscreet letters from 'Citron' among Cora's papers. The King would have found it credible that

[6] The Pearl from Plymouth, W. H. Holden; London: British Technical and General Press, 1950.
[7] The Empty House.   [8] The Final Problem.
[9] Holmes had quite lost sight of his old private tutor, and not until Holmes actually saw Moriarty again, did the former realize that Ex-Tutor and Arch-Criminal were the same.

such letters should have been written; that they had been found where Moriarty had claimed to have found them. But whether or not there were those dangerous letters hardly matters; Holmes either retrieved them from Moriarty or exposed Moriarty as a criminal trickster. The Dutch police, even in those days, had a well-earned reputation for efficiency; Holmes would have found them far more reliable than the average detective from Scotland Yard. Under Holmes's direction, the Dutch police could have – and most certainly did – make things very hot for James Moriarty.

Moriarty would not have used his right name in putting pressure on the King; how, then, did Holmes know that it was with Moriarty that he had to deal? As Holmes tried – but, one sees, ineffectually – to explain to Watson, the hunter (be he detective, confidence-trickster, general, admiral) soon learns to recognize his opponent's *pattern*. The 'signature' of Moriarty – or, indeed, of any other criminal – was as plain for Holmes to recognize in a crime as though Moriarty had openly claimed the guilt.

Besides, who but an ex-tutor, asked his name at Cora's funeral, could so quickly and so aptly have found, in his own name, a short, sharp pun on the first of the Four Last Things: 'Mori' – *memento mori* – 'Remember! thou, too, must die!'

Holmes returned from The Hague in the April of 1887 with a further mark of Royal approval: the Royal Order of the Lion of the Netherlands. Permission to accept these tributes from foreign monarchs was willingly given to Holmes by Queen Victoria.

There had been two cases in which Holmes had served the interests of Holland well; the second case, that of 'the Netherlands–Sumatra Company and the Colossal Schemes of Baron Maupertuis', to which Watson refers in the case of *The Reigate Squires*, did not lie precisely in the field of criminality, though it threatened irreparable harm to the destiny of Holland as a small, independent European nation with a large and rich overseas empire.

The trouble with the Baron, a Dutch subject of Walloon

extraction, was that he 'thought too big', too far in advance of his time. Rock-oil, discovered in the United States only thirty years earlier, had already laid the foundations of a vast industry, quite unforeseen when Edwin L. Drake literally 'struck oil' in Western Pennsylvania on 27th August, 1859.

Ten years after Drake drilled his first oil-well, rock-oil was being shipped to every country in the world, causing the profound economic change which came when the older illuminants, tallow candles and sperm-oil lamps, were abandoned in favour of the new kerosene, which was also adopted for cooking purposes. In 1874, the first trunk pipe-line was constructed, to carry 7,500 barrels a day from the oil-regions of Western Pennsylvania to Pittsburgh. Four years later, work started on the first pipe-line to cross from Pennsylvania into neighbouring states. This line was designed to carry the crude oil over the Allegheny Mountains to the Atlantic seaboard.

By 1886, when the Dutch government became exceedingly anxious over the activities of Baron Maupertuis, Oil had grown into Big Business, indeed; but kerosene remained the industry's principal product until the early twentieth century, when the Kerosene Age reluctantly gave place to the Gasoline Age.

Ten years before, as I mentioned on page 80, Gottfried Daimler had revived, though in its first really practical form, the internal-combustion engine, powered with that benzine[10] which was a distillate of American petroleum.

The modern motor-spirits did not really arrive until the introduction of the thermal 'cracking' process in 1913, a step forward which was as nothing compared with Houdry's catalytic cracking process for the refining of petroleum, introduced in 1938. This and other catalytic cracking processes opened the way to the production, in great quantity, of the modern high octane number aviation fuels.

'Petrol', itself – it was originally a trade-name of a London firm of oil-refiners, Carless, Capel & Leonard, who unwisely

[10] The use of this word here is somewhat metachronistic, since *Benzine* and *Benzene* (the latter a derivative of coal-tar) are both named after Benz. But there were highly volatile petroleum distillates before benzine.

omitted to patent the name – was not available until 1894; but there were more or less satisfactory high-volatility essences ready for the embryo automobilist on the introduction of Daimler's first horseless-carriages in 1877.

Maupertuis had the far-seeing eye of the really big operator. He not only formulated plans for the development of the already discovered East Indian oil, he foresaw what not even Daimler and Benz foresaw: the eventual displacement of all horse-drawn traffic in favour of the automobile. That is, he foresaw the huge world-market for petroleum products that a world changeover to the internal-combustion engine would inevitably create. There are those who say that the Baron foresaw the imminent achievement of powered heavier-than-air flight, with a further immeasurable extension of the petroleum market; but this has not been proved. However, he did foresee – and make appropriate plans for – the coming of the petroleum-driven motor-car. Watson is right to call the schemes of the Baron Maupertuis 'colossal'.

Already Oil, though hardly thirty years old, had evolved a characteristic marketing pattern, and – perhaps far more important – a type of thinking and acting which identified all the Big Boys more precisely than did ever their individual physical characteristics. They were all tough, ruthless, without pity or the possibility of satiation when it came to money; and already they had made so much money that they had – and all this well within thirty years – passed to the stage at which, though still insatiably greedy for money, they had come to love power even more. Flagler had not yet spent $40,000,000 of his own money simply to build a railroad into Florida; but the grand – and ruthless – gesture was already the hallmark of these oil-slicked bandits who were to replace the gun with the more powerful weapon of the corporation lawyer.

Maupertuis not only wished to develop the Dutch oil in the Far East, he wished also to create markets in the Far East which would further develop Dutch oil production. So far, so good. But, rather than go to the big European bankers for capital to develop Holland's far Eastern empire – the Barings, the Rothschilds, the Bischoffscheims, the Salamancas – Maupertuis proposed to avail himself of both the capital and the 'know-how' of the cormorants who had nested in the Pennsylvania oil-fields – and that politico-financial development the Dutch government could not permit. Pan-Americanism had not yet been adopted and proclaimed as a permanent imperial faith by Washington, but already the empire-building characteristics of American wealth were only too disturbingly apparent. It took no great prescience to foresee that in allowing Maupertuis to develop Dutch overseas possessions with American Oil capital, it would not be long before those possessions would be, *de facto*, if not *de jure*, dependencies of the United States of America.

Holmes dealt kindly but firmly with the Baron. Holmes was an admirer of, and a sympathizer with, the United States, but even Holmes could see how much more powerful such men as Rockefeller, Andrews and Flagler could be than any government – seeing that they might dispose of wealth on governmental scale, yet be free from those submissions to, and control by, public opinion that even the most autocratic and tyrannical governments must acknowledge. Holmes could understand how such as Flagler, who, after a 'health vacation' in Florida in 1883, had, three years later, purchased the Jacksonville, St Augustine and Halifax River Railroad, as the first step in developing a Flagler-dominated Florida, could upset the sensitive balance of political and economic power in the Far East. The secret history of the negotiations between Holmes and Maupertuis have never been published, but – since Holland's 'allies', Britain and the USA, joined up with the defeated Japanese to rob Holland of her Far Eastern empire (so as to hand it over to the Japanese-trained 'resistance fighter', Soekarno) – the relevant documents may be consulted in the Dutch State Archives.

In 1886, there were no playboys in the Swedish Royal House; Holmes was summoned to Stockholm on matters concerned solely with the welfare of the State – though, to be sure, there were strong emotional overtones in the opinions which had generated that dangerous situation in which Holmes's assistance had been invoked by King Oscar II.

The three Scandinavian kingdoms of Norway, Sweden and Denmark had, over the centuries, effected all the combinations possible to three basically similar social organisms: domination altering as power passed from one kingdom to the other. Each had fought the two others at least once: in 1788, Sweden declared war on Russia and invaded Finland; but, two years later, Denmark attacked Sweden, and forced her to sign a peace with Russia and retire from Finland. And so it went . . .

At the end of the eighteenth century, Denmark was a far bigger kingdom than it is to-day: it owned, besides the Home Country, Schleswig-and-Holstein, Norway, Pomerania, Iceland, Greenland, the Danish Virgin Islands and Bouvet Island in the sub-Antarctic, that African colony which is now called Ghana. Sweden, too, though it had lost power and influence in the Baltic, dominated by Sweden at the beginning of the century, made a recovery under Gustavus III (1771–1792), and was to emerge from the period of the Napoleonic Wars with greatly increased territory.

King Oscar II was the grandson of Jean Bernadotte and Desirée Clary, that Marseilles merchant's daughter who had been jilted by Napoleon in order that he might marry the tarnished but (as the parvenu genius thought) 'better connected' and more influential Joséphine de Beauharnais.

Bernadotte, brother-in-law to Napoleon through Joseph Bonaparte's marriage with Marie-Julie Clary, shared in Napoleon's greatness, rising from sergeant-major to Marshal of the Empire and Prince of Pontecorvo. In 1810, at the height of Napoleon's power and prestige – the year in which the Emperor married into the Imperial House of Austria – Bernadotte contrived to manœuvre himself into the heritage of the Swedish throne. The King of Sweden, Gustavus IV, was childless, and to secure the powerful assistance of Napoleon the Swedish Diet confirmed the succession of the new Crown Prince, Jean Baptiste Bernadotte, to the throne of Sweden.

On the defeat of Napoleon; a defeat to which Bernadotte,

as commander of the North German Army, decisively con-
tributed, as he smashed the French army at Dennewitz
(commanded by his fellow-Marshal and once companion-in-
arms, Ney); Sweden and Bernadotte were high in the list of
those for whom rewards were in order.

Denmark, having backed Napoleon, ranked for punishment.
The now completely victorious Allies sanctioned Bernadotte's
plan to unite Norway and Sweden under one crown –
eventually to be worn by Bernadotte; and desperate to end a
war that they had already lost, the Danes agreed to cede
Norway to Sweden, accepting Bernadotte's offer to cede
Swedish Pomerania to the Danes in exchange for Norway. As
it happened, the combined Russian and Prussian forces, recovering Swedish Pomerania from the French, made no
attempt, despite the Russio-Swedish alliance, to hand it back to
Sweden, but established a military government over the entire
territory. Eventually, the province went neither to Sweden nor
to Denmark, but to Prussia.

Sweden ended the war with Denmark by the Treaty of 14th
January, 1814; the Danes agreeing to cede Norway to the
winner.

In the end, despite the Treaty, Bernadotte had to take Norway by force. Prince Christian Frederick, the (Danish)
Governor-general of Norway, refused to give up his post, and
though the Allies made those protests which always seem
most particularly ineffective when voiced by those who have
just secured a decisive victory, the Governor-general declared
Norway's independence of both Sweden and Denmark, and
proclaimed himself king of an independent Norway as
Christian VII.

Bernadotte beat the Norwegians, of course; but he beat, too,
that opposition to his remaining in Sweden which had sprung
up with the restoration of the *ancien régime*, who chose to
forget that he had helped to bring about the downfall of
Napoleon and remembered only that Bernadotte, son of the
Town Bailiff of Pau, had worn the tricolour cockade, had
fought for the Republic of France and had received his
Marshal's baton at the hands of the Emperor.

The opposition was strong: it lasted almost to the end of Bernadotte's life. But it was never strong enough to dethrone him, nor impede his intelligent efforts to prove that it had been no mere love of windy rhetoric which had caused him to tell his predecessor, King Charles XIII: "No mortal ever received a stronger inducement, and no one was ever afforded a finer opportunity, to dedicate his life to the well-being of a whole nation."

This he did. He created modern Sweden; a state in which imperialistic ambitions were to have no place; which was to achieve internal and external peace by striving for the highest standard of living compatible with solvency. Sweden was to be the world's Great Neutral; friend of all, enemy of none; and supplier of the most sophisticated armaments and war *matériel* to any nation which could foot the bill.

It was a wonderful plan – especially for a man who had risen from nothing to a kingdom through the profession of arms. It is wonderful how history has vindicated his ambitions for Sweden; for they did not take into account two most important factors – that Bernadotte, King Charles XIV John of Sweden–Norway, had bitten the hand which had fed him; had turned on his master; had betrayed his benefactor; and that the Norwegians considered themselves subjects of the Dual Crown only by duress.

The Norwegians were the 'Irish' of Sweden–Norway; resentful of, and always mindful of, the fact that their independence had been taken from them by force. Much was done for them; they were never – in the view of the outsider – 'oppressed'. All that they were denied was their independence – and that was the one important thing which *was* denied them.

The bombing of the (principally London) British had been begun by the Irish with the blowing-up of Clerkenwell Prison in 1867; the campaign was to last for a quarter-of-a-century; being renewed later. The Norwegians adopted more passive expressions of revolt; the most effective of which was the deliberate and carefully-contrived development of a distinctive Norwegian speech, old forms being revived and new ones invented. The purpose was so to exaggerate the existing small differences between Swedish and Norwegian that they would become, in effect, two different languages. A heady nationalism swept Norway; in painting, music, literature, architecture, sculpture, no less than in modes of speech, a specifically 'Nordisk' sentiment was devised and passionately cultivated. Decade by decade, then year by year, then almost day by day, the differences widened and were further widened. 'There is between me and thee a great gulf fixed.'

By the time that Holmes went to Stockholm to see King Oscar II, practically any Swede could have said that to practically any Norwegian. And the uncomfortable persuasion was abroad that the widening differences between the two nations, bound in so uneasy a partnership, might not always remain on this mildly aggressive level – that, sooner or later, the dormant fighting impulses of the Norwegians might come to life in actual armed revolt.

We know now what Holmes advised. Twenty years before, Queen Victoria had permitted the Prussians to break the Protocol of London, and invade Denmark. Not all the lessons of that misguided decision had yet been learned; but some of them had – and what was now clear (after Prussia's defeat of every opponent and her raising herself to the dignity of an empire) was that civil war in Scandinavia would see the three kingdoms obliterated as completely by the rapacious Prussians and Russians as Poland had been obliterated at the end of the previous century.

Holmes, who had had some long conversations at the Foreign Office before leaving for Stockholm, advised that the Swedish Crown voluntarily divest itself of its Norwegian 'sister-kingdom'; that Norway be re-erected to what it had been for so many glorious centuries: a sovereign, independent state, entirely free of even the lightest treaty obligations to Sweden, and that a king be sought in a House historically-associated rather with Scandinavia than with Germany.

Had Holmes's advice been taken in 1886, much bitterness between the two unhappily-married nations might have been avoided; but there were questions of family pride which opposed the recognition of the *inevitability* of Holmes's solution. It was King Oscar's grandfather who had fought and beaten the stiff-necked Norwegians; it was he who had done so much for them : giving them schools, universities, good roads, industries, ports, Heaven knew what else. It was not easier for King Oscar than it has proved for many another man to give up – and voluntarily to give up – his patrimony. Indeed, the peaceful separation of the two kingdoms did not come until 1905, nearly two years after Holmes, taking a well-earned rest from his professional labours, had retired to bee-keeping and his books at Cuckmere Haven, on the South Downs, five miles from Eastbourne. He must have smiled as he read the report in *The Times* of the crowning of Prince Charles of Denmark as King Haakon VII of Norway, in the ancient cathedral of Trondheim, his Queen being Princess Maud of Connaught, grand-daughter of Queen Victoria. Through the windows he could hear that singularly Vergilian sound, the hum of bees about their skeps; and, farther off, the gentle susurrus of the Channel tide. Against an old wall, hollyhocks and lupins and sunflowers cast their polychrome brightness into the shadowed room. He shook *The Times* into a more 'readable shape', and, as he read on, he moved his head in a gentle reproof of that human obstinacy which could have delayed this happy inevitability for twenty years. But it had all come out as he had planned . . .

"Well, well . . ." he murmured, turning to the racing-page.

28 Holmes's greatest diplomatic triumph. King Christian IX of Denmark receives the deputation from his Storting (Parliament) to offer the throne of Norway to the King's grandson, Prince Charles, thus ending the unhappy union between Sweden and Norway: a peaceful outcome towards which Holmes had played an important part. *From the painting by Paul Fischer in the Frederiksborg Palace. Photograph made available through the kindness of the well-known Danish artist, Henry Lauritzen*

29 The Albert Hall. As it was when the affair of the Borgia Ring provided its own disastrous solution on the Hall's large stage. *(Contrad Research Library)*

Osborne Jan: 14– ۱۸۹۲ ج، ۱۴

اج ہم سب قدر اصل رہم اور اج کم کو اوہم اور اولاد
کو جو کبھی نہیں ہوا ۔ کیونکہ ہمارے جوان نواسی
پرنس البرت وکٹر آف ویلس اج صبح نو بجے فوت ہو گئے ۔

Today I and my family were almost in greater sorrow and grief than they had ever been before as my young Grandson Prince Albert Victor of Wales died this Morning at nine o'clock. V.

30 The end of 'Collar and Cuffs.' 'A merciful providence,' is how Sir Philip Magnus describes the death of Prince Albert Victor of Wales, Duke of Clarence, who, living, presented a constant threat to the Throne by his irregular behaviour. But, despite his faults, both the rigid Queen and his more tolerant parents were heartbroken by his death. Here is the relevant entry in the 73-year-old Queen's diary; the entry being both in Hindustani and English. It will be noted that the Queen does not give her grandson the ducal title of 'Clarence and Avondale,' conferred two years earlier (*Contrad Research Library*)

5

The Ripper and the Crown

In my *Clarence*, the first full biography of the Duke of Clarence and Avondale, eldest son of the Prince of Wales (later King Edward VII),[1] I have refuted the rumour that the Duke was the homicidal maniac known to history as 'Jack the Ripper', and I have named the Duke's tutor, the brilliant but insane James Kenneth Stephen, as 'the Ripper'.

I cannot follow my old friend William Baring-Gould in his solution of the 'Ripper' mystery, in which he names Inspector Athelney Jones, of Scotland Yard, as the infamous criminal. I think that I have presented convincing proof: not only did Stephen come of a family in which 'mental breakdowns' had been hereditary for at least five generations; not only did his father, Mr Justice Stephen, exhibit unmistakable signs of insanity even whilst judging a murder case;[2] not only does James Kenneth Stephen's death-certificate state plainly that he died insane; but also his poems reveal the woman-hating, homicidal obsessions of a deranged mind – just the poems, in fact, that we might expect from a murderous criminal (if insanity, of course, admit the concept of criminality) of 'the Ripper' type.

In those chapters of my book devoted to the identifying of J. K. Stephen as 'the Ripper', I have argued for a 'pattern' of ten 'Ripper' murders, from that of Smith on 3rd April, 1888, to that of Coles on 13th February, 1891. Other students of the 'Ripper' crimes put the total number at no more than five; but contemporary opinion was disinclined to accept this

[1] London : W. H. Allen & Co., 1972.
[2] That of Mrs Maybrick, an American, accused of having poisoned her husband by the administration of arsenic.

modest estimate of the maniac's total culpability. And one must admit that there were some murders which, though never attributed 'officially' to the Ripper (even by me), yet indicate the presence, in the East End, of a killer hardly inferior to 'Jack' in point of deliberate savagery. Such, for example, produced the mutilated female trunk – never identified – which was found under a railway-arch in Ruchin Street, Whitechapel, on 10th September, 1889.

More to the point is the fact that public opinion was inclined to attribute murders to the killer known afterwards as 'the Ripper' as early as 1887, and there is one small piece of evidence, not only that a 'Ripper' murder *had* been committed before the end of 1887, but that Holmes knew of it. There is no more record in the Holmes–Watson file than the brief mention, in *The Adventure of the Norwood Builder*, of 'The Case of Bert Stevens, the Terrible Murderer'.

Now, we know that Watson, not only in the interests of 'tact', to say nothing of the avoidance of expensive libel actions, but mostly because his professional training had conditioned him to discretion, always made some alteration, great or small, in the names of the *dramatis personæ*, in the locations of the adventures, and in even the dates involved.

But 'Bert Stevens' is so reminiscent of 'Jim Stephen' – especially when to both may be applied the dreadful title of 'the Terrible Murderer' – that it is difficult to resist the conclusion that Watson is referring to the man whom I have identified as one of the most dedicated and savage woman-mutilators in history.

It was in 1886 that James Stephen, according to his uncle's brief memoir in *The Dictionary of National Biography* (of which the uncle, Sir Leslie Stephen, was first editor), suffered that accident which 'affected his mental powers', a euphemism understandable in one of the Stephen family; in a man who, himself, did not go unscathed of the 'Stephen mental derangement'. There are several versions of this 'accident', which is supposed to have taken place at Felixstowe; so many versions – struck by the open door of a passing train, struck by the vane of a revolving windmill, and so on – that it is

possible that there was no accident as such, and that James
Stephen simply manifested, a little earlier than was customary in the Stephen family, the clear syndromes of the
hereditary mental complaint.

The difficult in treating James Stephen's insanity in the nor-
mal way came from the fact that he had been chosen by the
Prince and Princess of Wales, on the recommendation of Dr
Dalton, tutor-promoted-governor of Prince Eddy and Prince
George of Wales, to tutor Eddy through his two years as an
undergraduate of Trinity College, Cambridge.

If the British Royal Family of that time had been as 'respectably' bourgeois as, say, the Royal Families of Sweden–
Norway, Denmark or Saxony, it could have stood the revelation that an Heir to its throne had had a maniac – even an
homicidal maniac – for tutor. But there had been too many
scandals, notably around Prince Eddy's father, for it to be
hoped that any further scandal would not be magnified to
the augmented damaging of that Family's already diminished
reputation. It is often said, by those who should know far
better, that there were no scandal-giving 'Royal Dukes' in
Victoria's reign, as there had been in the latter Georgian days.
This is rubbish: with the exception of the Duke of Connaught and Strathearn, all Queen Victoria's sons were a wild
lot who had almost every vice in common with those which
had made the Georgian 'Royal Dukes' a scandal.

It would be hard to find three such dedicated and unscrupu-
lous pleasure-seekers as the Prince of Wales and his brothers,
the Duke of Edinburgh (later Duke of Saxe-Coburg-Gotha)
and the Duke of Albany. The one thing which may be said
of them, in their favour, is that their vices were all 'normal'
– women, drink, gambling, driving railway-trains, horseplay
in the streets and unkind practical joking. They chased 'respectable' women – especially the wives of their 'respectable' friends; they kept all the most notorious whores of
the day, from Cora Pearl to Lillie Langtry; they patronized
the most sinister elements of the Turf; they borrowed money
from Jewish moneylenders and 'repaid' the loans by introduc-
tions to Royalty, by making the lenders members of their 'ex-

clusive' clubs, by getting them lesser titles, and by inviting them, even, to their own homes.

The Prince of Wales had already made an appearance in the law court, in connection with the most unsavoury divorce case of the century, in the course of which the Prince's intimate friend, Sir Frederick Johnstone, admitted that he had suffered from gonorrhœa for several years ("too busy to cure it") and Lady Mordaunt had to admit that her child – declared illegitimate by herself – had been born with what appeared to be gonorrhœal ophthalmia. Untrue or not, it was widely rumoured that the Princess of Wales's non-healing affection of the knee, which left her with a permanent limp, had been caused by 'the bad disease', given to her by her husband.

The Duke of Teck, son of a morganatic marriage of Duke Alexander of Wurtemburg, was the father of Princess 'May', who married the man who was afterwards King George V. The Duke, married to a grand-daughter of George III, settled in England; but though he was raised, by Queen Victoria, to the rank of 'Highness', in the Jubilee honours of 1887, Teck enjoyed a very dubious reputation in the circles that he did *not* frequent. A devotee of the racecourse and its ancillary *milieus* – tented bars and railway-station buffets and seedy clubs such as the Pelican in Gerrard Street – Teck was hail-fellow-well-met with every shabby tipster and tout, every professional punter and tic-tac man; a world of friendships which seemed to accord oddly with even the vaguely military background that he affected: a major-general ('unattached') and two colonelcies, both of bank-clerk volunteers' regiments in London. No, the Duke, for all the undeniable dignity of his daughter, 'May', was no great shakes as an aristocrat. And even the Queen had her own dubious friendships; the most notorious, that with the openly offensive, permanently drunken ghillie, John Brown; but run, in point of unsuitable quality, a close second by the Queen's affection for the drunken, foul-mouthed Alexander Duff, whom she raised to a dukedom after having persuaded her grand-daughter, Princess Louise of Wales, to marry this appalling Scotch blackguard.

No, it was no time to be airing yet more of the Royal Family's dirty linen: James Stephen, because of his former intimacy with his Royal pupil – Eddy had dropped his old tutor pretty promptly on joining the crack 10th Hussars – had to be hushed up, not merely as a lunatic, but as a mass-murderer also. There were then, as there are to-day, 'discreet' nursing-homes, where well-heeled private patients might enjoy all the advantages of restraint without any of the humiliating inconveniences of such institutions as Broadmoor. And, just like the alienists of the more official lunatic asylums, the resident psychiatrists of the private 'homes' are often willing to decide that they have effected a 'total cure'. Stephen must have been taken into custody and released as 'cured', several – perhaps even many – times before, on 21st November, 1891, he entered a lunatic asylum at Northampton, from which he was never to emerge alive.

It is my opinion that, after the first revelation of Stephen's homicidal mania – the connection of a barbarous killing with James Kenneth Stephen as the killer – there was no mystery about the identity of 'the Ripper'. Certain additional facts have come to light since I finished my book, *Clarence*: the most important, to be found in the first volume of Professor Quentin Bell's life of Virginia Woolf (J. K. Stephen's first cousin), is that Stephen habitually carried a sword-stick – that is to say, Stephen went around London and Cambridge (where he was a Fellow) constantly *armed*. Professor Bell relates how, on one occasion, J. K. Stephen ran into the Stephen cousins' house at 22 Hyde Park Gate, drew the sword from his stick, and 'thrust it into a cottage-loaf'. In those days, the anthropomorphic – female – character of the cottage-loaf was even more evident by reason of a 'top knot' added to the 'second layer' of the loaf. Obviously, in its origins the cottage-loaf is a representation of the female human figure[3] – and Stephen was symbolizing his wish to kill all females (a wish openly expressed in his poems[4]) when he plunged the sharp point of

[3] The most ancient female fertility symbol, the 'Willendorff Venus', in an edible form.

[4] *Lapsus Calami*. Cambridge: Bowes and Macmillan, 1891.

his sword into the bulging 'bosom' of the cottage-loaf. There is not only the obvious female shape to explain Stephen's attack on the inanimate piece of baked bread; there is the sub-conscious reaction to a pun meaningful only to one familiar with the secret language of the contemporary homosexual underworld, in which a 'cottage' was a public urinal (usually of the cast-iron, kerb-edge, kind) and a 'cottage-loaf' was a male prostitute who loitered about – 'loafed' about – such malodorous places. In passing, we may remark that it was the attempt of one such 'cottage-loaf' to inflict mild blackmail on Labouchere, as the latter was on his way to the House of Commons, which inspired 'Labby' to propose the inclusion of homosexual offences in the list of those covered by the Criminal Law Amendment Act of 1884.

This brings us to another reason why it was essential that the identity of 'the Ripper' should not be revealed; he was a homosexual – or, at least, bisexual with a preponderantly homosexual urge[5] – and Prince Eddy's sexual tendencies shewed a similar pattern. In 1889, a male brothel was raided by the police on the initiative of the Editor of the *North London Press* – but only after the brothel-keeper, Hammond, had been allowed to decamp to France, *with his furniture*, and Lord Arthur Somerset, Superintendent of the Stables to HRH the Prince of Wales, had been advised to take the boat-train to Dover.

The affair was deplorably mismanaged – the hand of Holmes in this is apparent *nowhere*! – but some excuse may be found for the muddle and the muddlers in that there were several law-enforcing bodies at work, all stumbling over each other's feet, all working vigorously against all the others, and all with what appears now to be entirely different ends to serve. There were the Post Office police – the affair began when telegraph-boys were observed to be spending more than their meagre wages would justify; the ordinary Metropolitan

---

[5] He is said to have been 'madly in love' with Virginia Woolf's (then Virginia Stephen's) half-sister, Stella Duckworth, and to have been refused the house by her parents because of the nuisance that he was making of himself.

and City of London Police; the Yard itself, represented by the officious Inspector Abberline, who had already distinguished himself in the 'Ripper' affair by arresting *and charging* two patently innocent men; the Foreign Office's own undercover men, who arrested (if that's the correct word) all the telegraph-boys and took them, without relatives or legal representatives, to be examined in the FO's 'Star Chamber' in Whitehall. There were also several private detectives, all instructed by interested parties, including one 'tec with the dodgy monniker of Adolph de Gallo, working for a very sharp solicitor named Arthur Newton, who afterwards did time.

Doing its best with some badly arranged material, the Government initiated an elaborate legal farce,[6] in which Justice was seen to seem to be done, and the name of Prince Albert Victor of Wales (not yet Duke of Clarence and Avondale) was never mentioned.

It is when we consider the correct Christian name of Prince 'Eddy' that we can account for Watson's choice of 'Bert Stevens' as the name of 'the Terrible Murderer' noted earlier. Watson was so well aware of the intimate connection between Prince *Albert* Victor and his ex-tutor, James *Stephen*, and so well aware that it was this intimacy which forbade, at all costs, the identification of Stephen with 'Jack the Ripper', that, subconsciously or perhaps very deliberately, he drew on the names of both men to effect the slight alteration of 'James Stephen' to 'Bert Stevens'.

But there is another clue to Watson's knowledge in what has often been referred to as a misprint,[7] but which, in the light of our after-knowledge, appears to be rather what is called to-day a 'Freudian slip'. I refer to the misspelt name of the famous racehorse, *Isonomy*, winner of the 1878 Cambridgeshire, the 1879 Manchester Plate, and winner of the Ascot Gold Cup in two successive years – 1879 and 1880.

[6] Described in full in my *Clarence*, op. cit.

[7] It is so referred to by the late William Baring-Gould in the notes to his collection, *The Adventure of the Speckled Band and other stories of Sherlock Holmes: Sir Arthur Conan Doyle*; New York: The New American Library, 1965 (Paperback).

Isonomy's name was a familiar one even to those who never laid even a shilling annual bet on the Derby; yet Watson, referring to Isonomy in his account of one of Holmes's most memorable cases, *Silver Blaze*, curiously misspells the horse's name, 'Somomy', and though Watson's account of Turf activities in *Silver Blaze* shew him to have had the most lamentable ignorance of even the basics of racing (he quotes the odds against Desborough as 'five to fifteen' – Watson's unique version of 'three to one on'!), this hardly accounts for the subconscious rendering of 'Isonomy' as 'Somomy'.

Let us look at the dates. The case of *Silver Blaze*, which took the two friends down to King's Pyland, on Dartmoor, covered nearly five days – from Thursday, 25th September, to Tuesday, 30th September, 1890 – *exactly one year after* the first announcement, in the *North London Press*, that the 'West End Scandals' uncovered by the Editor's private detectives, working with the police, would result in 'startling revelations'. We know that, as Holmes and Watson 'flew along en route for Exeter', they read the newspapers – including the *Telegraph* and the *Chronicle* – that Holmes had bought at the bookstall at Paddington; and the talk must have gone on to mention that *cause* not so much *célèbre* as *terrible*, the news of which had 'broken' just a year before.

So, half-remembering that conversation, and being, at best, unfamiliar with the terminology of racing and the names of racehorses, Watson, thinking to write 'Isonomy', but recalling their discussion of the *sodomy* which had made 'the Cleveland Street Scandal' so unsavoury an affair, wrote 'Somomy', an unnatural word which may be explained only if we may suppose that, at the time of writing, Watson had unnatural vice on his mind.

James Kenneth Stephen – 'Jack the Ripper' – died in St Andrew's Hospital, Northampton, on 3rd February, 1892. He had been committed to the lunatic asylum on the preceding 21st November, a year to the day after he had consulted an eminent London alienist, and two years to the day after one of his more barbarous murders – or perhaps 'killing' is the juster word, seeing that Stephen, before he committed his first homicide, was undeniably insane.

He wrote to his family and to his friends, and he was allowed visitors. When his intimate, but neglectful, friend, 'Eddy', fell ill of that influenza which was to kill him, Jim Stephen wrote to him, and there is some evidence that Eddy either wrote – ill as he was – or caused a letter to be written to the wretched maniac, who could still remember an old friendship from the ultimate hopelessness of a barred-and-bolted cell.

Eddy died at Sandringham in the night of 13th–14th January, 1892: the not unexpected news of his death did not go out on the private telegraph-line from Sandringham to St Martin's-le-Grand until after the first editions of the newspapers had been printed and distributed. The news appeared in the 'fudge' of some of the later editions of the dailies, but was fully covered in the hundreds of evenings – London alone had eight – which, in those days, as at present, were on sale from about ten in the morning. By lunch-time on 14th January, James Stephen, 'the Ripper', would have learnt of the death of his ex-pupil, the man whose neglect of the ambitious Stephen must have helped to turn a brain already hereditarily disposed towards derangement.

What happened then, the death-certificate makes clear. The cause of death is given as 'Mania, 2½ months. Persistent refusal of food, 20 days.' The date of death is given as '3rd February, 1892'. If one subtract twenty days from 3rd February, one arrives at 14th January – James Stephen, having no more wish to live, began his fatal hunger-strike on learning that the faithless Eddy was dead.

They could have kept him alive; a patient in a hospital, a prisoner in a cell, may embark upon a hunger-strike of his own will; he continues only by permission of the authorities: a hunger-striker may always be forcibly fed . . .

But they let James Stephen go. His mind was unhinged, and with him mania had taken the most terrible form. For all their sakes – 'the Ripper's' especially – it was better, far better, that he should go.

For twenty days he endured the pangs of hunger and thirst; and on the twenty-first, release came. They kept the secret. In Eton College Chapel and in the Chapel of King's College, Cambridge, there are brass plates to commemorate the man who, as sportsman and scholar, had earned the admiration of his contemporaries.

Much more research than has, up to the present, been done is needed before we may know exactly how Holmes's services were employed in that hushing-up of maniac savagery that the prestige of the Crown rendered essential. But somewhere, somehow, Holmes was involved, as Watson's typically Watsonian reference to 'Bert[8] Stevens' the Terrible Murderer', makes clear.

[8] J. K. Stephen's elder brother was a 'Bert' too – Sir Herbert Stephen, Bart.

6

The Order of St Anne

Besides the vast collection of Sherlockiana assembled over many years by the late Adrian Conan Doyle at the Château de Luzens, in Switzerland, there exists a less well-known, though no less important, collection of the Count Arpad Apponyi von Karancs-Berény, formerly, among many diplomatic appointments, Third Secretary at the Austro-Hungarian Embassy in London, and first Hungarian Minister to Montenegro, in the few months between the re-establishment of Hungarian independence on 17th November, 1918, and the suppression of the mountain kingdom of Montenegro in November, 1920.

The Count, who had been educated in England (Summer Fields, Eton and Balliol), was of an ancient Hungarian family whose traditional religious allegiance had been untouched by any of the reformations centred about his homeland, and it was in connection with the 'Famous Investigation of the Sudden Death of Cardinal Tosca', in May or June, 1895, that Count Arpad first met the great investigator, Sherlock Holmes. An admiration strengthened by this and later personal contacts inspired the Count, whose family was of vast wealth, to initiate a collection of objects associated with Holmes. The collection, made over a period of many years, is to be visited in the Count's former town-mansion in Buda, where it is carefully maintained and guarded by the present Hungarian Government.

Inevitably, with the establishment of a Russian protectorate over Hungary, in 1946, the Count's Buda mansion, together with all his other properties, were 'nationalized', to become 'property of the People'. However, both the Buda house and its priceless collection of Sherlockiana escaped looting and bombardment, and Holmes's reputation behind the Iron Curtain is still such that nothing associated with him could fail to be treated with respect by the present rulers of Eastern Europe.

It is this respect that Holmes's memory commands which accounts for the fact that no fewer than four of Watson's accounts of Sherlockian cases are included among the works issued by the Red Army Publishing House, and are thus permitted reading for Russian soldiers and their families.

The four cases were introduced as Russian military reading-matter under the last Tsar; but, on the inevitable overhaul of military literature under the new régime, these four Sherlockian books received the Soviet *imprimatur*, and now perpetuate the fame of the Sleuth of Baker Street with new generations of Russians.

One of the treasures of the Apponyi Sherlockian Collection is the large morocco-covered, velvet-lined case in which lie the insignia of the Grand Cross of the Imperial Order of St Anne, presented to Sherlock Holmes by Alexander III, in January, 1887. The light red riband with its thin yellow borders is faded now, but the gold and enamel are as bright as when the Order was made, considerably before Holmes's birth. If one examine the backs of the enamelled-gold insignia, as I was permitted to do by the courtesy of the present Curator of the Magyar People's Sherlock Holmes Museum, Monsieur Istvan Batthyany, one sees that these delicate examples of the jeweller's art are all signed, *Keitel*,[1] *Bijoutier, à Petersbourg*, who was active before and after Napoleon the First invaded Russia in 1812.

The evidence of a history earlier than Holmes's indicates that these insignia were of unusual value, both intrinsic and associative. Monsieur Batthyany, some of whose ancestors had held high office under the Hapsburgs, and who has still

[1] Yes, I have often wondered, since I first came across the name of this Court Jeweller at the exhibition at the Musée Monétaire in Paris, in March, 1956, whether or not there was a connection between the Russian-based German bijoutier and Hitler's field-marshal.

some interesting memorials of his family in his own modest flat, suggested to me that these particular insignia may well have belonged to a Tsar – to judge by the date, Alexander I. But as all such insignia ought to be returned, on the death of the wearer, to the Sovereign, the grand cross might have been made for one of the great Russian generals of the day – Princes of the Russian Empire who are the heroes of modern Soviet hagiology: Suvorov, say, or Kutusov. That some historic insignia were presented to Holmes argues well that this high honour was awarded for no commonplace service.

And what was this service? Watson gives it a passing mention in his account of A *Scandal in Bohemia*, as 'The Summons to Odessa in the Case of the Trepoff Murder'.

Now, on first glance, this looks simple: the murder of (a presumably important Russian named) Trepoff; a murder which had baffled the Russian police.

Yes, but even had this 'Trepoff' been the Tsar's chief minister – he was not – the reward for the man who tracked down his assassin would not have been the Grand Cross of St Anne. We may, in fact, work backwards from the high award, and reason out the *probable* importance of the 'Trepoff' case from the value of the reward earned by Holmes.

In the first place, not only is 'Trepoff' no known Russian name – though it might sound like one to non-Russian ears – the name does not occur in the records of the time as being involved in any matter of importance.

Let us examine this name, assuming that it is, like the majority of the names that Watson gives *in his highly censored record of Holmes's detective adventures*, 'made up'.

Yes, but from what is it 'made up'? One can begin by analysing the (probably fictitious) name into its constituent syllables: thus – *Trep-off*. If the first syllable reminds us irresistibly of 'triple', of what does the second remind us? Of the word 'official' . . .? Possibly.

'Triple' – 'official' – Yes. What is it that is being echoed here . . . ?

Can it be simply Watson's not very subtle punning: 'Trepoff', a Russian-sounding way of writing the common German word, *Treppauf*, 'upstairs' – a well-known Anglicism for activities in the higher levels of society, especially of politics and diplomacy. But in punning thus, Watson was still hearing an echo of that 'triple'. For it is plain why Holmes went to Odessa, and why he afterwards received the grand cross of a Russian order usually given to foreigners who had been of service to the Empire. Holmes had gone 'upstairs' (*treppauf*) to meet the *three* emperors – of Russia, Germany and Austria-Hungary.

After the defeat of France in 1870–1, Prussia had headed what was, in effect, a completely federalized union of German states; this federation acknowledging the perpetual and irrevocable hegemony of Prussia, whose King now also bore the hereditary title of German Emperor.

Having beaten Austria decisively in the war of 1866 – 'The Seven Weeks' War' – Prussia now wished to re-strengthen her, and make her into a powerful (if subservient) ally.

On the initiative of Bismarck, architect of the new German Empire, a league uniting the rulers of the three empires of Russia, Austria-Hungary and Germany came into existence in 1872. Known – and gravely suspected – as the *Dreikaiserbund*, 'The League of Three Emperors', this triple alliance made no secret of its aims: to crush all revolutionary movements throughout their league-united territories (which meant from the Behring Straits to the Rhine and Danube) and to oppose the introduction of 'constitutional' government. All three Emperors believed in absolute rule – and said so.

But, in the fourteen years since the signing of the *Dreikaiserbund*, so many changes had taken place in Europe and in the policies of the three empires concerned that the League of Three Emperors may well have been said to be dead – this is the significance of Watson's use of the word 'murder' in association with the German word for 'upstairs'.

The first weakening of the *Dreikaiserbund* came with the German–Austrian Alliance of 1879, which left Russia once more on her own. Bismarck's conversion of this new Dual Alliance into a Triple Alliance, by inviting Italy to join with

Germany and Austria (1882), was hardly calculated to restore Russia's confidence in German intentions.

But, apart from all changes in policy, there was one fact of paramount importance to make the original *Dreikaiserbund* as ineffective, gone and dead as the Holy Alliance of 1815: the fact that the Emperor of Germany, being nearly ninety, and his heir obviously mortally ill with cancer of the throat, a young, obstinate, aggressive German Emperor was bound to ascend the throne within a matter of a few years. It was essential that this already proven go-it-aloner be presented with an irrevocable *fait accompli* – at least, so far as a self-defensive union of Europe's three Emperors was concerned. Bismarck wished to kill the old *Dreikaiserbund*, and replace it with a new and more permanent league, whilst the old German Emperor was still alive to sign all the necessary instruments.

The dates are eloquent. Speed was essential if the High Contracting Powers were to 'beat the clock'. It was already Christmas, 1886 (by non-Russian, non-Bulgarian and non-Greek reckoning). The new *Dreikaiserbund* – the so-called Treaty of Reinsurance – was signed in 1887. William I, Margrave of Brandenburg, King of Prussia and German Emperor, died on 9th March, 1888. The dying Emperor Frederick, who succeeded him, reigned only until 15th June – a reign of exactly fourteen weeks. On the same day, the dead Emperor's son, William II, took over; sealing all papers, imprisoning his English mother (eldest daughter of Queen Victoria) in her country house; banishing all the dead Emperor's servants of whatever class, and declaring, then and there, that 'he meant to reign as an Emperor'. The framers of the new *Dreikaiserbund* had 'beaten the clock' by just a year.

But why *Holmes* . . . ? Why not an officially accredited professional diplomat, rather than a self-denominated 'private consulting detective', even though he was now a Knight of the Order of the Polar Star of Sweden?

It is in Holmes's very lack of professional diplomatic qualifications that the three Emperors and their most astute adviser-manager, Prince von Bismarck, found their most compelling recommendations. Holmes represented nobody – no league, no government, no political party, no social or financial theory, no well-defined social class; as far as they knew, he hadn't even a religion (which fact stood well in Holmes's favour when the Pope needed a helper, trustworthy as well as efficient). And Holmes's activities in the present decade had gathered into his hands the threads of Europe's developing basic fabric.

The reason behind the ganging-up of the three Emperors, both as regards the first *Dreikaiserbund* and the second, was Turkey. The pious proclamations of the Absolutist faith were sincere enough, but all three Emperors could – and did – put its principles into practice without need for meeting to proclaim the Faith. The reason was Turkey, that several European nations – but principally Russia – had been nibbling at for, now, some three centuries.

What the three Emperors feared was not Turkey's strength – that was debatable, since the quality of the Turkish soldier was unmatched and the quality of the Turkish management and leadership contemptible – but Turkey's weakness.

Preserved more by stagnation and inertia than by sound administration, Turkey was still vast; sprawling across the Dardanelles, up to Austria and Russia on the north, taking in the ancient Greek colony of Ionia and all the Fertile Crescent on the south, and exercising a vague authority over Arabia as far as the Red Sea and the Persian Gulf. The three Emperors were meeting as their predecessors had met in 1772, 1793 and 1795 to carve up Poland among them. Now they were meeting to carve up Turkey; and they wished to know how Great Britain, which had 'leased' Cyprus from Turkey by the Britain-imposed Treaty of Berlin, 1878, and had already moved into that most important Turkish 'fief', Egypt, would do. Great Britain had not interfered with the dismemberment of Poland; she had not interfered when Tsar Alexander I had taken Finland from Sweden, and incorporated it, as the Grand Duchy of Finland, into the Russian Empire; she had not interfered when, thinking France powerless on its defeat by Germany in 1870, Russia had denounced the Treaty

31 The Foreign Office, from St James's Park. As it was in 1890, when both Sherlock Holmes and his brother, Mycroft – a member of the Foreign Service – were at the height of their, respectively, world-famous and completely undercover careers (*Contrad Research Library*)

32 One of the advertisements that Holmes saw. It was in Nevills' Turkish Baths in Northumberland Avenue that the affair of The Illustrious Client began (*Contrad Research Library*)

33 The Langham Hotel. In its day, London's most 'influential' hotel, to which all 'serious-minded' people, with business in view, came. It is now an office of the British Broadcasting Corporation, and Holmes and Watson would weep to see what had happened to 'their' Langham (*Contrad Research Library*)

of Paris, which forbade Russia to have a fleet in the Black Sea, *even though Great Britain had been a signatory of that treaty, no less than had France.* Yet Great Britain, through her ambassador in Petersburg, had not entered even a formal protest against this unilateral treaty-breaking. Did this mean, the three Emperors asked themselves, that Great Britain would stand aside and let them carve up Turkey, as, a century before, they had carved up Poland?

But one fact and one disturbing possibility gave them pause, and it was at this point of indecision that they called on Holmes for advice.

The fact was that the first purchaser of the highly practical Garrett-Nordenfeldt submarine, launched at Landskrona in 1885 – the so-callet *Nordenfeldt II* – was *Turkey.*

Did this mean that Turkey was undergoing or about to undergo one of those national recoveries which are, despite the 'Babylon, that great city, is fallen . . . fallen' pessimists, do happen quite frequently in the historical record?

In any case, the decade from 1879 to 1889 was a memorable one for the arms industry. There were new guns, both heavy and light – Hiram Maxim demonstrated his machine-gun, firing 666^2 Martini-Henry cartridges (at $1\frac{1}{2}$d. a cartridge) a minute, in 1887 – Jubilee Year. Two armament-buyers for the Chinese Government were the first to purchase the new gun – ' . . . a fine weapon . . . invaluable for subduing the heathen', said the American explorer, Stanley. There were new explosives, too – not only Herr Nobel's *Dynamite*, but the British Government's own high-explosives, including the very powerful *Lyddite* (because it was developed in the Royal Engineers' experimental laboratories at Lydd, in Kent).

But – and this should be noted with care – there wasn't a 'scientist' among the inventors. Almost all the military inventions came from engineers, whether military ones or not, and many came from persons who were neither soldiers nor engineers.

---

[2] It is curious – but is it altogether by coincidence? – that the fire-rate per minute of this truly diabolical contrivance should be the Number of the Beast in *Revelation.*

Lebel, Minié, Gatling, Lee, Metford, were all soldiers. Armstrong, the shell-proof steel, heavy-gun and torpedo man, was – of all things! – a Tyneside solicitor, who had taken over part-interest in a small engineering works in payment of a debt. Hiram Maxim was a French-Canadian engineer, self-taught, as, indeed, was Edison. Remington had already a flourishing arms business, and, anyway, turned to making his new typewriter with the same enthusiasm with which he continued to turn out his rifles.

So much for the fact that Turkey had bought a practical, fully-tested submarine, and that some new and remarkably inexpensive arms were available which might help many a weaker nation to recover lost ground in the arms-race. So much for the facts which were troubling the three Emperors into indecision.

Now for the disturbing possibility.

It was this. In all this wondering whether or not Great Britain would stand aside and permit the carving-up of Turkey, might not the three Emperors be facing the possibility that *they* might be asked to stand aside and watch *Great Britain* do the carving-up? It was not so wild a possibility. Great Britain had already acquired a Turkish possession so strategically situated that, from its shores, heavy guns might bombard the Turkish coast; Great Britain had already begun to take over another Turkish possession, Egypt; Great Britain, established in Aden (once a Turkish possession) since 1839, had controlled the Southern end of the Red Sea now for half-a-century, and was plainly extending her influence north to dominate those Arabian sultanates, emirates and sheikdoms which owed a nominal submission to the Sultan. A Turkey either 'neutralized' by a British protectorate or totally incorporated into the British Empire, would 'logically' provide a land-bridge connecting Egypt and India, over which what was later to be the dream of *German* Imperialism, a railway connecting Europe and Asia, could run its unhindered and empire-building length.

That Holmes, never so impartial as to sacrifice the long-term interests of his country for some immediate, if important, advantage elsewhere, advised the three Emperors well is a matter now of historical record.

He had (though they are understandably reticent at the Foreign Office, even about affairs now nearly a century past) consulted Lord Holdhurst as to his course of action. It was only a few weeks before Holmes's summons to Odessa[3] that he had successfully carried through the affair that Watson records as *The Adventure of the Second Stain*, in which Holmes not only met the Foreign Secretary on familiar, indeed on intimate, terms, but also gained further insight into the development of what was to prove one of the world's most significant weapons of war, the submarine warship.

Holmes was never in any doubt of the importance of this case of *The Second Stain*, but, in talking of it to Watson, he may well have had in mind the effects of that case on the future immediately following. Watson says of it: 'it was the most important case which he has ever been called on to handle' – an inaccurate judgement; but an understandable one when we consider Holmes's view of it *before he had solved the mystery*.

"It is a case, my dear Watson, where the law is as dangerous to us as the criminals are. Every man's hand is against us, and yet the interests at stake are colossal. Should I bring it to a successful conclusion" – he did, of course – "it will certainly represent the crowning glory of my career."

If he could think and talk like that about so relatively unimportant a case as *The Adventure of the Second Stain*, to what rhapsodies of self-congratulation must his vindicated reasoning have led him in discussing with Watson how he warned three Emperors to keep their hands off Turkey! (Twenty years later, a new Sultan remembered, and summoned Holmes to Constantinople.)

---

[3] I use Watson's rather loose phrasing here, but it was to the *port* of Odessa that Holmes took ship. From Odessa, he joined the Tsar, Emperor Francis-Joseph and Bismarck (acting as plenipotentiary for the aged German Emperor, too weak to make the long journey to the Black Sea) in the splendid summer palace of the Grand Duke Stanislas at Sochi.

7

Scandals in Clubland

Two social developments – both connected with building – profoundly affected the pattern of English life; the change beginning, of course, in London.

In 1851, an entirely new thoroughfare, Victoria Street, was driven from Westminster Abbey to Victoria Station through what were then the ancient, picturesque and (most of them) sadly neglected streets of Westminster.

The street was not immediately built up; but when, at last, buildings began to rise along its wide and straight length, those buildings were London's first flats, 'built on the Viennese model'. The flats were by no means cheap – which gave them the *cachet* needed to make the rich take to the new style of living: the flats, for instance, in Grosvenor Mansions (built 1866) cost £300 a-year, exclusive of rates. In addition to the blocks of flats – Sir Arthur Sullivan, famous partner of Sir W. S. Gilbert, lived in a Victoria Street flat – there were hotels affording unprecedented standards of luxury: the Westminster Palace (1866); the Windsor; the Grosvenor, adjoining Victoria Station; the Buckingham Palace Hotel, opposite the south side of Buckingham Palace; and the Belgravia, in Grosvenor Gardens. All are still standing as I write; though none save the Grosvenor has been an hotel for many decades.

The other fundamental social change – dwelling in flats ('to solve the servant problem') being the first – was the fashion of dining-out in the new hotels, especially in those palatial establishments in another new street, Northumberland Avenue, the cutting of which, between 1874 and 1878, through the gardens of the demolished Northumberland House, brought a much smaller hotel, *The Northumberland*, almost on to the Northumberland Avenue eastern frontage. This, no longer an hotel, was where Sir Henry Baskerville, Bart, stayed on the night that one of his new boots – bought from Harris & Son's shop in the Strand – was stolen. The hotel, which was familiar to Holmes, not merely because Sir Henry stayed there, but because the favourite turkish-baths of Holmes and Watson neighboured the hotel across the narrow width of Craven Passage, remains to this day; in honour of one of its most distinguished patrons, it has been renamed, *The Sherlock Holmes*, an upstairs room having been converted into a reproduction of the sitting-room at 221b Baker Street.

Three hotels of the very first class – the *Grand* (1880), the *Métropôle* (1885) and the *Victoria* (1890) – with a six-storey faience-fronted club, the *Constitutional* (1884), and a theatre designed on the most modern principles, the *Avenue* (since renamed the *Playhouse*), built in 1881, made new Northumberland Avenue one of the finest streets in the world; which it still is, if one may force the eye to detect the original splendour beneath the hopeless decay which comes over any building, not originally built for governmental purposes, but commandeered by any British Government for purposes quite unguessable by any taxpayer not dishonest or insane. The truth is that the faceless 'Departments' which seize the flourishing hotels of London and other cities are always acting as the plenipotentiary jackals of the equally faceless 'developers'. Sootily shabby without; hopelessly fouled within – meaningless paper notices thumb-tacked on the walls of rocaille panels ('in the Louis XV style'), and the great public rooms cut up by hutches of matchboard planking – these hotels are being deliberately 'run down', so that their removal will be 'justified' by the inspired articles in the press, welcoming the sweeping-away of 'eyesores' and their replacement by 'clean, modern buildings in a progressive, forward-looking style'.

But all this desolation and uprooting was decades in the seedy future when the grand hotels came to London and the other great cities, and effected a revolution in the habits of the Toffs. It became a habit to dine out; to receive unmatched service in surroundings of the greatest luxury, there to eat food prepared by chefs for whose skill kings and emperors and American millionaires would have been happy to compete.

It is said that the first Name to make a practice of dining out at one of the new hotels was Mrs Langtry, 'friend' of the Prince of Wales, and it is also said that 'Society was shocked' by her pioneering. If so, Society soon changed disapproval for imitation; and wives as well as mistresses began to frequent what had developed into a two-sex club with many of the attractions of a fashion-show.

An important result of this forsaking of the home for the restaurant or hotel grill-room was the 'redevelopment' of the Club. As an institution, the Club was already at least two centuries old; but now, challenged by the architectural splendour and matchless service of the new Hotel, the Club had, in a phrase as current then as now, to 'pull its socks up'. If the wives were flocking to the hotels, then the husbands wished for a wife-free environment as luxurious as that provided by the hotels. Queen Victoria might permit Macduff – intended for her grand-daughter – to get as drunk and foul-mouthed as he liked, but this tolerance was exceptional, even for HM, and certainly was not imitated by well-bred women of a lower social rank. To drink to excess, to talk freely (always remembering that We Don't *Ever* Discuss Politics, Religion or The Ladies); to be relieved, for a few hours, of the oppressive company of The Ladies; the Late Victorian Man needed his Club. There was enough capital about to see that he got it.

The Victorian club existed at all social levels, from the level of the *Pelican* in Gerrard Street to that of *White's* or *Boodles* in St James's Street. Think of the club as the physical expression of the escape from ever-pursuant Woman, and you have the reason why the Club, as an institution, underwent a renascence at the end of the last century.

Men formed clubs in order to see more of each other than their highly ritualized domestic disciplines permitted: the

Amphytrion, in Dover Street, flourished for a time because the Prince of Wales patronized it. Its *raison d'être* was its claim to provide the best cooking, the best wine-cellar in the world. It vanished when the Prince, easily bored, moved on to other establishments.

There were the specialized clubs, as there are to-day: for gambling, for prostitutes (Kate Hamilton's was the best-known of these), for racing-men, for nude shows, for drunks, for social climbers, and so on. But *not* to belong to a club was a social luxury that only the socially unassailable (and this didn't seem to include the Prince of Wales) could afford. Thus, Lord Rendel, an ennobled barrister, sports three clubs; Lord Rendlesham, the 5th baron of that title, is a member of only two; whilst the 5th Viscount Bolingbroke and St John was a member of only one club – W*hite's*.

The fact that the club-joiners are younger sons, untitled brothers and uncles and other male relatives, gives us the clue to the late nineteenth-century function of the club: to provide a bond uniting the unmoneyed members of the artistocracy and upper middle classes, and, in doing so, to provide them with those domestic comforts that their (relative) poverty denied them as outcasts from the family seats.

I have dwelt elsewhere on the harsh law of primogeniture governing Victorian heredity, whereby the heir inherited everything necessary to perpetuate the line and to maintain it in its proper splendour, and the younger sons had nothing but their background, their education, their connections and – sometimes – their titles, to help them on in the world. Sir Winston Churchill has recorded the fact that, at the time that his father was about to marry Miss Jennie Jerome, Lord Randolph could not have raised fifty pounds on his personal credit.

Naturally, then, the clubs attracted the sharks, for if the aristocratic pigeons had no money, they had valuable connections – and, in any case, the pigeons weren't above learning some of the hawks' flash tricks for conning the mug. ("Would you mind witnessing this family document?" Lord William

Nevill[1] asked a fellow club-member, Horace de Vere Cole. Lord William had cut a hole in a piece of the club's blotting paper, and indicated that Cole should sign there. "Sorry I have to hide the document, but it's very confidential, you understand?" "Oh, quite so," said Cole, a rich young man, signing his name to what he afterwards discovered was his own cheque for £20,000.)

And, because of the extensive growth of, and patronage of, clubs of every social type, the 'club mentality' began to make itself noticeable in the big private houses of the time, where the duty of the host (with or without hostess) was to provide perpetual entertainment for the numerous guests.

Gambling had always been a preoccupation of the English club-member; now, as the century drew to a close, it was to invade the private house as well.

A glance at Holmes's non-international cases after, say, the beginning of 1881, when he and Watson took the tenancy of the chambers in Baker Street, shews that he was inevitably caught up in the seamier side of London's club life. And, too, in those scandals which resulted in the extension of the 'club mentality' to include life in the great private houses.

Thus, somewhere between March, 1881, and October, 1886 – Watson is notoriously imprecise in his dating – we have Holmes performing what Watson calls 'The Service for Lord Backwater', followed soon after by 'The Arnsworth Castle Business', and – a year or so later – by what Watson calls 'The Saving of Colonel Prendergast in the Tankerville Club Scandal', of which, since it took place in the West End of London in the late 'Jubilee' summer of 1887, some details are available.

The clue by which I tracked down the identity of the 'Tankerville' Club was to be found in the fact that the family name of the Earls of Tankerville is Bennet – and it was in

---

[1] Lord William Beauchamp Nevill, 4th son of William, first Marquess and 5th Earl of Abergavenny, K.G. Lord William, born 1860, educated at Eton, and for some time *aide-de-camp* to the Duke of Marlborough when Lord-Lieutenant (commonly called 'Viceroy') of Ireland, married, in 1889, Luisa, daughter of Jose de Murrieta, Marquès de Santurce.

Bennet Street (which joins Arlington Street with St James's Street) that I sought the original of the 'Tankerville'.

I found it in a once much-frequented club, *The Walsingham*, which closed down only because of the scandal attaching to the unjust accusation made against Colonel Prendergast (his real name was Augustus Takeley – one sees that Watson is punning again here, as usual[2]). The word 'hell', for a club where gambling was the sole reason for its existence, had become obsolete by the late 1880s; but a 'hell' the *Walsingham* undoubtedly was. Colonel Takeley, an elderly regular officer who had purchased his commission, and was thus immovable until he had decided to retire on half-pay, stood in the way of several promotion-hungry officers junior to himself and not over scrupulous in achieving superior rank. To use a modern phrase, they contrived an ingenious plot to 'frame' the Colonel; and, but for the fact that Mycroft Holmes's head of department in the Foreign Office was Colonel Takeley's brother, Sherlock Holmes might never have stirred himself to intervene in the 'Prendergast' affair, and so clear the Colonel's name of the vile accusations which had been so ingeniously fabricated against him.

In November, 1886, Watson, who had gone to America and bought a small practice in San Francisco, a couple of years before, married Miss Constance Adams of that city. Shortly after, he returned, with his wife, to England, and acquired a perhaps even smaller practice in Paddington. It is clear from the record that the interruption of the domestic intimacy between Holmes and Watson had an important effect on Holmes's habits, no less than on those of Watson.

That, restless without his Watson-audience, Holmes began to frequent the new hotels of the grander class, is obvious from the fact, as related by Watson in the case of *The Noble Bachelor*, that Holmes, glancing at a waiter's bill and noticing that the charge for a sherry is 8d., knows at once that a charge of

[2] The pun, of course, consists in replacing the 'Take' of *Takeley* by 'Prender' (Latin *prendere* or French *prendre*, 'to take hold of, to grasp, to seize'), adding to this the 'gust' of *Augustus*, slightly changed to 'gast', to make the well-known English surname, *Prendergast*.

8d.[3] for a sherry could have been made only at one of the most expensive of London's hotels, and, what is more, suggests – correctly – the street in which such an expensive hotel is to be found.

It is clear that Holmes, besides meeting monarchs professionally, is enjoying that high standard of living to which his augmented income and now assured standing undoubtedly entitle him. He certainly knows what a sherry costs in the *Métropôle* . . .

But even the scandal of Colonel Takeley at the *Walsingham Club* paled, as they say, into insignificance, beside that far more scandalous affair of (I quote Watson here) 'The Atrocious Conduct of Colonel Upwood in Connection with the Famous Card Scandal at the Nonpareil Club'.

Watson, as usual when a case involves high personages, not only gives no details, but conceals the true identities of those involved under fictitious names. Fortunately, I had the facts of the case from the late Mr F. G. Thomas, KC, who, as a young barrister, was retained in the action which, though threatened, was avoided by the diplomatic skill of Holmes.

The 'Nonpareil' Club was, in reality, the *Marlborough*; Watson's fictitious name for this well-known Victorian club being inspired by the fact that, founded by the Prince of Wales, it was 'without equal' – 'nonpareil'. The 'atrocious conduct' of Colonel 'Upwood' was that – a detected cheat – the Colonel had the quick-wittedness and unparalleled audacity to 'defend' himself at the card-table by claiming that the Prince of Wales was an accessory to the Colonel's sharping.

No one, so the Colonel reasoned, would dare to do anything against him; he could not even be asked to resign from the *Marlborough*. But Holmes shewed how it was possible to prove, not only that the Colonel had cheated – in any case, the Colonel had admitted as much – but that, if the Colonel admitted that he had cheated *in such-and-such a manner*, then the Prince could not have been a party to the Colonel's fraud.

The matter was hushed up, of course; but Holmes was not astonished to read in *The Times*, a few weeks after he had

[3] Then 16 cents or 80 centimes.

shewn the Prince how to defy the Colonel's blackmail, that Colonel 'Upwood' had been 'accidentally shot' whilst out with Lord Lassiter's house-party in Norfolk.

It was the experience gained by Holmes in connection with these deplorable incidents at clubs' card-tables which enabled him to give expert evidence in the even graver scandal of the Tranby Croft affair, in which Sir William Gordon-Cumming, Bart, colonel of the Scots Guards, was accused, by one of his subalterns, of having cheated whilst playing *baccarat* (an illegal card-game) in a party which included the Prince of Wales.

The phrase, 'accident prone', had not then travelled from the insurance-company actuary to the ordinary citizen; in discussing the Prince of Wales's unfortunate capacity for becoming involved in scandalous affairs, Holmes remarked to Watson that "our friend, Tum-Tum, roots up trouble with all the brainless enthusiasm, as well as the unerring aim, of a hog rooting up truffles!"

He had disliked the Prince ever since May, 1887, when His Royal Highness had turned up at Holmes's chambers in a preposterous fancy-dress uniform, seeking to disguise his true identity under that of 'Count von Kramm,[4] a Bohemian nobleman'. It cannot be denied that Holmes's dislike of the Prince had its foundations in a sexual jealousy: Holmes was outraged that the Prince should seek his help in protecting himself against a discarded mistress – when that mistress, so little valued by the 'corpulent voluptuary', was, to Holmes, 'The Woman'.

However, when the prestige of the Empire was at stake, Holmes would not permit a personal prejudice to stand in his way. And, try as he might, even Holmes could not prevent the Tranby Croft affair from reaching, not merely the newspapers, but the law courts.

The Prince of Wales's son and heir, Eddy, was at York, with his regiment, the 10th Hussars. The Prince, who always attended, when possible, the Doncaster Races, used to stay

[4] A *nom de guerre* with curious future overtones, seeing what happened to Baron von Cramm in Hitler's Germany, over fifty years later.

with his always very numerous party at Brantingham, the country-house of the Prince's great friend and butt, Christopher Sykes. However, the Prince of Wales's 'friendship' had brought Sykes to the verge of bankruptcy, and, for all that the Prince was ('understandably', he remarked) irritated that Sykes had to refuse his Master the usual expected hospitality, the Prince made the best of a bad job and accepted, as alternative, the offer of Arthur Wilson, a rich North Country shipowner, that the Royal party should put up at Wilson's no-money-spared mansion, Tranby Croft.

The arrangement was that the Prince and party should stay at Tranby Croft, during the 'Leger Week', on the nights of 8th, 9th and 10th September, 1890. The Prince was to have brought his current mistress, Lady Brooke ('My Darling Daisy'), but a family bereavement, as the then phrase had it, prevented the Prince from adding adultery to the pleasures of horse-racing and *baccarat*,[5] and HRH was in a bad mood from the first night of his literally ill-fated stay with the shipowner.

Arthur Wilson's son and his friend, Berkeley Levett, a subaltern in the Scots Guards, 'happened' to be watching, with particular attention, some very odd manœuvres of Levett's colonel, Sir William Gordon-Cumming. It seemed obvious to these two young men that Sir William was dishonestly arranging the counters, *after having looked at his cards*, by that sleight-of-hand operation known in French casinos as *la poussette* ('the little shove'). After the game of *baccarat* had finished, and all had gone up to bed, young Wilson looked in on his parents, who were still awake, and told them what he *thought* that he had seen.

On the following morning, others were let into the 'secret' – notably, Mr and Mrs Lycett Green (the latter Arthur Wilson's daughter). All agreed to watch on the following even-

[5] Considerable confusion was caused in the minds of the honest British labouring classes by the introduction of the word, *baccarat*, into the proceedings. Pronouncing it 'back a rat', the humbler Briton took it to be a reference to a sport formerly popular with the Toffs – that of rat-catching in cellars, where two or three well-fancied terriers were let loose on sackfuls of the rodents.

ing, and see whether or not Sir William repeated the offence of which both Berkeley Levett and young Wilson declared him guilty.

They watched. They swore that they had seen Sir William cheat on two evenings (the nights of 8th and 9th September). They noted that Sir William, on these two nights, had won £225, mostly from the Prince of Wales – and they decided to tell what they claimed they had seen to Lord Edward Somerset (brother of that unhappy 'Podge' whose unwise patronage of telegraph-boys had made his flight to France mandatory two years before). Somerset decided that Lord Coventry and General Williams should be consulted.

Sir William Gordon-Cumming was then presented with the 'evidence', and, though he denied that he had cheated, foolishly consented to sign what was, in effect, an admission of guilt.

'In consideration of the promise, made by the gentlemen whose names are subscribed, to preserve silence with reference to an accusation made in regard to my conduct at *baccarat* on the nights of Monday and Tuesday, 8th and 9th September, 1890, at Tranby Croft, I will on my part solemnly undertake never to play cards again as long as I live.'

Of course, the silence which was the condition and consideration for Sir William's confessing was not observed; they said that 'the ladies' chattered; but from my own experience, I would not lightly assume that it was 'the ladies' who first betrayed the secret of Sir William's admission.

The story, with additions and alterations,[6] was in the pos-

[6] A highly dramatized version of the episode was, inevitably one supposes, current at the time and for long afterwards. It is this version that the late Captain F. Victor Hughes-Hallett prefers in his *Bran Mash* (London : Hutchinson, n.d., but about 1931): 'From Tranby I went on to stay with Arthur Wilson's son-in-law, E. Lycett-Green, a very cheery host, and then Master of the York and Ainsty. This was the man who sprang from his seat opposite the Prince, and, pointing at the culprit, called out, "You are cheating!"' I mention this quite improbable story to shew that I am aware of it, though, in fact, had matters turned out thus dramatically, Gordon-Cumming would not have signed the compromising document which ruined his career.

session of all 'in the know' within a matter of days; Gordon-Cumming wrote to the Prince asking that he be permitted to play cards with his brother-officers, in order to scotch the tale, but the Prince did not reply; and, in desperation, Gordon-Cumming brought an action for libel against his original accusers – the Wilsons, the Lycett Greens and Berkeley Levett (whom I met, as an elderly, humourless gentleman, when he had become Equerry to the Duke of Connaught).

Sir William lost – and how could it have been otherwise when he had signed so self-damning a document? But though the jury found for the defendants, it was not before both the Court and the Press had held the Prince up to public obloquy. Sir William, after he had lost the case, was dismissed the Army, expelled from his clubs, and, as Sir Philip Magnus says,[7] 'socially annihilated'. But the Prince of Wales suffered – although only temporarily – as much. 'It would be difficult,' says Magnus, 'to exaggerate the momentary unpopularity of the Prince of Wales; and Queen Victoria informed the Empress Frederick (12 June) that "the monarchy almost is in danger if he is lowered and despised".' Questions were asked in the Houses of Parliament; the Wowsers' Press came out hard against him; 'correspondents' to newspapers asked why the Prince was playing an illegal game at all, and why all the players weren't prosecuted? 'The Kaiser,' Magnus notes, 'had the effrontery to send Queen Victoria a letter (which has not been preserved) protesting against the impropriety of anyone's holding the honorary rank of a colonel of Prussian Hussars becoming embroiled with men young enough to be his children in a gambling squabble; and with unctuous rectitude, The Times expressed a wish (10 June) that the Prince of Wales himself would sign a pledge never again to play cards for money.'

Where did Holmes come in all this?

The late Sir Harry Poland, KC, told my Father many years ago the details of Holmes's involvement in this affair.

In the first place, Holmes's investigations were hampered

[7] *King Edward the Seventh*, Philip Magnus; London: John Murray, 1964.

by the fact that he had not been retained by Sir William Gordon-Cumming. He was 'retained' – if that is the word (and I am sure that it is not) – by Lord Edward Somerset, who had met Holmes whilst the latter was holding a 'watching brief' in the lamentable affair involving Lord Edward's uranian brother.

Lacking any 'official' position from which to direct the Tranby Croft affair, Holmes – according to Sir Harry Poland's account – yet succeeded in establishing the fact that Sir William was innocent of the charge brought against him, and was the victim of a plot to discredit him. (The same circumstances, almost exactly, as Holmes encountered in the matter of the 'Tankerville' Club and Colonel 'Prendergast'.)

Perhaps I should make the matter more clear were I to set it out in a tabulated form:

(a) Lieutenant-colonel Sir William Gordon-Cumming, Bart, formerly Major and Lieutenant-colonel, 2nd Battalion, Scots Guards, was an unpopular man. He was unpopular with:
1. The men under his command (*which didn't matter very much*) and
2. His social equals and superiors (*which mattered very much indeed*)

One could say here that Sir William had the reputation of being a pig. However . . .

(b) He had offended Lady Brooke.
(c) Lady Brooke was the current *maîtresse en titre* of the Prince of Wales.
(d) Lady Brooke asked for Sir Williams's head as – some time before – another whore, Salome, had asked for the head of John Baptist.
(e) The plot to discredit Sir William was hatched by Lady Brooke and her (non-royal) lover, Lord Charles Beresford. The simpleton marked to act as the 'stooge' was young Wilson, to whom Lady Brooke was prepared – in pursurance of the plan – to 'make up'.
(f) The Prince of Wales was *not* a party to the plot. So that,
(g) not being a party to the plot, the Prince accepted the

> 'evidence' of Sir William's culpability, thus unconsciously aiding and abetting the intention of the plotters.

Though, in some notes that I have seen, the word 'plot' is used more than once, it was Sir Harry Poland's view – and I find myself sharing it fully – that, certainly in the scheme's inception, 'plot' was far too harsh a word to describe what came out of the Tranby Croft house-party. The Victorian upper-class obsession with practical jokes should not only be borne in mind here; it should never be permitted to escape the historian's attention in seeking to know exactly what happened at Tranby Croft.

And has any historian of the Gordon-Cumming affair attached its proper importance to the presence, at that house-party, *of Christopher Sykes*?

In his book, *Four Studies in Loyalty*, Sykes's grandson has described what incredible humiliations the 'fun-loving' Bertie, Prince of Wales, put upon his 'friend' *and host*, Christopher Sykes. Reading of what his being cast for the position of perennial butt earned for Sykes makes it impossible to comprehend how any man could have endured such degradation without protest. Sykes's grandson has told how the butt was forced – by convention? by Bertie's iron will? by Sykes's craven desire to please his Royal master? – to stand completely still whilst Bertie poured a goblet of brandy over the wretched 'friend's' head – the Prince howling with half-witted laughter as the brandy flowed over Sykes's carefully parted hair, over his tall starched collar, over his 'boiled' shirt front and white piqué waistcoat with the white-jade-and-sapphire buttons, over the shoulders of the Poole dress-coat . . .

Holmes read and admired Poe. Had Holmes read that strange story, *Hop-Frog*, in which the patient, *uncomplaining* butt of the 'fun-loving' Prince endures the humiliations, the ceaseless ignominy, only so that he may seek and achieve a horrible revenge on the *unsuspecting* Prince? ("What . . . ? He *object* . . . ? The 'great Xtopher' . . . ? Are you *mad*? Why, he positively *loves* it – don't you, Christopher, old boy?")

34 Dovercourt Spa. It was here, in the Spa reading-rooms, almost
abandoned by the public even by 1914, that Holmes and Watson made
their *rendez-vous* before proceeding to foil the machinations of Von Bork.
This snapshot, from the mysteriously missing Watson files, is titled in his
handwriting. *(Contrad Research Library)*

35 The Great Eastern Hotel, Harwich. Principal hotel of that important
passenger port at which Holmes's last great adventure – the unmasking
and foiling of the infamous Von Bork – was successfully concluded. This
is Harwich as it was in 1914, on the eve of World War I *(Contrad
Research Library)*

36 Sir William Howard Russell, Dublin-born barrister, Doctor of Laws
and London militiaman, who, as military correspondent for *The Times* in
the Crimean War, may be said to have established the profession of 'War
Correspondent.' He was the first man to make the distant-from-war
civilian aware of what war really meant. *Photograph*: The Times

Brandy over one's head and dress clothes is bad enough; but add to this that the Prince's visits were as ruinous to the involuntary host as the first Elizabeth's 'visitations' had been to the involuntary 'hosts' of *her* day; to Sykes they were literally ruinous – only the personal appeal of one of the Prince's mistresses saved poor Sykes from bankruptcy; and though the Prince ordered Sir Ernest Cassell to 'help' Sykes, the Prince never 'forgave' his old favourite (and butt) for having, however accidentally, however obliquely, rebuked a Prince of Wales for a too-costly friendship.

It was an added humiliation for Sykes that he was included by Bertie's order in the Tranby Croft house-party. *He* should have been the host, not Arthur Wilson; it was only his poverty which had taken from Sykes the honour of entertaining his Prince. Reflecting on the possibilities inherent in the inclusion of the bitter, revengeful (yes, how could he, being human, have been otherwise?) Sykes in the party, I realized that, eighty years ago, Holmes must have reached the same conclusions that I was now reaching. The butt – faced with this last humiliation: hospitality at the hands of one who could afford what he could not – must have turned at last on his tormentor. And what made that more certain is that there was another in the party whose feelings the insensitive Bertie, we know, had outraged.

This was the rich Parsee, Reuben Sassoon, with whose specially designed counters – silver, marked with the three-feather crest of the Prince of Wales and values progressing from five shillings to ten pounds – Bertie was proposing to play *baccarat* that night. A few weeks before, Reuben, 'forgetting his place', had ventured to put his arm around Bertie's shoulder. In an abrupt reaction to this ill-bred insolence, Bertie had given Reuben a push which had sent the darkie stumbling down the stairs, narrowly escaping a broken neck. Reuben Sassoon, 'accepted' as a Royal Friend because of – and *only* because of – his lakhs of non-stinking rupees, was not likely to accept so very physical a snub in the submissive way in which the 'great Xtopher' had been receiving snubs. The presence of *two* thoroughly humiliated friends at the Wilson house-party could argue only some quite unusual happening.

Holmes may well have been too near, in time and place, to the disastrous events of the Tranby Croft affair to have seen instantly what had happened. But he did eventually see – and what he saw appalled him.

The 'plot' – and in the end it *was* a plot – had begun as a 'harmless' practical joke, with two, not merely one, marked as victims: Sir William Gordon-Cumming *and* the Prince of Wales. The aim of the 'practical joke' was to humiliate and terrify Sir William by a false (but apparently well-supported) accusation of cheating at cards, and to humiliate and terrify Bertie by tricking him into accepting the 'proofs' of Sir William's 'cheating'. It was not the first – and certainly would not be the last – Victorian practical joke which had run away with its designers.

That Sir William signed the 'confession' does not mean either that he was guilty as charged or that he was – as has been suggested to me – party to the practical joke. It simply means that he had lost his head for the moment. The cool-headed gallantry which had won him a clasp to his 1879 South African medal, a clasp and bronze star to his 1882 Egyptian medal, and two clasps to his 1884 Nile Expedition medal, failed him here. Faced with the contempt of his social superiors – none of them in the 'joke' – Sir William did what they asked him: behaved as though he were, indeed, guilty as charged.

Holmes disliked Sir William Gordon-Cumming even more than he disliked the Prince of Wales, but Holmes's sense of duty ordered him to inform Gordon-Cumming of the facts.

What Holmes had also to tell Sir William was that, by forcing the original 'joke' to the point at which Sir William had had to seek the remedial benefits of legal action, the plotters – we had now better call them that – had changed the relatively innocent pastime of 'practical joking' into the criminal activity of 'conspiracy'.

Sir William, Holmes pointed out, could easily turn the

tables on his persecutors by initiating a police prosecution against them for this conspiracy. When Gordon-Cumming asked Holmes if this could be done without the Prince's being involved in the general charge, Holmes was obliged to tell the baronet that the Prince would have to take his place in the dock with the other defendants – though that need not mean that the Prince would be convicted as a felon.

For all his faults, Sir William Gordon-Cumming had some principles inseparable from his class, his education and his profession of arms. He could not, even to save himself, cause his future King to be charged with the commission of a crime. He thanked Holmes, and indicated that he would pursue his (obviously hopeless) original plan. As we know, he lost.

On the day that he lost, his fiancée, the American Florence Garner, insisted on his marrying her. It would be pleasant, but untruthful, to record that the marriage was a happy one . . .

8

Continental Commitments

It may seem to us, our ears ringing with the nostalgic name-list of vanished greatness, that Holmes's services were so monopolized by those engaged in either provoking or avoiding war, that he had little time to spare for those humbler mysteries on which, in the early days of his professional career, he had been happy to try his skill. To have asked Holmes, fresh from the heavy atmosphere of a *Dreikaiserbund*; escorted, there and back, *en train de luxe* – or in the even greater splendour of an imperial steam-yacht – by the corseted elegance of *aides-de-camp* as stiffly formal as only Potsdam could make them; to attend to a problem in dusty, sunny, lower middle-class Croydon, would have been like asking the Royal solicitor, Sir George Lewis, to deal with a county-court summons for the rates. Well, perhaps Sir George might have handled the case; perhaps not – but Holmes would, and did. He walked with kings and greater than kings; but he never lost the common touch.

Indeed, the cases for which he is famous – note that these are the cases that Watson describes for us in detail – are those which take him to the as-yet-unspoiled, only slightly urbanized, countryside of Esher, Reigate, Stoke Moran; the still completely non-urbanized countryside of Donnithorpe, Hurlstone, King's Pyland; the perfectly suburbanized 'dormitory' districts of Norbury (Sydenham), Croydon, Lee (Kent), Oxshott, Woking. It is almost as though Holmes, in throwing himself so wholeheartedly into the case of, say, Miss Violet Smith, the 'typewriter', wished to force himself to swim with the main current of normal human existence, rather than pant to death, like some gaffed fish, in the too-rarefied, insufficiently human, Top Levels.

The fact is that, for Holmes, *any* problem was an addictive fascination; and the social status of the victim of some irregularity mattered little or nothing (usually nothing) to Holmes. His 'practice' began to assume *Debrett*-and-*Gotha*-like qualities simply because there were victims of irregularity at high – indeed, the highest – levels, as well as at the lowest, and with the means to command Holmes's services, the rich and powerful obviously had what to-day we call an 'edge'.

Nevertheless, even a cursory glance through the Watson-compiled list of cases, from 1874 ('The "Gloria Scott"') to 1914 ('His Last Bow'), makes it clear that the majority of Holmes's cases were acted out at a level in the social structure somewhat under the middle. When Holmes tells Watson, with unmistakable self-satisfaction, that "I cannot recall any case within my experience which looked at the first glance so simple, and yet which presented such difficulties", he is not recalling the happy solution of some Imperial intrigue, but the case of two pathetically pretentious suburban villa-dwellers – their 'fancy' name sufficiently indicates both their social pretensions and their social limitations: Mr and Mrs Neville St Clair – one of whom, the wife, is characteristically suspicious of her husband (and so goes to Holmes); the husband, incapable of living up to the standard of a Lee villa, has taken to begging (in the disguise of a man with a twisted lip).

At no point in Watson's very detailed account of this case is it even suggested that Holmes feels that his talents are being put to inadequate use in solving the problem of what happened to Mr Neville St Clair. To Holmes, it is another problem; and thus, something to be solved. It was as well that kings and emperors – as well as the odd duke – should have needed Holmes's services so urgently and so frequently: the kitty at Baker Street would have looked pretty empty had the Neville St Clairs and the Violet Smiths been the only supplicants for Holmes's kindly and efficient offices.

There must have been many cases involving Holmes that Watson does not mention, even by so much as a fugitive line. There was, for instance, after 1880, a lot of (obviously imitative) action on the free-lance anarchist front. On 19th April, 1882, Roderick MacLean shot at the Queen; as he missed, from a distance of a few feet, the assailant was held to have been insane. On the other hand, Albert Young, a little over a month later – 26th May, 1882 – merely *threatened* to shoot the Queen. This was held to be the felonious act of a sane man; and Albert the Bad copped ten penn'orth oakum-picking; a sentence exactly equal to that awarded to Charles Brookshaw, six months later – 21st November, 1882 – for *threatening* to kill the Prince of Wales.

And when these late Victorian oddities were not shooting at, or threatening to shoot at, the Nobs, they were engaged in even more unseemly activities. On 24th October, 1882, Charles Soutar received five years' penal servitude at Edinburgh for having stolen the body of the Right Honourable Alexander William Crawford, 25th Earl of Crawford, 8th Earl of Balcarres, and 33rd Lord Lindsay of Crawford, who had been buried, with considerable feudal pomp, two years earlier. The fact that Mr Soutar was unable – or merely unwilling – to explain why he had 'snatched' the greatly decomposed body of his late Lordship did not prevent the Scots jury from finding the defendant guilty.

What with one irregularity and another, Holmes must have been kept remarkably busy. It is (at least, to me) not hard to understand that he took unwisely to such powerful stimulants as cocaine . . .

Money – and the peremptoriness which grows on the moneyed – could not be denied, for all the Violet Smiths and Mary Sutherlands and Henry Bakers. We find the French cropping up frequently – privately or officially – as consistent clients of Sherlock Holmes, just as we find his services more than once requested by official France's official enemy, the Vatican. But let us consider these French cases, the first of which has so far escaped my solution.

Watson mentions no fewer than six cases related to France or the French, to which we shall add whatever problem took Holmes, in his capacity of research-chemist, to Montpellier, from November, 1893, to March, 1894.

Let us list them, as given in Watson's record, with the dates as supplied by the ingenuity and dedication of that master-researcher into matters Sherlockian, the late William Baring-Gould. Here, then are the 'French' cases in chronological order:

1. The Rather Intricate Matter from Marseilles — Mid-October, 1887

2. The French Will Case — Week of Monday, 10th September, to Saturday, 15th September, 1888

3. The Unfortunate Mme Montpensier — Between Saturday, 20th October, and late November, 1888

4. The *second* part of the intricate affair of *The Second Stain*. 'I still retain an almost verbatim report of the interview in which Holmes demonstrated the true facts of the case to *Monsieur Dubuque, of the Paris Police,*[1] and Fritz von Waldbaum, the well-known specialist of Danzig.' — July, 1889

5. The Matter of Supreme Importance to the French Government — Late December, 1890, to March, 1891

6. The Tracking and Arresting of Huret, the Boulevard Assassin — April–December, 1894

In this list – this *pattern* of detective consultancy – we must, of course, include Holmes's activities, covering the five months between October, 1893 and April, 1894; that period which, probably, was spent in 'researches into coal-tar derivatives at Montpellier', but which cannot have been devoted

[1] My italics – M.H.

exclusively to analytical chemistry, since it can hardly have been by coincidence that Holmes continued straight on from the Montpellier research to tracking down Huret, the assassin.

Watson's 'tact' is sometimes, I think, confused with Watson's ignorance, especially of the *minutiæ* of aristocratic relationships. One feels that it was never Watson's hand which reached up and took down a *Debrett* or an *Almanach de Gotha* 'from our bookshelf', and the fact – as Mr Baring-Gould has established – that Watson spent his boyhood in Australia may have inoculated him with a certain prejudice against Toffs – especially Toffs with handles to their name.

So, for 'Madame de Montpensier', we ought to read ('Her Royal Highness) la duchesse de Montpensier', daughter-in-law of King Louis Philippe, and herself the sister of Queen Isabella II of Spain. The Orleans family, together with the Bonapartes, had once again been expelled from France – 13th July, 1886 – and though the Duc de Montpensier was safely settled in Spain, of which country he had become a national in 1859, the majority of the other members of the exiled Orleans family returned to England, where they had long since acquired several magnificent houses.

Watson's reference to 'The French Will case' only a month or so before the case of 'the Unfortunate Madame Montpensier' makes it obvious, I think, that these were not two separate cases at all, but merely two 'phases' of the same case.

The latest expulsion of the former Royal Houses from France had been provoked by a Royalist demonstration in 1886, the Comte de Paris – son-in-law of the Duc de Montpensier – having married his daughter, Marie Amélie, to Don Carlos, Duke of Braganza, heir to the Portuguese throne. In the previous year, Princess Marie of Orleans, daughter of the Comte's brother, the Duc de Chartres (the prince who had served in the National Guard during the 1870–1 war) had been married, also from the magnificent *château* of Chambord, to Prince Waldemar of Denmark, *nephew of Alexandra, Princess of Wales.*

The first of these two marriages had been marked with expressions of Royalist fervour which had taken little account of Republican sensibilities, but the second marriage affronted the Republicans even more.

A week before the second marriage, the Comte de Paris had 'scandalized' the Republicans by a grand reception that he had given, at which every name of importance in Royalist circles was present.

The marriage itself was carried through with so much traditional splendour, so much Royalist defiance of Republican prejudice, that the Republicans in the two Chambers went to work immediately to expel the 'dangerous' Royalist element from France.

The necessary Bills were rushed through, and five days after the second wedding, all members of any former Royal Family of France were ordered to leave the country – *and* leave their goods behind them. Only with difficulty had the 'authorities' been persuaded to allow both the Royal families time to arrange their affairs in France. Not until the re-occupation of Paris by the troops of De Gaulle was the Act of 11th June, 1886, repealed, and the exiled princely families permitted to return to their homeland.

All property belonging to the exiles in France was sequestrated, and put into what is euphemistically called 'State care'. It was property 'frozen' under this sequestration that Holmes was asked to get the French Government to release; and here again we seem to see that 'The Matter of Supreme Importance to the French Government' cannot be separated from Holmes's activities on behalf of the exiled Orleanist princes.

The 'matter of supreme importance to the French Government' must have been, in my opinion, the problem that the Princes were making in exile for that Government. The French, whether Royalist or Republican, whether devoutly Catholic (like the Marquis de Gallifet) or anti-clerical (like Léon Gambetta), were all, it seemed, equally dear to the Francophile heart of Bertie, Prince of Wales. Ever since, as a child, he had told the beautiful Empress Eugénie how much he liked France, he had never wavered in his affection, nor abandoned

169

that enduring ambition to see the two countries united in
something more than the bonds of a formal treaty. His 'un-
official diplomacy' took no account of the change in France
from an empire to a Royalist republic; from a Royalist to a
socialist, anti-Royalist republic; he did not let his deep affection for his aristocratic, Roman Catholic, Royalist friends –
Gallifet, as a prime example – prevent his carefully cultivat-
ing the friendship of the republican socialist Gambetta. To
Bertie, friendship with France was something to be striven for
at all costs – and when one considers that the French were
as disliked in his own family (not individually, but as an ab-
straction with dangerous political overtones) as throughout
the British Empire, it says much for Bertie's unsuspected
powers of diplomacy that he did, before he died, achieve what
he had been working for over a period of some forty years:
the *Entente Cordiale*.

The trouble was that the French, who badly needed some
'insurance' against the Triple Alliance, were not so sure that
they wanted it from the British, whom – and not without
reason – they mistrusted. It was true that, unprecedented in
the long, common history of the two nations, there had
been no war between them for now seven decades, but there
had been plenty of snarling, and if there had been no war, it
would have been an exaggeration to claim that there had
been peace.

On the other hand, the French weren't positively against
the idea of the *Entente Cordiale*; and – although under a
Royalist President, Marshal McMahon – the French had
shewn themselves most co-operative in the matter of the Channel Tunnel, which was abandoned only because of the stupid
alarmist campaigning of General Sir Garnet Wolseley. (It was
by the Act authorizing the Tunnel – an Act of 1875, *which
has never been repealed* – that the boundary between Britain
and France was declared to be at a point equidistant between
the two coast-lines; an important decision in view of the
modern agitation to extend 'territorial waters' far beyond the
old three-mile limit.)

The trouble was that the French Government could not

exactly shelve a decision about the *Entente* whilst the Princes were making themselves so popular in Britain. Not only were all of them popular with all the members of the Royal Family; not only were they now related by marriage to the most popular member of that Family – the Princess of Wales; but they were immensely popular, also, with the British people.

The British Royal Family treated these grandsons and great-grandsons of the regicide 'Philippe Egalité' as 'one of Us'. The Duc d'Aumale was always 'Cousin Aumale', and the other Princes were on not less familiar terms with Queen Victoria and her immense family.

The Duke had found that certain way to the hearts of the English common people; active patronage of the racecourse.

At his splendid palace of Chantilly, the Duke had established both racing-stables and a well-laid-out racecourse; and his visits to Britain, after he had returned to France (following the collapse of the Empire in 1870), always included a look-in at Tattersall's, as a buyer of bloodstock for Chantilly. English jockeys, including the famous and immensely popular Fred Archer ('The Tinman'), rode for, and were entertained by, the affable Duke, so that Chantilly became, under his benign and sporting rule, another Ascot or Goodwood, as full of English horses, English jockeys and British persons of distinction – among them the future Queen Mary's turfite papa, the Duke of Teck – as Goodwood or Ascot themselves.

When the republican government of France so brutally expelled this hippophile Duke, every British newspaper – though the leader, on this occasion, was the *Sporting Times* (*The Pink 'Un*) – came out with banner headlines, denouncing the barbarous and unsporting French. Had some politician at that moment had a need for a war with France, it would have been a conflict highly popular with the British.

'The matter of supreme importance', then, must have been a decision connected with the continued exile of the Princes, as that exile affected the proposed *Entente* with Great Britain. It must not be forgotten that the expulsion of the Princes and other more violent demonstrations of French Republican sentiment were inspired by the 'Monarchist scare' centred about the flamboyant personality of General Georges Boulanger, who, though not officially a Monarchist, was fervently anti-Republican, and considered (I believe unreasonably) so dangerous that the Republicans charged him, in 1889, with high treason. Boulanger fled to Brussels, where he committed suicide on his mistress's grave.

It is possible now to see what Holmes gave, as advice, to the French Government. It was this: The exile of the Princes, if it will help that Government to achieve internal peace, need not be ended, since the 'forces' working for the *Entente* in England really consist of only one man, Bertie, Prince of Wales, whose affection for France and for the *Entente* cannot be modified, no matter what France do – certainly no matter what she do to Princes. Thus, Holmes, argued, the Republican Government could have its cake and eat it too: enjoy all the advantages of an *Entente* – by leaving the care of France safely in Bertie's hands – without the political disadvantages of a formal commitment to treaty obligations.

But that, *secretly*, Holmes, as 'undercover plenipotentiary' for (not Britain or France, but specifically) the *Entente*, brought it into being, over ten years before the formal signature of the Anglo-French Agreement (8th April, 1904), is clear from the fact that – as was said earlier – he consented to experiment in the production of new armaments; poison-gas or high-explosives, or both; in a French Government laboratory. Sir Philip Magnus, in his *King Edward the Seventh*, says, in talking of the *Entente* after its formal signing in 1904:

> Foreign policy is an organic growth which changes continuously in response to changing national interests and aspirations; but British public opinion disliked the *entente* with France, which was still regarded crudely as the corrupt and traditional enemy. It disliked the *entente* so much that the leading members of the British Liberal Cabinet, which took office in December, 1905, felt justified in concealing from most of their colleagues, as well as from Parliament and the country, the fact that conversations had been initiated between the British and French General Staffs.

Holmes could have pointed out that, practically speaking, 'conversations' had been initiated between the British and French 'war cabinets' a great deal earlier.

And what of Huret, who seems, in time at least, to be a part of this lengthy and complicated French involvement?

Watson calls Huret, 'the Boulevard Assassin', as though the man had been not only a repetitive killer but also one who chose to kill only on the various boulevards – or perhaps it was one special boulevard – of Paris. But is that what Watson, often as crudely imprecise in his language as in his 'facts', actually means?

Take that word *boulevard*, which certainly now means a (usually wide) street. But the word *boulevard* is the same word as English 'bulwark', and had originally that meaning. The modern French streets called *boulevards* are so called because they occupy the sites of the fortifications which formerly encircled Paris and other ancient cities. Is it in this original sense that Watson uses the word *boulevard* – 'bulwark', 'rampart', etc?

We have no details of how Holmes tracked down Huret, but, if the tracking occupied the world's great sleuth for some eight months – April to December, 1894 – and President Casimir-Perier not only awarded Holmes the cross[2] of an Officer of the Legion of Honour, but acknowledged Holmes's services in a personal letter of thanks, the tracking down and arrest of Huret can have been no ordinary achievement; no question of keeping watch in a Parisian boulevard to catch a killer whose *modus operandi* was known.

Assassination was popular at that time: a Russian Emperor, an Austrian Empress, an Italian King, a French President, an American President – these were only some of the eminent victims of the assassin's knife, pistol or bomb. Other attempts on eminent life failed – Queen Victoria and her son were shot at several times. I think that the French police, having got wind of an attempt on the life of Casimir-Perier, asked Holmes to track down the assassin before he could strike. With precious little in the way of a clue to aid him in his search,

[2] Description changed by Louis XVIII from the original 'star'.

Holmes found Huret by inviting the French President – with the consent of the French police, but without the consent of the President – to act as 'stalking horse' for the well-hidden assassin, by visiting Holmes at the Montpellier laboratory. Holmes knew that this visit would fetch Huret out of hiding, and it was so – the man had hardly raised his hand to discharge the pistol when the concealed French detectives leaped on him, disarmed him, and put an end to the threat to the President's life. Huret had hidden himself in a culvert within the outer ramparts of the old fortifications – the *boulevards* – and it was this fact which caused Watson to call him 'the Boulevard Assassin'.

9

Pope and President

Leo XIII was a worldly, shrewd Pope whom it was
the fashion amongst worldly, but not always so
shrewd, Protestants to admire. Leo – after whom the two sailor
sons of the Prince of Wales named their little dog – did a
number of novel things, used by his involuntary admirers to
justify their thinking well of him; but the fact is that his
admirers approved what Leo did because they already admired
him; he was not liked merely because of the novelties that he
introduced into Papal conduct.

In his reign, for instance, the practice of castrating boys
intended for the Sistine choir (so that their youthful treble
should not break with puberty) was discontinued: though
not, fortunately for the historical record, before the bleating
soprano of a *castrato* could be immortalized on the wax cylinder
of a phonograph. He has earned a sort of grudging respect
from dedicated socialists because he published a Bull telling
Christian employers that their workers had rights.

He was greatly admired by Queen Victoria, who once sent
him, as a present, a sack full of walnuts, inside each nut
being a golden sovereign. The symbolism of this odd but
princely gift escapes me . . .

He did not, however, admire the people over whom Queen
Victoria ruled, and when the bisexual Prince Eddy, heir to
the throne after his father, Bertie, Prince of Wales, wished
to marry Princess Hélène of Orleans (niece of the Duc de
Montpensier), and she went to Leo to ask his blessing on the
proposed union, the Pope refused, and warned Hélène that,

were she to marry a heretic, she would be skating dangerously near eternal hell-fire. The fact is that the Pope considered that he had been insulted by the British Government, and was not averse to having a human revenge on his humiliators.

In this way.

On the forcible annexation of the temporal dominions of the Pope by King Victor Emmanuel II in 1870, which left the then Pope – Pius IX – a sovereign without a kingdom, Great Britain refused to acknowledge a political change brought about by force, and continued to refuse recognition to the new United Italy's annexation of the Papal States. (Even to-day, Great Britain refuses, 'officially', to recognize the fact that the once independent states of Latvia, Lithuania and Estonia have been forcibly incorporated into Soviet Russia.)

Thus it was the Vatican continued to maintain its consulates at Malta and Gibraltar, with Great Britain accepting Papal passports and visas. So the situation continued until 1884, when a tardy realization that the Papal States were no more, and that Italy now ruled in Rome, caused Mr Gladstone's government to withdraw 'recognition' from the purely temporal aspect of Papal power, and request the Apostolic Delegate in London to close the two remaining Papal consulates on British territory. Leo XIII took the snub, as he saw it, hard. Though the British – and, in particular, the London – people cared little for the Papacy and its exotic and (to the British generally) effeminate customs, the Catholic Church in Britain suffered none of those inconveniences which seemed so greatly and so constantly to trouble it in 'Catholic' countries. Long before the Risorgimento had really got into its stride, the coldly realistic appraisal of British social stability and that British mental laziness to which has been given the euphemistic name of 'tolerance', had convinced the directors of Church policy that the time had come to begin the transfer of capital from revolution- and war-threatened Europe to Protestant but tolerant Britain.

No difficulty was placed in the way of the Roman Church's acquisition of land, and an ingenious exploitation of the then

37 Victorian efficiency was inseparable from Victorian energy. Collecting filled mail-bags from the shoot at the General Post Office, St Martin's-le-Grand, at 8 p.m. *Date about 1887: a contemporary drawing by Gordon Browne, R.I. (Contrad Research Library)*

38 De Blowitz, the other 'greatest of all *The Times*'s correspondents'. His talent, unlike Russell's, lay in the subtle, often tricky extraction of the truth from those least willing to reveal it. His most spectacular coup was to send *The Times* details of the clauses of the Treaty of Berlin (1878) before the High Contracting Parties had published them. *Photograph: courtesy of* The Times

Duke of Norfolk's superstitiousness brought half-a-million pounds' worth of fine churches as a sort of 'dowry' for the Roman Church's Second Coming. *Punch* hated the Roman Church; hated even more its English cardinals. But what was a little sneering to an institution which had weathered the persecutions of Decius and Diocletian, and, within fifty years of Diocletian was persecuting the pagans even more savagely itself?

Leo didn't like the English; but he had no objection to the employment of Holmes, mostly because Holmes's skill was unrivalled, and the 'Little Affair of the Vatican Cameos' – again I use Watson's terminology – had demonstrated to the Papacy how very convenient, at times, the famous British 'phlegm' could be. As this was the first of the cases which associated Holmes with Papal Rome, we shall return to it shortly. In the meantime, it will be useful to list, in chrono-logical order, the five known cases in which Holmes worked professionally for the Pope.

1. The Little Affair of the Vatican Cameos   Late April–early May, 1888
2. The Bishopsgate Jewel Case   Before September, 1888
3. The Famous Investigation of the Sudden Death of Cardinal Tosca   May or June, 1895
4. The Case of the Two Coptic Patriarchs   July, 1898
5. The Disappearance of the Famous Black Pearl of the Borgias   Around Saturday, 20th May, 1899

Let us take the cases *seriatim*, observing the dates. In 1888, agitation on the industrial front had assumed grave propor-tions, not at all minimized by the fact that the year 1887 had marked the Queen's Golden Jubilee: an illegal procession of unemployed (with a strong reinforcement of unemployable) had marched to the West End, where, the police being unable to restrain them, the Horse Guards dispersed the mob – though only after it had broken windows in Pall Mall clubs and done other damage. In the following year, another mob invaded Hyde Park, thoughtfully arming itself with the Park railings;

and in that same year, the Dockers and Bryant & May 'match-girls' struck; the first to secure a guaranteed sixpence-a-day; the latter in protest against the slavish (and dangerous) conditions in which they worked.

In these uprisings, two 'religious' leaders, representing – apparently – the opposite extremes of theological belief, took an active and, indeed, provocative part: Edward, Cardinal Manning, ex-clergyman son of a bankrupt London banker, and Charles Booth, 'General' of the Salvation Army – *both extremely popular with the 'socialist' Prince and Princess of Wales*, whilst Queen Victoria had a special affection for Booth.

In 1884, as part of the new programme for 'liberalizing' the Monarchy, the Prince of Wales had been invited to permit himself to be nominated as a member of the Royal Commission on the Housing of the Working Classes – a subject in which the Prince's father had interested himself, in a highly practical way. Contemporary 'Big Names' which are of no interest to us now were represented on the Commission; an absence being a nominee of the Prince's – Octavia Hill. Dilke supported this departure from precedent, but Gladstone vetoed the appointment of a woman, however eminent, to a Royal Commission. But another precedent the Prince *did* manage to establish: he insisted that Cardinal Manning, as a Prince of the Roman Church, should take precedence after himself, and *before* the Marquess of Salisbury. (No wonder that the ordinary Protestant Briton wondered how true were the stories that the Prince had secretly 'gone over to Rome'!)

Both the Prince's support of Manning, and Manning's support of the dockers – with 'General' Booth, Manning and some other eminent zealots marching through the City and into the well-guarded West End – had earned Manning and his Church much enmity of a highly-organized sort. The ranks of British Protestantism – both of the Established Church and of the (generally more-or-less Republican) Nonconformity – began to close up, and an anti-Prince movement, already scandalized by his womanizing, card-playing, horse-racing and patronage of rich foreign Jews, now set out to 'gun' him for the far more serious offence of 'bowing the neck to the Scarlet Woman of Rome'.

Manning had already had to fight a ludicrous libel action, to scotch a statement made in the *National Police Gazette*, repeated in *Town Talk* and copied by a number of less well-known but equally libellous journals, that, whilst still a Church of England clergyman, he had married the notorious murderess, Mrs Manning ('heroine' of a popular ballad – which, of course, immortalized her), divorced her in order to become a Roman priest, though not before he had given her a son whom Manning had allowed to grow up 'a common docker' – the notorious Tom *Mann*, leader of the striking dockers.

Preposterous as this myth was, it had to be challenged in open court (just as, some ten years later, the Duke of York – afterwards King George V – had to bring a libel action against a journal which had accused him of having secretly married, and then deserted, Admiral Tryon's daughter); and in the course of his examination, Cardinal Manning had to admit that his banker father had 'failed' – as the euphemism of those more decorous times had it.

It was the fact that the prestige both of the Prince and the Pope was involved now with that of the Cardinal which caused Holmes to be summoned to deal with 'The Little Affair of the Vatican Cameos', which could not have been anything but a *big* affair had Holmes not smartly nipped the mischief in the bud.

Briefly, when the French bombarded Rome in 1849, a trooper of the first regiment of Hussars entered and looted – with a number of his companions – the palace of the Cardinal Settimana-Bardolini, Commissary of the Great Seal to His Holiness. What the trooper took were some cameos from a cabinet whose doors had been knocked open by a fragment of shell. The cameos, Alexandrian work of the second century AD, were of exquisite workmanship, though that was not the prime reason for the trooper's having taken them. It was the obscenity, not the workmanship, which attracted him.

After nearly forty years, the cameos, described as having

been 'in a private collection', came up for auction at Christies, were bought for a large sum, by the London art-buying agent of Mr Pierpont Morgan, the American millionaire, and put on show at Burlington House before going to America.

At the exhibition, they were recognized, by a poverty-stricken amateur of such things, as having been formerly in the possession of Cardinal Settimana-Bardolini. It was fortunate that the connoisseur was an ardent Roman Catholic; instead of going to either the newspapers or the police, he went to Manning, whom the connoisseur had known from days before the Cardinalate, and Manning, realizing the explosive nature of the connoisseur's discovery, reported secretly to Rome, and explained matters to Holmes.

The situation called for some delicate handling. The Pope had no wish to recover the obscene cameos; he would much rather have the American millionaire's money – but the secret of the former, the true, ownership, must never be revealed; certainly not now, with all the anti-Roman forces of Great Britain and France collaborating to associate the Church's name with any scandal. This Holmes was able to conceal.

In the course of his enquiries into the means by which the cameos had passed from the illegal possession of a French trooper to that of an English collector of *vertu*. Holmes's attention was called to an expensive, 'exclusive' City jeweller's, having a profitable connection amongst those bankers and stock-brokers whose *amies* had to be kept sweet and pliant with gifts of costly jewellery. This elegant and discreet *bijoutier* of Bishopsgate, with branch-shops in Burlington Gardens, the rue du Fauborg St Honoré and the via Princiana, closed down, its owner being sent to ruin his finger-nails with ten years' oakum-picking.

The sudden death of Cardinal Tosca, as he was speaking at an Albert Hall meeting organized for the purpose of 'making a solemn act of Reparation for the Reformation', not incredibly caused what the contemporary news-sheets called a 'tremendous sensation'. The fact was that, as the Cardinal was speaking, crowds of militant Protestants were being batoned away from the many entrances to the Albert Hall;

and since it was known that Protestants had been buying tickets of admission to the meeting; the collapse and death of the Italian on the flower-decorated stage were at first connected, by the angry Roman Catholics, with the presence of their hysterically-agitated enemies both inside and outside the great Hall. The meeting had already shewn signs of being uncontrollable even before the Cardinal rose, with every evidence of nervousness, to address the gathering in Latin – since he could speak no English, and had been told that all English persons of education had spent up to ten years at school and university learning the *lingua franca* of the Church.

Cries of 'Hokey-pokey, penny a lump! That's the stuff to make you jump!' greeted the Cardinal's Latin, mistaken for Italian by Englishmen who pronounced the tongue of Catullus and Ovid in quite a different way. "Where's the monkey, Antonio?" shouted one rude pillar of the Established Church – upon which a section of the Antis broke out into a rollicking rendition of "Oh, oh, Antonio . . ." discorded by the rising of the whole body of the Hall (the Others) in a brave if quavering rendition of *Faith of Our Fathers* . . .

The Cardinal, indeed, had hardly had time to utter more than a formal 'God bless you, Good people', in Latin, when he gave a gasp, clutched his side with a jewelled hand, turned purple, and collapsed, frothing, on the red Oetzmann carpet. Before a man, shouting, "Let me pass: I'm a physician!" could climb up on the stage, His Eminence was dead.

The angry scenes before him, Holmes was able to prove, had caused the Cardinal to twist, in his nervousness, the ring – not his Cardinal's ring – that he wore. (Yes, many persons, now that Holmes mentioned it, had remarked upon that nervous trick!) What Holmes proved was that the ring, a present from an English admirer of the Cardinal's work for the Faith, had once belonged to Lucrezia Borgia, and what had poisoned the Cardinal had been the notorious Borgia poison, *acqua tofana*, still potent to work its mischief after nearly four centuries. Holmes acquitted the present-giver of guilt; but where was the black pearl which had fallen from the Borgia ring as the Cardinal's hand crumpled beneath his falling body?

Holmes afterwards found it, mounted as the knob of a Suffragette's hat-pin: it proved to be one of the least easy of Holmes's professional tasks to take possession of the pearl which had been adopted by the formidable lady on the ancient principle of 'Finders, keepers!'

The tracking down of this lady from among the eight thousand people – all more or less hysterical – who were that night within the Albert Hall, was recognized as a triumph of the detective art.

The Two Coptic Patriarchs come into the Vatican–Holmes chronicle only by accident; they were carrying neither indecent Alexandrian cameos – though they did come, at least one of them did, from Alexandria – nor lethal Renascence rings.

As part of its campaign for the pacification of an Egypt that General Sir Herbert Kitchener – with some later-to-be-greatly-over-publicized help from a young cavalry officer named Winston Churchill – was about to conquer in the final battle of Omdurman, in September, 1898, the British Government had been extending the smile of patronage and the hand of generosity to the leaders of Egypt's 'representative' political, religious, philosophical and cultural groups.

The two Patriarchs, on one of those paid-for holidays better known to generations of holiday-subsidizing mugs as 'fact finding missions', decided to take a paid-for trip around Europe. Vaguely hinting to the Cardinal Secretary of Propaganda that the Coptic Church might be 'exploring' the Œcumenical possibility – as the Jacobite Church of South India was known to be doing – the Patriarchs enjoyed lavish Roman hospitality for several weeks, not only at slap-up luncheons and dinners at the Vatican, but at Archbishops' and Bishops' palaces all over Italy. In the end, looking at the expense-sheets, the Cardinal Secretary of Entertainments arranged with the British Ambassador to the Quirinal to invite them to England. "It would greatly assist the development of cordial relations between England and Egypt," the pliant cleric pointed out.

The Patriarchs took off; but instead of coming up the expected way, by the Rome–Paris express, and so, by Calais, to Dover and London, they decided, for reasons which were never made plain, to take a tramp-steamer from Genoa, which, after touching at almost every port in the Mediterranean, landed them at Surrey Docks, and let them emerge from Finland Yard into a meeting of idle dockers called by a professional agitator to protest against the immigration of foreign (and worse, *unskilled*) labour, which was threatening the jobs of such of the British as were lucky enough to get even casual employment.

The cobbled streets, laid with shining tram-lines; the dirty white horse-trams, drawn by even dirtier (and always heavily moustached) white horses; the soot-blackened brick of industrial dwelling, factory, dock-wall and warehouse; the tiny, over-stocked shops with *Fry's Chocolate* in stuck-on porcelain characters on every small-paned shop-window; the clatter of iron-shod wheels – of rattling milkman's chariot, of lumbering dray (drawn by the huge-hooved beasts descended lineally from those who had borne the armoured knights at Cressy and Agincourt and Flodden), of towering dust-cart and vast six-wheeled pantechnicon . . . For all these exotic sights and sounds (to say nothing of the home-brewed Canning Town smells) the two oddly dressed strangers had little or no time. The crowd, inflamed by speaker's rhetoric, idleness and sixty-shilling bitter, mistook the two Patriarchs for Hassidic rabbis or Russian archimandrites – it was all the same to the British, and mattered little either way, seeing that the strangers were foreigners.

Holmes came into the affair, not to apologize to the Patriarchs for the severe beating-up that they had received at the hands of the British – the smoothies from the Foreign Office had seen to that – but as one commissioned by the British Government to find the *portmanteaux* full of valuable antique ecclesiastical vessels and other sacred objects which, so the Patriarchs claimed, they had been carrying when they came out of the dock-gates and hit the crowd (or, rather, when the crowd hit them).

In one way this not very important case represented a total failure for the world's greatest detective: for he failed to find any trace of the valuable *portmanteaux*, nor could anyone on the SS *Charlie Peace* remember ever having seen such objects. The bluebottles of Canning Town, the sensitive inhabitants complained, hadn't never give 'em no rest since them two monkeys in the black nightshirts had come out of Finland Yard . . . *They'd* never seen no two porty-mantles or even tatchy-cases, the indignant Canning Townians swore. Ask *them*, they said, they'd take their bleedin' davy them two foreign coves 'adn't never 'ad no porty-mantles . . .

Holmes reported to Lord Salisbury that, following his most searching enquiries, he found himself forced to agree with the majority opinion in Canning Town. "In this case, my Lord," said Holmes, gravely, "*vox populi* is most certainly *vox Dei* . . ."

"Very possibly," said the man who was, that year, doubling in the *rôles* of Prime Minister and Foreign Secretary; "but *vox populi* here is going to make us pretty unpopular in Egypt – at least, with the Copts. What do you suggest?"

This case, which was the most total failure that Holmes could ever acknowledge, was also his most complete success.

"I have, sir," he added, as gravely, and drawing a paper from his pocket-book, "a detailed list of the treasures which were lost when the two *portmanteaux* disappeared. I thought that it would save time if I called in at Messrs Garrard, the jewellers, in Haymarket, and obtained from their Mr Rowbotham a rough estimate of the cost of replacing the missing articles. Of course, the priceless antiquity and sentimental associations of these missing objects are not matters for a jeweller's estimation; but the gold, silver, gems . . ."

"Of course. How much, Mr Holmes . . . ?"

Holmes glanced at the list.

"Some garments are missing, of course; some articles of the toilet . . . soap-box, razor-case, hair-brushes . . ."

"Trifles, to be sure. The – er – *sacred* objects, Mr Holmes . . . ?"

"An estimate only, my Lord, but . . . but Garrard's regret

that they cannot possibly oblige us with replacements at a cost of less than . . . *forty thousand pounds.*"

"I . . . see . . . ee . . . ee. A round figure, Mr. Holmes?"

"There are some odd pounds, shillings and pence. Yes, I made it a round figure."

"And you think, Mr Holmes, that Her Britannic Majesty's Government should commission the replacements from Messrs Garrard . . . ?"

"Unless, my Lord," said Holmes, staring out of the window at the hansoms and four-wheelers going both ways along King Street, "Their Exalted Beatitudes might prefer to take the cash and replace the missing objects a little nearer home . . . ?"

"Yes . . . I see. 'Their Exalted Beatitudes', eh? I must remember to mention that to Lady Salisbury at dinner tonight; my wife, Mr Holmes, has an odd interest in magniloquent titles of honour – foreign, of course. And . . . have Their Exalted Beatitudes suggested that they would prefer the cash . . . ?"

"Only, sir, in explaining that they would prefer not to hang about London whilst Garrard's are preparing the replacements, which, in any case, they could obtain, they tell me, much more expeditiously in Alexandria."

"Just so. Their religious duties must keep them very busy, Mr Holmes. We must take example from these industrious prelates, and see to it that we do not waste *our* time. You recommend that this sum be paid to them?"

"I do, sir – all things considered."

"Very well, then; it shall be as you suggest. You are prepared, despite your unrivalled reputation, Mr Holmes, to admit total failure in your endeavours to trace the missing bags . . . ?"

"Yes, my Lord, unreservedly."

"Oh well, Mr Holmes, I really cannot see that an occasional failure of this sort could possibly harm your reputation."

"I thank your Lordship," said Holmes, bowing.

"They will not be returning to Egypt from – where was it? – ah, yes, the Surrey Docks? No, I imagine not. Two elegant young messengers in the Foreign Service – and a reserved first-class compartment in the Boat Train from Victoria. Yes, well now, Mr Holmes, let us trust that Their Exalted Beatitudes will return to Egypt full of benevolence towards the British. You saw, by the way, that General Kitchener trounced those natives at – where was it? Ah yes, Omdurman? Good thing, too. Finishes our troubles *there*; for a bit, anyhow. Randy's son managed to get into the finish. Hm. 'Their Exalted Beatitudes . . .' Well, well . . . Forty thousand pounds, eh? The Treasury won't like it, Mr Holmes; they certainly won't. Still, see if I can't smuggle it through the Army Estimates . . ."

10

The Washington Records

We pause here to note that 'The Service to the Royal Family of Scandinavia', in late December, 1890, and what Watson calls 'The Summons to Norway', in the early July of 1895, are both connected with the decision of King Oscar's government to let Norway regain her independence – observing, too, that Holmes is 'summoned to Norway' in July, 1895, and that, on 22nd July, 1896, HRH Prince Christian Frederick Charles George Waldemar Axel of Denmark, a lieutenant in the Royal Danish Navy and a Knight of Justice of the Order of St John of Jerusalem in England, was married to HRH Princess Maud Charlotte Mary Victoria, third daughter of TRH the Prince and Princess of Wales. With this marriage between the future King of Norway and the daughter of a future King of Great Britain and Ireland, the independence of Norway was assured; more important, the foundations of a lasting peace between Sweden and Norway had been assured as well.

The gazetting of Holmes as a Knight of the Order of the Seraphim – Sweden's supreme order of chivalry – is dated 22nd July, 1896. The 'King of Scandinavia' was recognizing Holmes's private services to three neighbouring nations in the most public way possible. The 'Seraphim', the Swedes rightly think, is the 'Garter' of English, the 'Golden Fleece' of Hapsburg royalty. Holmes, the King felt, deserved the 'Seraphim' – and more . . .

To Holmes, however, the most important work that he had ever undertaken, covering the period between April, 1895, and October, 1903, were those important labours, twice – and briefly – referred to by Watson (in the course of his narratives of *The Adventure of the Priory School* and *The Adventure of the Three Students*) as 'The Case of the Ferrers Documents' (early May, 1900) and 'The Striking Results of Some Laborious Research in Early English Charters', which covers the period – 1895–1903 – mentioned above.

It has astonished me that the real nature of this research has not been noted, especially by American Sherlockians, or even by less erudite students of Anglo-American relations, and notably in view of the fact that the name 'Ferrers' provides the certain clue to the nature of the research undertaken, over a period of eight years, by Holmes; since the House of Ferrers is united by marriage to what the German genealogists call the *Stammfamilie* of the House of Washington.

General George Washington, first President of the United States, was a collateral of John de Ferrers, only son of Robert de Ferrers, 8th and last holder of that earldom of Derby which was created by Stephen in 1138, the year of the Battle of the Standard. The title was forfeit, but Robert's son, John, was summoned to Parliament as Baron FERRERS of Chartley, in the county of Stafford; this title being of the older type of 'barony by writ'. In 1677, King Charles II, in recognition of the fact that Sir Seymour Shirley, 5th baronet, had died in the Tower, a prisoner of Cromwell, called out of abeyance, in favour of Sir Seymour's brother and heir, Sir Robert, 6th baronet, one of those ancient peerages of which Sir Robert's grandmother, Lady Dorothy Devereux, daughter of the 2nd Earl of Essex, had been co-heir. This was the barony of Ferrers of Chartley, and by sign-manual under the Great Seal, Sir Robert Shirley now became the 8th Baron Ferrers of Chartley in the peerage of England.

Sir Robert, still but a baronet, married, 1671, Elizabeth, only daughter of Sir William WASHINGTON of Garnsdon, of the main branch of the Washingtons, Sir William being a younger brother of the Reverend LAURENCE Washington, MA, great-grandfather of President George Washington. This marriage united the Shirley and Washington families. Governor Shirley of Virginia was thus a near-relative of George Washington, to whom Shirley refused to grant a 'regular' Army commission, in 1758, with results which would alter the power-structure of the world.

It was this Shirley-Washington marriage of 1671 which introduced the 'Washington' names into the Shirley family.

In 1711, Sir Robert Shirley, Baron Ferrers, was further advanced in the peerage – though now that was of Great Britain, and no longer that of England (to which no further titles could be added after the Act of Union, 1707). He was raised to the dignities of Viscount Tamworth and Earl Ferrers. He died, full of years, in 1717, when, the ancient barony of Ferrers of Chartley passing to his grand-daughter, the newer titles passed to his second son, WASHINGTON, 2nd earl, who died without children. He was succeeded by his nephew, LAURENCE, 4th earl, who died unmarried in 1745, and was succeeded by another LAURENCE, son of the Honourable LAURENCE Shirley, 4th son of the first earl. The 4th earl, LAURENCE, died in an unusual way: in a paroxysm of rage, he killed his land-steward, Mr Johnston; was tried before the bar of the House of Lords by his peers; and hanged with a silken rope at Tyburn, 5th May, 1760. He was succeeded, as 5th earl, by his brother, WASHINGTON, a vice-admiral in the naval engagements against the French, Spanish and rebellious British North American colonists. The 8th and 9th earls also bore the name of WASHINGTON.

There were, as I have written, many other Washingtons besides the heirless George; one was at Wellington's side on the day before Waterloo; another – Vice-Admiral Sir George Washington, KCB – fought on the American Station as a boy during the War of 1812.

What Holmes sought, amongst 'early English charters', generally and amongst 'the Ferrers documents' in particular, were the archives of the Washington family, to be handed over to the United States as a gift on the hundredth anniversary of the death of General George Washington in 1799. We shall see, presently, why this research continued until 1903.

What was the sentiment which inspired the British Government to commission Holmes to undertake this antiquarian and genealogical research? A hardly concealed fear of the United States; a fear all the more potent to alarm British politicians and 'statesmen' since nothing – or, rather, nothing that their fatuous complacency was likely to observe – had warned them of the sudden, vicious but politically calculated attack that 'Our Cousins', speaking through Cleveland and Olney, were about to make on 'the Old Country'.

Because British foreign policy had, even before the end of the Revolutionary War of 1769–83, 'demanded' a 'neutral' United States, the British Foreign Office had continued to believe what it *hoped* was true – and that it knew to be quite untrue – that the successive American governments had an affection for 'the Old Country'. What affection there had been had quite disappeared after the end of the Civil War; not only had British political folly – perhaps dictated by the dying Prince Consort, perhaps not – alienated the triumphant, revenge-hungry North, and the brutally despoiled South; but the ethnic elements of the new nation had changed their proportions – the dominant strain was no longer White Anglo-Saxon Protestant. To what was soon to be a majority of Americans, Britain was no longer 'the Old Country'.

Wooing of the Americans had begun early in the history of the young republic; Americans – painters, engineers, 'inventors' – flocked to London before 1790; and in 1797 – for reasons which were certainly not clear to the British people; least of all to the merchants of Britain – valuable concessions were made to the Americans, in respect of the Indian trade, then the jealously-guarded monopoly of the Honourable East India Company. But by this still mysterious concession to a nation of ex-British subjects, the Americans were permitted to carry on trade with the Company's territories in India, in articles not prohibited by law, on paying only the duties paid by British vessels. 'The advantages,' says the anonymous author of *The Extraordinary Black Book*,[1] 'were not neglected by the Americans. In a few years, the trade of the United

[1] London : Published by Effingham Wilson, Royal Exchange; 1831.

States in India equalled nearly one-half the trade of the Company. It was singular policy to admit a foreign state to the participation of the India trade while our own merchants were excluded.' 'Singular', maybe; but it was an early expression of that cloud-cuckoo-land dream of some British politicians that, if 'we' were sufficiently tender to the Americans, they would return to the fold.

Imagine, then, the alarm and terror in the Be-Nice-To-America-At-All-Costs party when, on two occasions in 1895, Official America – President Cleveland and Secretary of State Olney – threatened to settle a dispute with Great Britain 'if necessary by war'.

The two occasions had their origins in disputes of a trivial nature, in neither of which was the United States directly involved – only by the tenuous ethics of that British invention, the Monroe Doctrine, and by the 'solemn responsibilities' of the inevitable development of that Doctrine : the new, now unashamedly imperialistic 'Pan-Americanism'.

The first anti-British blast of the wind of American change came with the United States' intervention in a dispute between Great Britain and revolution-torn Brazil. I have told the story elsewhere; but here I need only say that the threat of war, accompanying Richard Olney's Note to Lord Salisbury, was concerned with the trivial subject of Britain's 'occupation' of the island of Trinidad, a barren, rabbit-and-land-crab-infested rock forming part of the Martin Vaz Group, some 600 miles east of Bahia, then the capital of Brazil.

As for the other blast . . .

'Venezuela,' writes Sir Philip Magnus,[2] 'had laid claim, on historical grounds, to a large part of British Guiana, and while negotiations were in progress President Cleveland of the United States sent a blustering and provocative message to Congress on 17th December, 1895. Pleading the Monroe Doctrine, and focusing his gaze on the next Presidential Election, he announced that he proposed to settle the Anglo-Venezuelan dispute himself and to employ force, if necessary, to impose his decision; and that vigorous twist administered to

[2] *King Edward the Seventh*, op. cit.

191

the lion's tail caused a transport of unseemly belligerent enthusiasm to convulse America.'

One could argue that the Prince's open friendship for rich
Jews was about to pay off.

'That utterly unexpected but imminent prospect of war
with the United States aroused bewilderment and horror in
Great Britain; and at the height of the crisis, the proprietor
of the *New York World*, Joseph Pulitzer, cabled an invitation
to the Prince of Wales to state his views. The Prince composed a perfect reply which he shewed to Lord Salisbury, who
reminded him that it was his constitutional duty to be silent;
but the Prince felt so strongly about the wicked absurdity of
an Anglo-American war that he rejected that advice and
cabled (23rd December, 1895) to Pulitzer: "I thank you for
your telegram. I earnestly trust, and cannot but believe, present crisis will be arranged in a manner satisfactory to both
countries, and will be succeeded by same warm feeling of
friendship which has existed between them for so many
years."

'Published on Christmas Eve, that message could not possibly have done harm, and its effect was, in fact, conciliatory
and helpful. The dispute was later referred to an arbitral commission composed of two Englishmen, two Americans and a
neutral chairman, whose award, in October, 1899, was sub-
stantially in favour of Great Britain.'

Sir Philip Magnus could have added that the affair was
evidently cooked up – and not by the Venezuelans. For the
boundaries between Venezuela and British Guiana had been
settled by a boundary commission fifty years earlier, sitting
under a Swiss as neutral president. As for the restoration of
'that warm feeling of friendship', the *National Police Gazette*
(American proprietor, Richard Fox) reported in 1897 that the
top-billing English comic, Dan Leno, was hissed and booed
off the stage of a New York music-hall for having incautiously
uttered the words, 'dear old England'.

Of course, if Britain was amazed by the belligerency – in
words, at any rate – of Cleveland and his dog, Olney, it was
as nothing compared with the amazement of the two Ameri-

can 'statesmen' when they realized that their irresponsible threats, uttered merely for the noble purpose of vote-catching, and never meant to be taken seriously – least of all by Great Britain – had actually *frightened* their British 'opposite numbers', and that the British 'statesmen' were now – incredible as it seemed – fawning on Cleveland to beg him to be merciful.

He had more sense than to attack Great Britain – the timorous, half-witted Salisbury, played-out descendant of an Elizabethan 'statesman', who, in any case, had risen in favour less by intelligence than by a grovelling pliancy, would have been, sooner or later, thrust aside by some bolder character (the still young Herbert Kitchener, for instance) – but, full of the confidence that an undeserved reputation for power and ferocity always inspires, he launched attacks on two weaklings with possessions of great strategic importance: Hawaii and Spain. Queen Liliuokalani was deposed by this good man's successor for her 'moral turpitude'; Spain's Caribbean and Far Eastern possessions were taken from her with an even less plausible excuse. Yet another nation had staked its claim to Empire . . .

There were probably hundreds of scholars in the Britain of 1895, all far more competent than Holmes to trace the history of the Ferrers and Washington families back to their remote and modest beginnings. But Holmes had something that few contemporary genealogists and antiquaries in Britain had: a passionate affection for the United States – for the country, for the people, for what the great republic seemed to him to symbolize – and, perhaps more important to the world, Holmes dreamed of a day when the two nations, old and new, split at Boston Harbour, would be re-united under one flag; a single nation, with one language, a single Law, and the world-conquering power of the matchless Anglo-Saxon ethic to bring peace to mankind . . .

Curiously enough, the dream was to come true; not, of course, as Holmes had dreamed it – dreams never 'work out' – quite the same as the dreamer dreamt but near enough: though not, one feels, in a way which would altogether have gladdened the heart of Holmes.

Still, it was for that dream that he so willingly went about his archivist's task, dredging up from the all-forgiving, the all-obliterating past the names of so many nonentities, memorable now only for the fact that they had lived centuries ago. Old charters yellowing and drying out in the muniment-chests of decaying church-lofts, in the attics of mediæval colleges, on the never-looked-at shelves of country houses' store-rooms: Holmes sought them out, wherever they were to be found. And on George Washington's Birthday, 1899, a magnificent set of volumes was presented to the American President by Her Britannic Majesty's minister to Washington. A similar set of volumes was presented to both Queen Victoria and her son, the latter the person most responsible for this peace-seeking gesture towards the new transatlantic imperialism, and the one who (despite his unhappy realization that Holmes was one of the few persons completely proof against the famous Edwardian charm) had personally commissioned this work from the great detective.

The title of the work, as given in the *Catalogue* of the British Museum, and in the *Catalog* of the Library of Congress, is as follows:

THE FERRERS DOCUMENTS
Being a Genealogical and Historical Account of the Ferrers, Washington and Allied Armigerous Families, with Special Reference to that Branch of the Allied Families which Terminated in
GEORGE WASHINGTON
General of the Continental
Army
&
First President of the United States
of America
Published by Her Majesty's
Command

The name of the author is not given, though a pencilled note, in the Washington copy, remarks that 'The author is well-known to be the famous Mr Sherlock Holmes. The work was suggested and commissioned by the present King of England'. The note is dated '1.6.'02.' – oddly so, if it be a coincidence, since 6th January, 1902, was Holmes's forty-eighth birthday.

The three presentation sets of *The Ferrers Documents*, one of which I was permitted to examine at Windsor by the kindness of the late Sir Owen Morshead, the Librarian, were illuminated by hand throughout; all the coats-of-arms having their various tinctures added by the heraldic artist commissioned through the College of Arms.

One hundred other sets, each numbered, were printed on a heavy, hand-made Whatman paper. None of these was for sale, though occasionally a set comes on the market. The work was not, surprisingly, entrusted to Eyre & Spottiswoode, Printers to Her Majesty, but to Henry Frowde, MA, Publisher to the University of Oxford. The printer's name is given as 'Horace Hart, MA, Printer to the University'.

The President who came after the assassinated McKinley – who succeeded Cleveland in 1897 – was of a very different type: just as ambitious to make the United States rich, strong and respected, but imaginatively prepared to build up his great country's prestige in more subtle ways.

A young sprig of the British nobility – Winston Churchill – had met and liked this new President when the latter was still an already-bigger-than-life colonel of Rough Riders in the easy-meat Cuban campaign. Lieutenant Winston Spencer-Churchill, 'veteran' of Omdurman, had been, at his own request, 'detached for special duties', as an 'observer' of the Spanish–American war. Now Roosevelt began to 'take an interest in the Old Country' – an interest all the easier to take in that his own 'Old Country' was rather Holland than England. *The Ferrers Documents* interested Teddy Roosevelt and, at King Edward's request, Holmes undertook the – to him now by no means distasteful – task of doing for the Roosevelt family what he had done so brilliantly for the Ferrers-Washingtons. On his necessary visits to Holland, Holmes was pressed by the young Queen Wilhelmina – still unpopular in Britain because of the shelter that she gave to the fleeing

President Kruger (as she was to give still more unpopular shelter, in 1918, to the abdicated and fleeing Kaiser William II) – to be her personal guest.

Soon, Teddy Roosevelt's correspondence with the King began to take on a personal, warmly amicable note: 'Dear Mr President'; 'My dear King Edward'. What had commenced with the King's commissioning a Roosevelt pedigree for 'Teddy', developed into a sincere friendship. On 24th March, 1905, the British Ambassador in Berlin wrote to Lord Knollys: "You tell me that the King is full of mistrust of the Emperor, and this is only natural after what we know of his attempts to sow distrust of us in other nations, and more especially in America. These attempts have signally failed . . ."[3]

Holmes, having refused a knighthood from the new King, offered for 'The Services Which May Perhaps Some Day Be Described', as Watson says, had accepted from King Edward a 'founder-membership' of that Order of Merit specially created for such cases as Holmes's. Relations between the two men, monarch and subject, though they might never develop to cordiality, had grown less tart; the King was never backward in acknowledging the important international benefits of Holmes's work, and Holmes's unselfconscious patriotism knew an honest pride in work which had strikingly justified itself in the cause of peace.

Though the work on the Washington family history was undertaken and carried through with all Holmes's usual assiduity, he welcomed it – as did the British Foreign Secretary, the Secretary of State for the Indian Department: the Right Honourable Lord George Hamilton, PC, MP; and the Viceroy of India – as a convenient explanation of his absence from public view. This unpublicized work, undertaken at the express solicitation of Government, originated in what students of Sherlockian history[4] call 'The Great Hiatus' – that period

[3] Royal Archives, W.45/146. Quoted by Magnus.
[4] I was interested to read in *The Times* (28th July, 1972) that a wealthy manufacturer of optical instruments – notably magnifying glasses – Sir Sigerson Holmes-Verner (obviously related to Sherlock

between Holmes's apparent death at the Reichenbach Falls, on Monday, 4th May, 1891 and what, without disrespect to the Deity, the same Sherlockians call 'The Return', on Thursday, 5th April, 1894. In the course of this three-year period, the history of which has never been publicly recorded, even in part, Holmes visited, amongst many other then remote places, the 'Forbidden Land' of Thibet, barred to Europeans since the expulsion of the last of the Jesuit missionaries in the seventeenth century.

The question of whether or not Holmes left Thibet in 1892 or 1893 a true Ahanta was learnedly discussed in *The Baker Street Journal*[5] between the Reverend Henry T. Folsom (*against*) and Mr A. Francis Harris (*for*). I found the arguments, not so much inconclusive – they were – as unnecessary. Just as mountaineering expeditions in nearby Sikkim and Nepaul – I cite that of Lieutenant-colonel L. Augustine Waddell, in 1891 – were the 'semi-official' attempts of British or British Indian governments to spy on Thibet, so Holmes's invitation to Lhasa is claimed to have originated in the Panchen Lama's desire that Holmes should track down – and thus prove or disprove the existence of – the *metoh-kangmi*, which has been somewhat inaccurately but picturesquely rendered into English as 'The Abominable Snowman'. (Colonel Waddell saw, photographed and reported the footprints of a 'Snowman' in his mountaineering.)

But the plain fact is that Holmes procured an invitation from the Panchen Lama to visit Lhasa because Holmes was an accredited though 'undercover' agent of the British Government. The report on which he was involved between 1900 and 1903 – when he was apparently working full-time on the Roosevelt archives – concerned Thibet, and its immense value to the British Government and the Government of India was apparent when, in 1903, Colonel Sir Francis Younghusband led the first military expedition into Thibet since the Ghurkas had been defeated there in 1844. Had Younghusband accepted

Holmes) had founded a Chair of Sherlockian Studies at the new University of Keele.

[5] Vol. 15, No. 4, New Series, December, 1965.

all of Holmes's recommendations, and abandoned the military aspect of the expedition, not only would the killing of many Thibetans have been avoided, but the expedition would not have left behind it a bitter memory of British perfidy. The award of the CSI to Holmes, in recognition of his help in making the invasion of Thibet possible, was accepted by him only because Holmes no longer wished to offend the King.

One last contact with overseas Power before Holmes retired, in late October, 1903, to his books and his bee-keeping in the peace of the sea-girt Sussex Downs, came in the January of that year: 'The Commission for the Sultan of Turkey'.

The year 1903 was to prove the busiest of Holmes's life, no fewer than thirteen cases, besides that of Turkey, claiming his effective attention – and this activity in addition to the completion and revision of *The Roosevelt Archives* and Holmes's confidential report on Thibet.

Though never what Byron called a 'clubbable' man, and congenitally averse to 'Society', Holmes's fame had brought him both social invitations and official commissions that he now, in his fiftieth year, found it almost impossible to refuse. Though neither Watson nor Holmes says so, it seems evident to me that the retirement in October, 1903, must have been forced upon Holmes by a burden of inescapable duties that he no longer had the physical strength to bear.

For 1903 was a 'social' year as well as a busily professional year, for the reason that so many diplomatic 'puddings', in the stirring of which Holmes had had more than a single finger, were now coming to the boil. On 30th April, 1903, a telegram, re-routed through the Foreign Office, arrived at Baker Street from Sir Charles Hardinge, commanding Holmes, in the King's name, to meet the Royal train in Paris, and to be present with those attendant upon President Loubet when he greeted Edward VII.

That night, Holmes was a guest at dinner at the British Embassy, where it was noticed that King Edward took him aside, and spoke to him in what was evidently a most friendly manner. Holmes went on, with the Royal and Presidential party, to the Théâtre Français, to see the significantly titled *L'Autre Danger*. It was here that the King's felicitous compliments to Jeanne Granier on her acting changed the reserve of the Parisians to a warmth of welcome which astonished even the King – used, not only to charming people, but to assessing and changing the moods of crowds.

Holmes did not stay in Paris for the State performance at the Opera, after the President had given a dinner for the King at the Elysée Palace; but Holmes did attend the review at Vincennes in the morning, and took luncheon at the British Embassy with the King, after which His Majesty drove to a race-meeting at Longchamps, and Holmes returned to London by the afternoon boat-train.

Holmes was also commanded to the Royal Box at Covent Garden, on Tuesday, 5th May, when the King and Queen, the Prince of Wales (later King George V) and the Princess, with other members of the Royal Family, attended a 'gala' performance. A delicate compliment was paid to Holmes by the King in that – even though the gala performance was known to be an anticipatory celebration of the about-to-be-signed *Entente* – His Majesty had chosen to hear Wagner's opera, *Das Rheingold*, because he had learnt that Wagner was Holmes's favourite composer.

The 'Commission for the Sultan of Turkey' had been executed over four months before when Holmes's work was irritatingly – if agreeably – interrupted by these social occasions. Holmes himself has emphasized the importance of this 'commission': it 'called for immediate action, as political consequences of the gravest kind might arise from its neglect'.

From our almost omniscient position of hindsight, we can see some of the more immediate of those grave political consequences clearly: insurrection of the Bulgarian minority in Macedonia, then a part of Turkey-in-Europe; intervention by Russia or Austria–Hungary or both to 'protect the lives of the Christian subjects of the Sultan'; a 'temporary occupation' of Macedonia – 'until things had quietened down' – as permanent as the temporary occupation by Great Britain of Malta;

a formal annexation of Macedonia; and – worst prospect of all – a Poland-style carve-up of, first Turkey-in-Europe, and then, when that part of Turkey had been digested, a seizure of Turkey-in-Asia, with Russia dominating the Black Sea and the overland road to Persia and India, and Austria–Hungary dominating the Adriatic and Aegean, and so the whole of the Eastern Mediterranean, posing a threat to British-protected Cyprus and, beyond, to British-protected Egypt.

Six years before, as Great Britain and her 'enemy', Germany, were signing a secret agreement to carve-up the African possessions of Portugal, 'Britain's Oldest Ally', Russia and Austria–Hungary were also coming to terms – again secretly – on the position to be adopted over insurgent Macedonia, by now in a state of almost constant revolt.

The Bulgarians believed that sufficient anti-Turk agitation would provoke one or more of the Great Powers to intervene, and cause Macedonia to be added to Bulgaria, a principality (ruled by a Hohenzollern), still nominally under Turkish suzerainty.

Tsar Nicholas II and the Emperor Francis Joseph agreed that, though it would be pleasant to divide Turkey-in-Europe between their respective empires, the strategic importance of Macedonia was so obvious that it could not be seized – for the present, at any rate – without the danger of intervention by a group of Powers: Britain, France, Germany, and possibly even Italy, all uniting, despite their differences, to protect the territorial integrity of Turkey-in-Europe. Reluctantly, then, the secret agreement of 1897 was realistic in that it held both the High Contracting Parties to work for the maintenance of the *status quo ante*; and realistic, too, in that it sketched out the steps to be taken in the event of the present uneasy situation's being – forcibly or otherwise – ended.

At the beginning of 1902, rumours, very vague at first, began to circulate around the tea-parties and dinners of the lesser European diplomats – those second, third and fourth secretaries who are at once the source and gatherers-up of 'informed gossip' – that Austria–Hungary and Russia were planning some move to end the *impasse* over Macedonia.

Pressed for details, the rumour-mongers shrugged their shoulders. "Can't tell you a thing more, dear fellow. Just a hint that all may not be so peaceful in the Balkans not so very far ahead . . . No, word of honour, not a dashed thing more . . . Promise !"

The rumours came to that most sociable of Asiatics, Rustum Pasha, Ambassador to the Court of St James from the Sublime Porte. Rustum, though a Turk, was also a Christian; a fact which had not prevented his having been appointed to what was then the 'plum' diplomatic post in the Sultan's gift. Rustum – 'Rusty' to the jolly dogs of the Diplomatic – was immensely popular in London, attending the Greek Orthodox Church in Moscow Road, Westminster Abbey or the Jesuits' church in Spanish Place as indifferently as regularly. He was a superb horseman, and played polo at Roehampton. He also drank, owned racehorses, played whist and the new bridge, and even played cricket. His son was at Eton. He was okay.

During the greater part of 1902, Rustum, who well understood the historical pressures which were acting to change the world-position of his country, used his own secret service to prove that, in the first place, Russia and Austria–Hungary were considering a move to end the *status quo* in Macedonia, and, second, that in consequence they had now made a secret pact, superseding that of 1897, to act in the Macedonian affair together – presumably splitting the swag. What Rustum's agents could not discover were two highly important facts: the plan by which the allies were to move against Macedonia (and so against Turkey) and the date on which the now inevitable ultimatum to Turkey would be presented jointly by Russia and Austria–Hungary.

Faced with the realization that his efficient agents could learn no more, and aware that a crisis was upon his country, Rustum sent an embassy servant to Baker Street with a note: could Mr Holmes come to Chesham Place as soon as possible? The records of the Turkish Embassy in London shew that Holmes ordered the embassy messenger to wait whilst the Great Detective changed into dress-clothes, and took the messenger's four-wheeler back to Chesham Place. There, over dinner with Rustum Pasha, the Counsellor of Embassy and the Military Attaché, the well-named General Fahir Kavi (*kavi* means 'strong, solid', in Turkish), Holmes learnt of the Sultan's fears that his Macedonian provinces would soon be plotted into, not merely insurrection (that, alas, had been going on for some time), but civil war so violent that Russia and Austria–Hungary would need no further excuse to intervene.

By the end of the year, professional agitators had fanned Macedonian insurrection into a blaze so fierce that Britain, alarmed that such a key-territory should fall into anarchy or – worse – should be divided up by the Russians and Austrians, approached all the Powers involved, asking that some steps be taken to restore order to rebellion-torn Macedonia.

It was for this that the two plotting Empires had been waiting. Turkey, on Holmes's advice, had already introduced some reforms in Macedonia; but these were insufficient to still the agitation, and on 25th February, 1903, Russia and Austria–Hungary produced what is now known as the *February Programme* (of Reform). Its most obvious quality was its respect, not for the mentioned 'understandable patriotric aspirations' of the insurgent Bulgarians, but for the traditional and legal rights of their Turkish overlord, the Sultan. The principal proposal – of a type which had become traditional in modern European diplomacy; and thus now acceptable to most as being completely precedented – was that a consortium of the Great Powers should appoint an Inspector-general for Macedonia, with plenary powers to suppress disorder and promote internal harmony. Moreover, this Inspector-general would be responsible rather to the Great Powers than to Turkey. This was a most broad-minded – indeed, generous – proposal; for it would remove from the Sultan the odium of imposing discipline on non-Turkish subjects, and transfer that task to a faceless international body, which could well ignore the prejudice which would, as a matter of course, be transferred from the Sultan to the new *de facto* 'ruler' of Macedonia.

The world was not astonished that the Sultan warmly welcomed the new plan for the pacification, within Turkish sovereignty, of his Macedonian dominions. It was believed that he had not been consulted in the drafting of the plan; and this is literally true. On the other hand, as was suspected even at the time, the Sultan was in full possession of the facts of the plan even before the drafting reached its final stages; and this, also, is true. The secret intermediacy of Holmes saw to it that the plan was modified to make it acceptable to the Sultan and to the Turkish people; and that the Sultan – whose gratitude caused him to confer the Order of the Osmanieh (1st Class) on Holmes[6] – was satisfied that Holmes had extracted what good he might from an intrinsically bad situation is evident from the willingness to co-operate that the Sultan shewed.

Unfortunately – and this was something that both the Sultan and Holmes knew and feared – two of the Great Powers, Austria and Russia, had a vested interest in seeing that trouble was *not* suppressed in Macedonia; though they still had a vested interest in pretending that they *did*.

Stirred up by both Russian and Austrian agitators, the already inflammable Macedonian Bulgars continued their disorder even under the new Inspector-general. (The post was offered to Holmes; one wonders how differently history might have been written had he accepted!)

Holmes retired in October, 1903 – and many have asked, 'Why October?'; 'Why not see the year out . . . ?'

It was in October that the true nature of the Russo–Austrian plan was revealed. The *February Programme* having 'demonstrably failed' to restore order in Macedonia, the two Powers now produced their own so-called *Muerzsteg Programme* which, against the strongest protests of the Sultan, they proceeded, on their own authority, to apply to Turkish Macedonia. The *Muerzsteg Programme*'s principal 'reform' was to place all Turkish Macedonia under an *international* gendarmerie, with inspectors to be appointed by *all* the High

[6] This, too, may be seen in the Apponyi Sherlock Holmes Museum in Buda.

Contracting Parties, those inspectors to be responsible, not to an Inspector-general (and, through him, even though nominally, to the Sovereign Power, Turkey), but each to the Power which had appointed him. This plan not only removed, in practice, if not in theory, Macedonia from the authority of the Sultan, but left the territory free to be plundered by the two land- and power-hungry allies, who, twelve years later, were to be fighting each other in a war from which neither would emerge in its original form.

The Sultan had no reproaches for Holmes that his first, moderate, plan had not worked; there are some forces so powerful that – as we have seen more than once in this present century – the goodwill of common humanity cannot, for the moment at least, combat them.

Holmes was tired – with that exhaustion to which undeserved disappointment, far more than any physical over-exertion, contributes. He was tired, and he needed a rest. He found it in the still unspoiled Sussex, rusticity by the sea, of an England which has now gone.

He returned, of course, but not 'professionally'; only for rare 'busman's holidays' to enhance the pleasure of retirement by an occasional interruption of its calm rhythm.

Once his old powers were invoked by accident – the sight of a dead body lying on the beach beneath his house; but it was no accident which took him to Chicago in 1912 and 1913, to build up the false identity of 'Mr Altamont', the fanatical hater of Britain. That the first Great War was imminent, all in power knew; and Holmes had to come out of retirement to give his beloved country what help he might.

How brilliantly he took the stage of international *Realpolitik* for the final appearance has been recorded by Watson, in *His Last Bow*, an adventure that Watson, too, came out of retirement, both to be Holmes's helper in, and to record.

The Blue Blood of the Holmeses

A Genealogical Note

This monograph, here introduced as an Appendix, originally appeared as an article in *The Baker Street Journal*, the exceptionally well-produced organ of *The Baker Street Irregulars* (of New York), a body whose 'scion societies' now literally span the entire globe. For many years *The Baker Street Journal* has been edited by Dr Julian Wolff, MD ('The Commissionaire'), and I take this opportunity to voice the admiration that I and all my fellow-Sherlockians feel for Dr Wolff's dedication to that nobly 'Irregular' task of 'keeping the memory of the Master green'.

I have always thought that Holmes's acknowledged attitude towards acknowledged aristocrats – indeed, towards Aristocracy generally – had always something not a little ambiguous in it. When Holmes encounters an aristocrat the Master appears to be almost ill-at-ease. He is not only uncomfortable himself; he contrives to make the well-bred man equally uncomfortable.

Holmes, face-to-face with what Watson evidently regards as Holmes's 'betters', is usually at his most formal; any hint of the casual or informal in the other man's manner, and Holmes's back is up – at once. Holmes is so ill at ease with Baron Adalbert Gruner that he reminds the Baron to call him 'Mr Holmes'; and the Great Sleuth is hardly more at ease with 'the King of Bohemia' or the Duke of Holdernesse.

It is true that Holmes told Watson, soon after their first meeting, that the Holmeses were of 'yeoman' stock – and so, indeed, they were. What Holmes did not add was that, like so many other British families of yeoman origin, his had been ennobled, and that the actual peerage had failed for lack of 'heirs male of the body'. Holmes – our Holmes – was a plain 'Mister' who, but for that missing link in the chain of descent, should have been 'My Lord'.

The peerage in question was that of Holmes of Kilmallock – an Irish barony created in the first year of King George III.

In view of the fact that this barony was one of the first to be created by George III after his accession in 1760, we may take it for granted that the title was awarded in respect of some very special service rendered to the Crown.

Before I go on to give details of this barony, I should like to point out that the presence of a barony in his pedigree sufficiently explains Holmes's 'awkwardness' in his relations with titled persons. Holmes is not abject, as one might be who is conscious of social inferiority; yet Holmes does not claim equality with the bearers of titles of honour. He is – let us admit this – somewhat sullenly conscious of the fact that he *ought to be able* to claim equality with the Peerage; and the knowledge that he *cannot* puts our Mr Holmes at something of a moral disadvantage.

There is another point, too, to be noticed: in the descent of the Holmeses before the grant of the *first* barony, there is mention of illegitimacy – please observe this: I am sure that it troubled Mr Holmes who, for all his virtues, was always something of a prude.

Thomas Holmes, of Newport, Isle of Wight, was – for special services, the nature of which has still to be determined – raised to the peerage of Ireland, as BARON HOLMES OF KILMALLOCK, in the County of Limerick.

Thomas was the son and heir of Henry Holmes, of Yarmouth, Isle of Wight, of which ancient 'kingdom'[1] (the Roman *Vectis*) Henry Holmes was the Lieutenant-governor. Henry

[1] The Isle was raised to the dignity of a kingdom by King Henry VI of England, in favour of the contemporary Earl of Warwick, who thus became Wight's first and last king.

(died 23rd June, 1738) was the husband of Mary (buried 7th May, 1760, aged 82, at Yarmouth), illegitimate daughter of Robert Holmes, Governor of Wight – and uncle of Lieutenant-governor Henry, who thus married his illegitimate first cousin.

As the peerage, granted to Thomas Holmes in the year in which his mother died, was an Irish one, this meant that, even after his elevation to the peerage, he could still retain his seat in the English House of Commons, where he had sat as Member for Newtown, Isle of Wight, from 1743 to 1747, and as Member for Yarmouth, Isle of Wight, from 1747 onwards. He continued to represent Yarmouth until 1764, in which year (on 21st July), he died without heirs male of the body, and the peerage became extinct.

Thomas, first Baron Holmes, married, firstly, Anne, widow of Colby Apsley, esquire, and daughter of Henry Player, esquire, of Weevil House, Alverstoke, Hampshire. Anne was born in February, 1694–5, at Alverstoke, and died there, 29th September, 1743. (Thomas was born, 2nd November, 1699.)

His second wife was Catherine Leigh, who lived until 4th March, 1784.

We come now to the *second* barony of Holmes.

Thomas, first baron Holmes of Kilmallock, left no son, but one daughter, Elizabeth, who married Thomas Troughear, Doctor of Divinity, of Northwood, Isle of Wight.

Dr Troughear, by Elizabeth his wife, had one son, Leonard, like his father a clerk in Holy Orders.

Leonard Troughear matriculated at Queen's College, Oxford, on 22nd March, 1749–50 – being then seventeen years of age – and became a demy of Queen's, 1750–3.

At some time during his undergraduate days, Leonard Troughear assumed, by Royal Licence, the surname of *Holmes* in lieu of his own patronymic of Troughear, and it was as the Reverend Leonard *Holmes* that he married, almost certainly in 1760 (the year in which old Mrs Henry Holmes died, King George III ascended the throne of Great Britain, Ireland and

France,[2] and Uncle Thomas was created first Baron Holmes), Elizabeth, daughter of the Reverend Thomas Terrell, Rector of Calbourne, Isle of Wight.

This Leonard Troughear-Holmes must have been a distinctly unusual parson, even in the eighteenth century – that Golden Age of Unusual Parsons.

For, by a King's Letter of 25th October, 1797, the extinct barony of Holmes, which had lapsed with the death of Leonard's maternal uncle, Thomas, in 1764, was revived in Leonard (Troughear) Holmes's favour, and he was created, by the patent of 4th March, 1798, Baron Holmes of the second creation.

Why the title, most mysteriously motivated in the first instance, was revived for a parson-nephew of the original peer, I have not yet been able to find out; but the date of the second creation is significant – taken in conjunction with the place in which Mr Leonard Holmes exercised his priestly functions. For the Isle of Wight, in 1797, was the centre, on the English side of the Channel, of the vigorous French 'Resistance' movement sponsored by Pitt; the Dutch Emigrant Brigade joining the various French 'Resistance' units in 1799. It seems likely to me that the Reverend Mr Leonard Holmes had become a figure of importance in this undercover activity.

Leonard, Lord Holmes of the second creation, died about May, 1804, without having left a male heir; so that his two daughters became the co-heirs of his estate (though not of the barony, which descended, according to the patent, only in *tail male*). And these two daughters bring the story of the Holmes barony up to the time of Sherlock Holmes himself.

The elder daughter was Elizabeth (born about 1762?); she married twice. By her second husband, Sir Henry Worsley (*a marriage which unites the present Duke of Kent, grandson of King George V, with the family of Sherlock Holmes*), she left a son and heir. On his marriage to the Honourable Elizabeth (Troughear) Holmes, Sir Henry adopted, by Royal

[2] A traditional claim, by Kings of England and – later – Great Britain – to the throne of France was not abandoned until, with the signing of the Treaty of Amiens in 1802, George III agreed to forego for himself and his successors, the British monarch's ancient 'claim' to France.

Licence, the additional patronymic of Holmes, becoming Sir Henry Worsley-Holmes, baronet.[3]

The daughter of Sir Leonard Worsley-Holmes, the 9th and last baronet, Elizabeth, Baroness Heytesbury, brought the estates and name of Holmes into the noble family of a'Court; the 2nd Baron Heytesbury, William Henry Ashe a'Court, who had been Conservative Member of Parliament for the Isle of Wight (1837–47), adopting the additional surname of *Holmes* on his marriage, in 1833, with Sir Leonard Worsley-Holmes's daughter and heiress.

The present peer, William Leonard Frank Holmes-a'Court, 5th Baron Heytesbury, was born in 1906, and succeeded to the title in 1949. It is not without significance, surely, that Margaret a'Court-Repington, a member of a collateral branch (grandchildren of Sir William Pierce Ashe a'Court, 1st baronet) should have married, in 1881, Major Edwin Frederick Wodehouse, Assistant-commissioner of City Police at the time when Sherlock Holmes, his not-so-distant cousin-in-law, was busy hushing up the threatened scandal centring about the dark alleys of the East End?

Sherlock Holmes, then, was connected with the peerages both of Great Britain and of Ireland, not only as of the past but, through the then Lord Heytesbury, of the present. This consciousness of noble blood it was which, in my opinion, made Holmes so often so very 'difficult'. The diffidence of his ambivalent character prevented his calling attention to his peer-studded pedigree that, since he lacked any title himself, was generally unknown to others; yet, irrationally, he expected others to know that he was not quite the 'yeoman' that he claimed to be; and the anger that he felt at being treated, by those whom he considered his social equals, as their social inferior, too frequently led him into solecisms of conduct which can have done nothing to assert his claim to gentility.

[3] The present Worsley baronetcy, of Hovingham, Yorkshire; creation of 1838; represents the senior branch of this ancient family. It was into the junior branch, the Worsleys of Appuldercombe, that the Honourable Elizabeth (Troughear) Holmes married. The family (in the direct line) of Worsley of Appuldercombe became extinct with the death of the 9th and last baronet in 1825.

APPENDIX II

Holmes and the Vatican

Maintaining an old connection ...?

The choice of Sherlock Holmes as mystery-solver by Pope
Leo XIII, in at least five cases over a period of eleven years –
1888–99 – is only partially (and, to my mind, not at all satisfactorily) explained by the pontiff's highly-publicized 'broad-
mindedness'. It was a time in which Britain was unpopular
with the Vatican, and the Vatican was decidedly unpopular
with the mass of the British. When the bisexual 'Eddy', Duke
of Clarence and Avondale, elder son of the Prince of Wales
and thus a future King of Great Britain, had fallen madly in
love with the beautiful Princess Hélène of Orleans, everyone
of influence, from Queen Victoria downwards, welcomed and
encouraged the mutual love of the two young people. 'Eddy'
had figured (though not, Heaven was thanked, in the newspapers) as the central character in an unsavoury scandal involving a male brothel; and in this marriage his parents and
grandmother saw the total 'redemption' of their sexually
erratic son.

As a good Roman Catholic, Princess Hélène went, as I have
described in this book, to get the Pope's blessing. She did
not get it; and I have suggested that His Holiness was working
off some spleen against the British in refusing his consent to
Princess Hélène's marriage to a heretic.

Then why the calls to Holmes, that very English Englishman, when the Vatican, which had shewn such hostility to
Britain and its Royal Family, found itself in trouble?

The answer, I think, must be sought, not in any contemporary relationship between the Vatican and Great Britain, or
between the Vatican and Holmes, but in a relationship be-

tween Holmes's family and the Vatican dating back to the middle of the previous century, when the then Pope's then extensive temporal dominions had an extensive seaboard, and that seaboard called for a powerful and efficiently run navy.

Sir Edwin Sherrinford, Holmes's maternal grandfather, had married Violette, daughter of Antoine Charles Horace Vernet (1758–1835), better known as 'Carle' or even 'English' Vernet, from his obsession with English manners and modes – especially with English horse-racing, that he was amongst the first to introduce into France. Vernet was the son and father of artists no less distinguished than himself; indeed, the Vernets had been successful artists in France since the latter part of the seventeenth century. Holmes's great-uncle (Emile Jean), Horace Vernet, born in 1789, did not die, full of honours, until Sherlock was nine. The lad must have met his handsome old great-uncle, with moustaches and beard à l'impériale, several times on the Holmes family's journeys through France.

But this marriage between a Vernet and an Englishman was not without a precedent; and the Vatican records – faultlessly complete and instantly accessible in those pre-Computer days – shewed that a Vernet had married, in the previous century, an Englishman with what must be the most improbable appointment in history: John Parker, Commander-in-Chief of the Naval Forces of His Holiness the Pope.

Sherlock, as we know from Watson, was proud of his descent from the Vernets – even in the earliest days of his acquaintance with Watson, Holmes's natural reserve cannot prevent his mentioning to Watson that 'my grandmother was a sister of Vernet, the French painter'. What more natural, then, that the Vatican, knowing of Holmes's family relationship with its former naval commander-in-chief, should appeal to Holmes's sense of family loyalty to get the late Commander Parker's still-surviving employers out of several messes?

Holmes had a long – a very long – memory. The Vatican's memory was even longer . . .

Acknowledgments

Once again, it is my pleasure, no less than my duty, to record the help that I have received from both friends and strangers, in the preparation of this book. Not only have Sherlockians from the Old World and the New rallied to assist me with information and advice; but many with little or no interest in the Master have given noble assistance in answering my questions, begrudging neither time nor labour in order to make their replies as full and as informative as possible.

In particular, I wish to put on record my deep sense of obligation to the following:

Dr Sven Järpe, of Linköping, Sweden, for information on the Swedish and other Scandinavian Royal Families, and for a most useful (though not yet used) suggestion as to *another* reason for Holmes's having been summoned to help 'the King of Scandinavia'.

The Right Honourable Earl Ferrers, for referring me to the history of his family, as set out in *Stemmata Shirleiana*, which records the marriage uniting Lord Ferrers's family, the Shirleys, with that of George Washington, Founding-father of the United States of America.

My fellow-Sherlockian, Hr Henry Lauritzen, of Aalborg, Denmark, for his consistent friendly support, generally, and – in regard to this book – for information on, and pictures of, the several Scandinavian Royal Families, as well as for his setting-up and decorating my dedication to yet another fellow-Baker Street Irregular, Hr A. D. Henriksen, of Bagsværd, Denmark.

And two more Irregulars: Dean Dickensheet, of San Francisco, for research and encouragement (to say nothing

of the finest picture of Holmes in my possession), and Peter
Blau, of the American Geological Institute, for help, as swift
as ungrudged, in researching pictures for this book.

Once again my thanks to Sir Philip Magnus-Allcroft, Bart,
for permission to quote from his unrivalled *King Edward the
Seventh*, the only biography of the King which, in my
opinion, relates the Monarch to his world, as in this book, I
have tried to relate Holmes to the world in which he rose from
obscurity to immortality.

Research into the history of the Washington Family, both
in Europe and in America, made me greatly indebted to the
following:

Fellow-Irregular Heer Cornelis Helling, of *The Dutch
Sherlock Holmes Society*, Amsterdam;

Drs R. A. D. Renting, Chief Archivist, Rotterdam City
Archives;

Drs G. J. Mentink, Chief Archivist, Gelderland State
Archives;

Heer J. A. van Zelm van Eldik, Secretary of the Chancery
of the Netherlands Orders of Knighthood;

Heer C. W. Delfortie, *Centraal Bureau voor Genealogie*, The
Hague;

Drs H. M. Mensonides, Director, Municipal Archives of
The Hague;

Drs R. E. O. Ekkart, Keeper, Leyden University Historical
Museum;

Herr Dr Puechler, Director, Bavarian State Archives,
Munich;

Herr Walter von Hueck, Archivist, Deutsches Adelsarchiv,
Marburg a.d. Lahn;

The Keeper of Archives, Leicester Museums & Art Gallery,
Leicester, England;

The Secretary, Northamptonshire and Huntingdonshire
Archives Committee, Northampton, England;

The Secretary, Central Chancery of the Orders of Knighthood, London;

The Keeper of the Archives, Public Record Office, London;

Acknowledgments

The Chief Librarian, Ministry of Defence Library (Central and Army), London.

Lastly – and most warmly – to Mr David Spink, Chairman of the world-famous jewellers and fine-art dealers, Mr Spink collected for me the several Orders and Decorations from amongst those awarded to Mr Sherlock Holmes – awards which are illustrated in Plate 23.

To all the above, and to those who have helped me in other ways, my sincere thanks!

M.H.

Bibliography

As I have said before, the bibliography of Sherlock Holmes is 'immense'; I make no apologies for quoting once again the judgment of Ellery Queen in the introduction to his suppressed anthology, *The Misadventures of Sherlock Holmes* (1944): 'Someone has said that more has been written *about* Sherlock Holmes than about any other character in fiction. It is further true that more has been written about Holmes *by others* than by Doyle himself.' If it were possible to paint the lily by adding truth to truth, then the years since Ellery Queen stated the above truths have merely 'added truth' to the unchallengeable veracity of his statement. The books *about* Sherlock Holmes continue to proliferate, and, as I said in introducing the Bibliography of *The London of Sherlock Holmes*, 'it would be impossible to list even a thousandth of what has been written – articles and books – on the perennially fascinating subject of Sherlock Holmes.'

The books, then, that I have listed below are, not so much source material – though they are that, of course – as books to which I recommend the reader desirous of pursuing further information on the two linked subjects of this present work: Holmes himself and the world-in-change-and-dissolution against the background of which he rose to international stature as The Greatest Detective of Them All.

Again as I have pointed out, the principal sources of information for the research scholar dealing with modern times are the products of the periodical press and – where they survive – public archives and the files of private correspondence. I have more than once called the reader's attention to the value of those 'illustrated journals which, in the days before the "telly", provided the eagerly-sought comment on the news:

such journals as *The Queen, The Graphic, The Sphere, The Illustrated London News, Country Sport, The Field, Madame, London Letter, The King, Black & White*, and – at a lower but still successful end of the scale – *The Penny Illustrated Newspaper*[1] and *The (National)Police Gazette* (both invaluable for the student of Victorian Crime).'

On *Sherlock Holmes* ('The Higher Criticism')

Baring-Gould, W. S. *The Chronological Holmes*; New York: Privately printed, 1955.
— *Sherlock Holmes of Baker Street, A Life of the World's First Consulting Detective*; New York: 1962; London: 1963.
— *The Annotated Sherlock Holmes*; New York and London: 1967.
Bell, H. W. *Sherlock Holmes and Dr Watson: The Chronology of Their Adventures*; London: 1932; (Paperback – private – reissue by the Baker Street Irregulars of New York, 1953).
Blakeney, T. S. *Sherlock Holmes: Fact or Fiction?* London: 1932; (Baker Street Irregulars reissue in paperback, 1954).
Brend, G. *My Dear Holmes*; London: 1951.
Christ, J. F. *An Irregular Chronology of Sherlock Holmes of Baker Street*; Ann Arbor, Mich.: 1947.
Hall, T. H. *Sherlock Holmes: Ten Literary Studies*; London: 1969.
Harrison, Michael. *In the Footsteps of Sherlock Holmes*; London: 1958; New York: 1960; (revised) London and New York: 1971.
— *The London of Sherlock Holmes*; London, New York: 1972.
Holroyd, J. E. *Baker Street By-Ways*; London: 1959.
— (Ed.) *Seventeen Steps to 221B*; London: 1965.
Morgan, Robert S. *Spotlight on a Simple Case, or, Wiggins, Who Was That Horse I Saw With You Last Night?*; Wilmington, Delaware: 1959.
Roberts, Sir S. C. *Doctor Watson: Prolegomena to the Study of a Biographical Problem*; London: 1931.
— *Holmes and Watson: A Miscellany*; London: 1953.
Simpson, A. Carson. *Simpson's Sherlockian Studies*; Philadelphia: 1953–1960.

---

[1] Whose 'illustrated' week-by-week coverage of, e.g., the 'Jack the Ripper' murders must set the all-time standard of misapplied journalistic ingenuity.

Bibliography

Smith, Edgar W. *The Napoleon of Crime*; Summit, New Jersey: 1963. (This is the standard Life of Dr James Moriarty.)

Starrett, Vincent. *The Private Life of Sherlock Holmes*; New York: 1933; London: 1934; (*revised and enlarged*) Chicago: 1960. (The first important – and still, in my opinion, the greatest – comment on The Sacred Writings.)

Van Lier, E. J., MD. *A Doctor Enjoys Sherlock Holmes*; New York: 1960.

Warrack, Guy. *Sherlock Holmes and Music*; London: 1957. (Presents Holmes as the Musician.)

As I said, the list is endless, especially were we to seek to ihclude the essays, reference-books (e.g. S. Tupper Bigelow, QC: *An Irregular Anglo-American Glossary of More or Less Unfamiliar Words, Terms and Phrases in the Sherlock Holmes Saga*; Toronto: 1959), short-stories, pastiches, etc – and these, not in *one* language, but in most of the tongues of the modern and ancient – you may read Holmes both in Latin and Greek – world.[2] In this fascinating 'ancillary Holmesian literature', I instance two of its most delightful manifestations:

Wolff, Julian, MD. *Practical Handbook of Sherlockian Heraldry*; New York: Privately printed, 1955.

Titus, Eve. *Basil of Baker Street*; New York: 1958. (Perhaps the last word – or the High-Water Mark – of Sherlock-inspired fantasy. The wonderfully illustrated – by Paul Galdone – adventures of Basil the Mouse, who models his life on that of the Master.)

Historical – Political and Strategic

Of the very many historical studies of the latter nineteenth century and early twentieth century, I recommend the following for a condensed but comprehensive survey of the period.

Gomme, Sir L. *London in the Reign of Victoria, 1837–1897*; London: 1897.

Harrison, Michael. *London by Gaslight: 1861–1911*; London: 1963. (*Far more world-embracing than its title suggests.*)

[2] As well, of course, in both Braille and Pitman's Shorthand !

Jarman, T. L. *Democracy and World Conflict, 1868–1965*; London: 1964.

Leslie, R. F. *The Age of Transformation, 1789–1871*; London: 1965.

Tull, G. K. and Bulwer, P. *Britain and the World in the 19th Century*; London: 1966.

— *Britain and the World in the Twentieth Century*; London: 1966.

Western, J. R. *The End of European Primacy, 1871–1945*; London: 1963.

Historical – Modes and Manners

Anonymous: *Fifty Years of London Society*; London: 1923.

Battiscombe, G. *Queen Alexandra*; London: 1969.

Davis, Lt-Col. R. Newnham. *Diners and Dining-Out*; London: 1913.

— *The Gourmet's Guide to London*; London: 1910.

Handbook to London As It Is (1879). Anonymous: *published by John Murray*. London: 1879.

Harper, Charles G. *A Londoner's Own London, 1870–1920*; London: 1924.

Harrison, Michael. *Fanfare of Strumpets*; London: 1971.

—*Clarence: The Life of H.R.H. the Duke of Clarence & Avondale, K.G.*; London: 1972.

Holden, W. H. *They Startled Grandfather –Gay Ladies and Merry Mashers of Victorian Times*; London: 1947.

— *The Pearl of Plymouth*; London: 1950.

Laver, James. *Victorian Panorama*; London: 1948.

Magnus, Philip. *King Edward the Seventh*; London: 1964.

Nevill, Lady Dorothy. *Under Five Reigns*; London: 1925.

Nevill, Ralph. *The Life and Letters of Lady Dorothy Nevill* (ed. Ralph Nevill); London: 1930.

— *Night Life: London and Paris Past and Present*; London: 1926.

'One of the Old Boys'. *London in the Sixties*; London: 1928.

'One of Her Majesty's Servants'. *The Private Life of the Queen* (i.e. Victoria); London: 1897.

Osgood Field, Julian (published as 'Anon'). *Things I Shouldn't Tell*; London: 1923.

— *Uncensored Recollections*; London: 1924.

— *More Uncensored Recollections*; London: 1925.

'Resident, A Foreign'. *Society in London*; London: 1899.

Bibliography

— *Society in the New Reign* (i.e. of Edward VII); London: 1903.

Shirley, E. P. *Stemmata Shirleiana*; London (2nd edition): 1877.

Smalley, Geo. W. *Anglo-American Memories*; London: 1910.

Tisdall, E. E. P. *Queen Victoria's John Brown*; London: 1938.
(Whilst a detailed and – so far – the best account of Queen Victoria's Scots personal attendant ['Friend more than servant; loyal, faithful, brave . . .'], the book is also a succinct but admirably comprehensive survey of the Queen's reign, both at home and throughout her world-wide Empire.)

The Washington Ancestry and Records of the McClain, Johnson and Forty Other Colonial American Families; prepared for Edward Lee McClain by Charles Arthur Hoppin; (3 vols), Greenfield, Ohio: Privately Printed, 1932.

Index

Index

Index

Index